The Khartoum Campaign

The Khartoum Campaign
A Special Correspondent's View of
the Reconquest of the Sudan by
British and Eygyptian Forces
Under Kitchener—1898

Bennet Burleigh

The Khartoum Campaign: a Special Correspondent's View of the Reconquest of the Sudan by British and Eygyptian Forces under Kitchener—1898
by Bennet Burleigh

First published in 1899 under the title
The Khartoum Campaign, 1898, or the Re-Conquest of the Soudan

Published by Leonaur Ltd

Text in this form copyright © 2008 Leonaur Ltd

ISBN: 978-1-84677-528-4 (hardcover)
ISBN: 978-1-84677-527-7 (softcover)

http://www.leonaur.com

Publisher's Notes

The opinions expressed in this book are those of the author and are not necessarily those of the publisher.

Contents

Preface	7
Review of Field	9
Days of Waiting and Preparation	20
Mustering for the Overthrow of Mahdism	34
By the Way—From Cairo to Dakhala	41
Dakhala Camp: Gossip and Duty	54
From Dakhala to Wad Habeshi	63
Wad Hamid to El Hejir	75
El Hejir to Um Terif	84
Skirmishing With the Enemy	95
The Battle of Omdurman—First Phase	107
The Battle of Omdurman—*Continued*	**129**
Stories of the Battle—Omdurman	152
Close of Campaign	172
The Official Despatches	195
The Fashoda Affair	224
Postscript	256

Preface

By the overthrow of Mahdism, the great region of Central Africa has been opened to civilisation. From the date of the splendid victory of Omdurman, 2nd September 1898, may be reckoned the creation of a vast Sudan empire. At so early a stage, it is idle to speculate whether the country will be held as a British possession, or as a province of Egypt. "The land of the blacks," and their truculent Arab despoilers, has the intrinsic qualities that secure distinction. Given peace, it may be expected that the mixed negroid races of the Upper Nile will prove themselves as orderly and industrious as they are conspicuously brave. Whoever rules them wisely, will have the control of the best native tribes of the Dark Continent, the raw material of a mighty state. This, too, is foreshadowed; the dominant power in Central Northern Africa, if no farther afield, will have its capital in Khartoum, "Ethiopia will soon stretch out her hands unto God."

The recent events which have so altered the condition of affairs upon the Upper Nile, deserve more than ephemeral record. A campaign so full of inspiriting incident, a victory which has brought presage of a great and prosperous Sudan, merits re-telling. Through half a score of battles or more, from the beginning to the death of Mahdism, I have followed British and Egyptian troops into action against the Dervishes. I knew General Hicks, and had the luck to miss accompanying his ill-fated expedition. In the present volume, *Khartoum Campaign*, the narrative of the reconquest is completed, the history being carried to the occupation of Fashoda and Sobat, including the withdrawal of Major Marchand's French mission. I have made use of my telegrams and letters to the *Daily Telegraph*, London, and the full notes I made from day to day during the campaign. Besides, I have quoted in certain cases from official sources, and given extracts from verbal and written communications made to me by distinguished officers engaged in the operations.

For use of maps, sketches, and photographs, I am indebted to the proprietors of the *Daily Telegraph*, to Mr Ross of *Black and White*, Surgeon-General William Taylor, Colonel Frank Rhodes, Lieutenant E. D. Loch, Grenadier Guards, Mr Francis Gregson, Mr Munro of Dingwall, N.B., and others.

Bennet Burleigh
London
December 1898

CHAPTER 1

Review of Field

It is an easier and kindlier duty to set forth facts than to proclaim opinions and pronounce judgments. Before Tel-el-Kebir was fought in September 1882 and the Egyptian army beaten and disbanded, the insurrection headed by the Mahdi or False Prophet had begun. In the disrupted condition of affairs which succeeded Arabi Pasha's defeat by British arms the Dervish movement made further rapid progress. To Sir Evelyn Wood, V.C., at the close of 1882, was assigned the task, as Sirdar or Commander-in-Chief of the Khedivial troops, of forming a real native army. It was that distinguished soldier, aided by an exceptionally able staff, who first took in hand the re-organisation and proper training of the *fellaheen* recruits. By dint of drill, discipline and stiffening with British commissioned and non-commissioned officers he soon made passable soldiers of the "Gippies." The new army was at first restricted to eight battalions of Egyptian infantry, one regiment of cavalry, and four batteries of artillery. Although there were Sudanese amongst Arabi's troops, they were mostly gunners. It was not until May 1884 that the first "black" regiment was raised. Yet it had been notorious that the Sudanese were the only Khedivial soldiers who made anything of a stubborn stand against us in the 1882 campaign. The blacks who came down with the Salahieh garrison on the 9th of August 1882, and joined in the surprise attack upon General Graham's brigade then in camp at Kassassin, were not easily driven off. The large body of Egyptian infantry and cavalry, although supported by several Krupp batteries which, issuing from the Tel-el-Kebir lines, assailed us in front, were readily checked and pushed back. It was our right rear that the "blacks" and others forming the Salahieh column menaced, and it required some tough fighting before Sir Baker-Russell with his cavalry and horse artillery was able to drive them off. In truth, the "blacks" held on long after the main body of Arabi's force had abandoned their intention of driving the British into the Suez Canal or the sea.

The first Sudanese battalion was recruited and mustered-in at Suakim. It got the next numeral in regimental order, and so became known as the "Ninth." Many of the blacks who enlisted in the Ninth—Dinkas, Shilluks, Gallas, and what not—were deserters from the Mahdi's banner, or Dervishes who had been taken prisoners at El Teb and Tamai. It has never yet been deemed advisable to enrol any of the Arab tribesmen in the Khedivial regular army. Hadendowa, Kababish, Jaalin, Baggara, and many other clans, lack no physical qualifications for a military career. Their desperate courage in support of a cause they have at heart is an inspiration of self-immolation. But they are as uncertain and difficult to regulate by ordinary methods of discipline as the American Red Indian, and so are only fitted for irregular service. In March 1885 General Sir Francis Grenfell succeeded to the Sirdarship. With tact and energy he carried still further forward the excellent work of his predecessor. Four additional Sudanese battalions were created during his term, and the army was strengthened and better equipped for its duties in many other respects. Sir Francis had the satisfaction of leading his untried soldiers against the Dervishes, and winning brilliant victories and, in at least one instance, over superior numbers. He it was, who, at Toski in August 1889, routed an invading army of Dervishes, whereat was killed their famous leader Wad en Nejumi. That battle put an end to the dream of the Mahdists to overrun and conquer Egypt and the world. The Khalifa thereafter found his safest policy, unless attacked, was to let the regular Egyptian forces severely alone.

BENNETT BURLEIGH

It was shown that, when well handled, the *fellaheen* and the blacks could defeat the Dervishes. Lord Kitchener of Khartoum became Sirdar in the spring of 1892. His career in the land of the Nile may be briefly summarised: first as a Lieutenant, then successively as Captain, Major, Colonel and General, that Royal Engineer Officer from 1882 has been actively employed either in Egypt proper or the Sudan. He has, during that interval, been entrusted with many perilous and delicate missions and independent commands. Whatever was given him to do was carried through with zeal and resolution. In his time also little by little the Khedivial forces have been increased. A sixth Sudanese battalion was raised in 1896, and in that and the following year four additional *fellaheen* battalions were added to the army. When the Khartoum campaign began, the total muster-roll of the regular troops was eighteen battalions of infantry, ten squadrons of cavalry, a camel corps of eight companies, five batteries of artillery, together with the customary quota of engineers, medical staff, transport, and other departmental troops. There was a railway construction battalion numbering at least 2000 men, but they were non-combatants. As the whole armed strength of Egypt was, for the occasion, practically called into the field, the peace of the Delta had to be secured by other means. A small armed body called the Coast Guard and the ordinary police, apart from the meagre British garrison, were responsible for public tranquillity. The re-organisation and increase of the Coast Guard, which was decided on, into an army of 8000 men, was a brilliant idea, and one of the recent master-strokes of Lord Cromer and the Sirdar. It is ostensibly a quasi-civil force, and it was formed and equipped without the worry of international queries and interference. The Coast Guard is mainly composed of picked men, including old soldiers and reservists. Their duties carry them into the interior as well as along the sea-coast, for, partly on account of the salt tax, there are revenue defaulters along the borders of the Nile as well as by the Mediterranean and Red Sea. They are dressed like soldiers and are armed with Remingtons.

Mohammed Achmed, who called himself the Mahdi, or the

last of the prophets, whose mission was to convert the world to Islamism, was a native of Dongola. He was born near El Ordeh, or New Dongola, in 1848, and was the son of a carpenter. In person, he was above the medium height, robust, and with a rather handsome Arab cast of features. During 1884 I saw his brother and two of his nephews in a village south of El Ordeh. All of them were tall stalwart men, light of complexion for Dongolese, courteous and hospitable to strangers. Mohammed Achmed, from his youth, evinced a taste for religious studies coupled with the ascetic extravagances of a too emotional nature. From Khartoum to Fashoda he acquired a great reputation for sanctity. Religious devotees gathered around him and followed him to his retreat upon the island of Abba. There he, in May 1881, first announced his claims as the true Mahdi. His barefaced assertions of special divine command and guidance found credulous believers. With the wisdom of the serpent he had added to his influence and security as a prophet by marrying daughters of Baggara sheiks, *i.e.* chiefs. Mohammed Achmed was a vigorous and captivating preacher, learned in all the literature of the Koran, ever ready with apt and telling quotations. His early teaching was decidedly socialistic, including a command for the overthrow of the then existing civil state. His principles have been summed up officially as "an insistence upon universal law and religion—his own—with community of goods, and death to all who refused adherence to his tenets." Unfortunately, "opportunity" played into his hands. The misrule of the Pashas, the burden of over-taxation coupled with the legal suppression of the slave trade, and the demoralisation of the Egyptian forces enabled Mohammed Achmed to rebel successfully. Troops sent against him were defeated and annihilated. Towns capitulated to his arms and within a period of two years the inhabitants of the Sudan were hailing him as the true Mahdi, their invincible deliverer. With the capture of Khartoum, on the morning of the 26th of January 1885, and the abandonment of the Sudan and its population—the Egyptian frontier being fixed by British Government order at Wady Halfa—the over-lordship of that immense region from the Second Cataract to the Equatorial Lakes was yielded to the so-called Mahdi Mohammed Achmed did not long enjoy his conquests. Success killed him as it has done many a lesser man. For a season he gave himself up to a life of indolence and the grossest lust. On the 22nd of June 1885, less than six months after Gordon's head had been struck off and brought to him, the Mahdi suddenly died. It is said by some that his death was due to smallpox, by others that one of his women captives poisoned him in revenge for the murder of her relatives. His demise was kept secret for a time by his successor Abdullah, the chief Khalifa, and the other Dervish leaders. It was given out that the Mahdi's spirit had been called to Heaven for a space but would soon return to lead his hosts to fresh triumphs and further fat spoils. A tomb was erected over the place where his body lay, and the legend of his mission was taken over by Abdullah, who also in due season had visions and communicated reputed divine ordinances to the Dervishes. Abdullah, who was ignorant, illiterate and cruel, far beyond his dead master—"the cruellest man on earth," Slatin Pasha dubbed him,—by his exactions and treacheries soon overreached himself. Events were hastening to the overthrow of Mahdism. Sheiks and tribes fell away from the Khalifa and returned to the fold of orthodox Mohammedanism. By 1889, as an aggressive force seeking to enlarge its boundaries, Mahdism was spent. Thereafter, stage by stage, its power dwindled, although Omdurman, the Dervish capital, remained the headquarters of the strongest native military power that North Africa has ever known.

Lord Cromer has been blamed for many things he did, and much that he left undone, during the earlier days of Mahdism. A fuller knowledge of the whole circumstances justifies my saying that, as custodian of *British interests*, he acted throughout with singular prudence and great forbearance. It was not with his wish or approval that several of the untoward expeditions against the Dervishes were undertaken. It is permissible to regret that, from a variety of causes, the British Government engaged in more than one ill-considered and irresolute campaign for the destruction of Mahdism. Much treasure and countless thousands of lives were foolishly squandered and all without the least compensating advantage. The barren results of the Sudan campaigns directed from the War Office in Pall Mall form too painful a subject for discussion. It is only fair to say, that the military officials' hands may have been much hampered from Downing Street.

HEADQUARTERS, WADY HALFA

As I have stated elsewhere, it was not until 1896 that the serious reconquest of the Sudan was begun. Before then there had been, as Mr Gladstone after all appropriately termed them, "military operations," but not a state of war. He might have called them "blood-spilling enterprises," for they were only that and no more. The re-occupation of the province of Dongola in 1896, freed the Nile up to Merawi, and gave the disaffected Kababish, Jaalin and *riverain* tribesmen a chance of reverting to their allegiance to the Khedive. It also enabled the Sirdar to pass his gunboats farther up the river. Another gain issuing from the forward movement was that his right was secured from serious attack. Then followed the building of the wonderful Wady Halfa direct desert railway towards Abu Hamid, Berber, and Dakhala at the mouth of the Atbara. It was the 1897 campaign which put all these places into the Sirdar's hands. During that year's high Nile, he passed his gunboats over the long stretch of cataracts betwixt Merawi and Abu Hamid, and ran them up the river where they co-operated with the land forces, regulars and friendlies. Nay more, the steamers were set to do a double duty: convey stores to the advanced posts and assail and harass the Dervishes, pushing as far south as Shendy and Shabluka, the Sixth Cataract. By prodigies of labour and enterprise the railroad was speedily constructed to Abu Hamid, then on to Berber, and thence to Dakhala. The whole situation became greatly simplified the moment the line reached Abu Hamid. From the first, the question of dealing a death-blow to Mahdism with British-led troops had turned upon the solution of the transport problem. The through rail and river connection once established from Cairo *via* Wady Halfa to Abu Hamid put an end forever to all serious difficulty of providing adequate supplies for the troops. From Abu Hamid the Nile is navigable far south for many months during the year. Then again, the occupation of Abu Hamid unlocked the Korosko desert caravan route and drew more wary and recanting Dervishes away from the Khalifa. Following the capture of Abu Hamid, Berber was promptly taken for Egypt by the friendlies, and the Suakim-Berber trade route, which had been closed for many years, was re-opened.

The end was slowly drawing near, for the Sirdar was closing the lines and mustering his forces for a final blow. Railroad construction went forward apace. At the rate of from one to two miles a day track was laid so as to get the line up to Dakhala. Meanwhile, workshops were being erected at suitable points, and three additional screw gunboats, built in England, were re-fitted for launching. The flotilla was becoming formidable; it comprised 13 vessels, stern-wheelers and screw-steamers, all armed with cannon and machine guns and protected by bullet-proof shields.

Believing there was a chance to wreck the railroad and capture outposts and stores, Mahmoud, a nephew and favourite general of the Khalifa's, led a powerful Dervish army from Shendy north to raid the country to and beyond Berber. In spite of the gunboats, after disposing of the recalcitrant Jaalins, Mahmoud crossed the Nile at Metemmeh to the opposite bank. Accompanied by the veteran rebel, Osman Digna, he quitted Aliab, marching to the north-east with 10,000 infantry, riflemen and spearmen, ten small rifled brass guns and 4000 cavalry. It was his intention to cross the Atbara about 30 miles up from the Nile, and fall upon the flank and rear of the Sirdar's detached and outlying troops, killing them in detail. He reckoned too confidently and without full knowledge. Using the steamers and the railways the Sirdar quickly concentrated his whole force, bringing men rapidly up from Wady Halfa and the province of Dongola. The entrenched Egyptian camp at the junction of the Atbara with the Nile was strengthened, and General Gatacre's brigade of British troops was moved on to Kunur, where Macdonald's and Maxwell's brigades also repaired. Mahmoud had ultimately to be attacked in his own chosen fortified camp. His army was destroyed and he himself was taken prisoner. So closed the unexpected Atbara campaign in March last. Thereafter, as the Khalifa showed no intention of inviting fresh disaster by sending down another army to attack, the Sirdar despatched his troops into summer rest-camps. Dry and shady spots were selected by the banks of the Nile between Berber and Dakhala. One or another of the numberless deserted mud villages was usually chosen for headquarters and offices. With these for a nucleus, the battalion or brigade encampment was pitched in front and the quarters were fenced about with cut mimosa thorn-bush, forming a *zereba*. All along the Upper Nile, wherever there is a strip of cultivable land, or where water can be easily lifted from the river or wells for irrigation, there the natives had villages of mud and straw huts. In many places, for miles following miles, these hamlets fringe the river's banks, sheltered amidst groves of mimosa and palms. The fiendish cruelty and wanton destructiveness of the Dervishes, who, not satiated with slaughtering the villagers—men, women and children—further glutted their fury by firing the homesteads and cutting down the date palms, resulted in depopulating the country. Ignorant and fanatical in their religious frenzy to convert mankind to their new-found creed, the Mahdists held that the surest way to rid the world forthwith of all unbelievers lay in making earth too intolerable to be lived in.

These native dwellings, when cleaned, were not uncomfortable abodes. As the flat roofs were thickly covered with mats and grass whilst, except the doorway, the openings in the mud-walls were small, they were even in the glare of noontide heat, pleasantly cool and shady. The troops found that straw huts or *tukals* afforded far better protection than the tents from the sun and from dust-storms. So it came about that, copying the example set by the *fellaheen* and black soldiers, "Tommy Atkins" also built himself shelters, and "lean-to's" of reeds, palm leaves and straw. Drills and field exercises were relaxed, and the troops had time to rig up alfresco stages and theatres and to enjoy variety entertainments provided by comrades with talent for minstrelsy and the histrionic arts. Meanwhile the preparations for the final campaign against Mahdism were not slackened. Vast quantities of supplies and material of war were stored at Dakhala. Outposts were pushed forward and Shendy was occupied, whilst Metemmeh was held by friendly Jaalin tribesmen, who had suffered much at the Khalifa's hands. The Bayuda desert route also had been cleared of Dervishes by these and by neighbouring tribesmen. On the direct track from Korti to Omdurman, outlying wells and oases were in possession of the Kababish and their allies who had broken away from Abdullah's tyranny. The whirligig of time had transformed the equality preachings, and "unity in the faith" of Mahdism into the unbridled supremacy of the Baggara and especially the Taaisha branch of that *sept* over all the people of the Sudan. They alone were licensed to rob, ravish and murder with impunity. It was the natural sequence of lawless society. Once the foe they leagued to plunder and kill had been disposed of, they turned and rent each other. Abdullah being a Taaisha, he, as a prop to his own pretensions, set them in authority over all the races of the Sudan. One by one, however, Arab clansmen and blacks repented and deserted Mahdism.

The time was ripe for ending the mad mutiny against government and civilisation. July is the period of high Nile in the upper reaches, and the Sirdar planned that his army should be ready to move forward by then. At that date all was in readiness. The Egyptian army which was to take the field consisted of one division of four brigades, each of four battalions with artillery, cavalry and camelry. Besides these there were two brigades of British infantry—Gatacre's division—a regiment of British cavalry, the 21st Lancers, and two and a half English batteries, with many Maxims. It was known that Abdullah had called into Omdurman all his best men and meant giving battle.

CHAPTER 2

Days of Waiting and Preparation

"Everything comes to him who waits," but the weariness of it is sometimes terrible. Oftentimes waiting is vain, without accompaniment of hard work. The Sirdar made deliberate choice to carve out a career in Egypt. He did so in the dark days when the outlook was the reverse of promising, in nearly every aspect, to a man of action. Abdication of our task of reconstruction was in the air, the withdrawal of the British army of occupation a much-talked-of calamity. Through every phase of the situation, Kitchener stuck to his guns, keeping to himself his plans for the reconquest of the Sudan. He wrought and watched while he waited, selecting and surrounding himself with able officers, and exacting from each diligence and obedience in the discharge of their duties. The Dongola campaign and the fortuitous one of the Atbara against Mahmoud greatly strengthened his position. There might be further delay, but his triumphal entry into Omdurman and the downfall of the Khalifa were certain. The Sirdar had but to ask, to receive all the material and men he wished for. He adhered to his early decision to employ only as many British troops as were actually necessary to stiffen the Khedivial army, and no more.

After the battle and victory of the Atbara in the spring, the British troops, or Gatacre's brigade, marched back from Omdabiya by easy stages to the Nile. The wounded and sick were conveyed into the base hospital at Dakhala, whence they were afterwards sent down to Ginenetta or, as it then was, Rail-head. From that point they were, as each case required, forwarded by train and steamboat to Wady Halfa and Cairo. It was at Darmali, 12 miles or more north of Dakhala, that the British soldiers went into summer-quarters. On the 14th of April the brigade mustered 3818 strong, made up as follows:—833 Camerons, 826 Seaforths, 969 Lincolns, and 665 Warwicks. Two companies of Warwicks had been left in the Dongola province when the advance was made. Besides the muster of battalions enumerated, the brigade included a Maxim battery, detachments of the Army Service Corps, and other details. The Tommies settled down in camp, living under peace conditions, for with the rout of Mahmoud's men, the nearest Dervish force worth considering was as far off as Shabluka Cataract. Everybody was bidden to make himself as snug as possible. Outlying houses and walls were thrown down to secure a free circulation of air. As for sunlight, that was shut out wherever practicable. The first home drafts to make up for losses arrived at Darmali on the 23rd of April. About 130 men then joined. It was thought desirable to maintain the British battalions at their full strength, and some of them mustered nearly one thousand strong. As the percentage of sick was continuous, and the rate increased as the campaign progressed, the actual roll of men "fit for duty" grew less as we neared Omdurman. Of course, "youths," and all the "weedy ones," were in the first instance rejected by the army doctors, and were never permitted to go to the front. Men over 25 years of age were preferred, and it so happened that both the Grenadier Guards and the Northumberland Fusiliers had a high average of relatively old soldiers, and consequently few sick. From the end of April until the end of May, dull hot days in the Sudan, leave was granted to officers to run down to Alexandria and have a "blow" at San Stefano, by the sea-side. There were quite a number of deaths in the brigade shortly after the men got into camp, the customary reaction having set in on account of the exposure and strain precedent to the victory of the Atbara. To reduce the numbers quartered at Darmali, the Lincolns and Warwicks, on the 19th of April, were marched a mile farther north along the Nile, to Es Selim, where they formed a separate encampment, the Camerons and Seaforths remaining at the first-named place. The average daily number of sick in the brigade at that period was 100 to 150. On one occasion there were 190 men reported unfit for duty. Most of the cases were not of a serious nature, and the patients speedily recovered and returned to their places in the ranks. There was no lack of stores and even dainties at the camps, for supplies were carried up by caravan, escorted by Jaalin friendlies, from Berber and elsewhere. Much of the sickness in the army was probably due to the men recklessly drinking unboiled and unfiltered Nile water. At that season the river had sunk into its narrowest bed, and there were backwashes and sluggish channels full of light-green tinted water. More filters were procured, and extra care was taken with all the water used for domestic purposes.

In May there were route marches twice a week, the brigade going off at 5.30 a.m. and returning about 7.30 a.m., all in the cool of the morning or such bearable temperature as there was in the 24 hours' daily round in that month. During these exercises the troops had plenty of firing practice, being taught to blaze away at bushes, and occasionally at targets representing Dervishes. In that way the remainder of the million of tip-filed Lee-Metford bullets were disposed of, for it had been arranged that there was to be a new cartridge case for the Omdurman campaign. The latest pattern "man-stopper" was a bullet fashioned with a hollow or crater at the point, the nickel casing being perforated.

So the days droned past for the British soldiers, with little to do beyond essaying the impossible of trying to keep cool. It was often otherwise with the Egyptians, for they had to assist in getting the railroad through to Dakhala from Ginenetta, in forwarding boats and stores, and later on in establishing wood stations and cutting fuel for the steamers. The first of the tropical summer rain showers fell at Darmali on the 27th of May. On the 18th of June Major-General Gatacre went off on a shooting excursion up the Atbara, taking with him a party of ten officers and a few orderlies. They found relatively little big game but plenty of gazelle and birds. The bodies of the slain in Mahmoud's *zereba* at Omdabiya still lay where they fell, unburied, but dried up and mummified by the sun. Natives had stripped the place and carried off everything left behind by us. A number of Dervishes were seen lurking about, part of the defeated army of the enemy, who were afraid to return to Omdurman, anticipating that the Khalifa would have them killed. Indeed, it appeared that numbers of the runaways had settled down at New Hilgi, and were attempting to cultivate. As for the four or five thousand Dervish cavalry that Mahmoud had with him, they also never returned to Omdurman. Quite probably they made their way back to their original homes in small bands, rightly believing that Mahdism was doomed. Assured of pardon and good treatment at our hands, fourteen of the Mahdists and a number of women came in with General Gatacre's people. No attempt was made by the Dervishes in the neighbourhood to "snipe" the party. They returned to Darmali on the 27th of June. With the sun gone north came the rising of the Nile and fresh breezes. The gunboats kept diligently patrolling the river, watching for any signs of movement on the part of the Khalifa and his forces. The enemy were reported to be gathering in large numbers at Omdurman for the coming conflict. As Shendy was held by a small force of Egyptians, and Metemmeh nominally by the Jaalin for us, frequent visits were made to those posts. Later on, other shooting parties went up to Omdabiya and found that there was an increase in the numbers of natives about, and that flocks and herds were to be seen grazing in the vicinity. The tribesmen showed that they had abandoned the Khalifa by tearing the Dervish patches off their clothing. All being quiet, and peace assured in the Dongola province, the two detached companies of the Warwickshire left Korti and joined their comrades in Es Selim camp.

July was a very busy month. The river flotilla and transport service had all to be thoroughly organised for the impending advance. Gunboats received the final touches and completed their armament. The steamers, barges and *giassas*, native sailing craft, underwent thorough repair. More and still more munitions of war and provisions were sent forward and stored at Dakhala. That post grew into a formidable camp. The three new twin-screw gunboats built on the Thames, besides other ship-work reconstruction, were put together near Abadia, a village above the Fifth Cataract and north of Berber. The railroad had been hastily laid and completed to Abadia after the battle of Atbara. Thither the sections of the barges and steamers needed for the campaign had been sent by rail from Wady Halfa. Before that date, engineering and other workshops had been erected at Abadia, which, because of its favourable position, was chosen for a permanent camp and industrial centre. Base-hospitals, too, were built there, in order that the wounded and sick might travel as far as possible by water. Astonishing as had been the rapidity with which the Wady Halfa Abu Hamid portion of the desert railroad was laid, smarter work still was done carrying the line through to the Atbara. The utmost energy was put forth, after the defeat of Mahmoud, by the Director of Railways, Major Girouard, R.E., to get the track completed to Dakhala, the junction of the Atbara with the Nile. Not only the railroad battalion, which was nearly 3000 strong, but every available Khedivial soldier, laboured in some way or other at the task. They put their hearts and thews to the toil, for it was recognised that its completion not only solved the transport problem, but was a swift and sure means of return to Egypt. The railroad battalion worked wonders in grading and laying. Fellaheen and negro, they showed a vim and intelligence in track-making that Europeans could not surpass. Native lads, some in their early teens, clothed with little beyond a sense of their own importance and "army ammunition boots," many sizes too big for their feet, adjusted the fish-plates and put on the screw nuts. Then, for those who bore the heavy burden of rails and sleepers and carried material for the road bed, there were licensed fools, mummers, and droll mimics, who by their antics revived the lagging spirits of the gangs. There is an unsuspected capacity for mimicry in what are called savage men. I have seen Red Indians give excellent pantomimic entertainments, and aborigines in other lands exhibit high mumming talent. In the railroad battalion there was an eccentric negro who was a very king of jesters. From the Sirdar and the Khalifa downwards—for he was an ex-Dervish and had played pranks in Omdurman—none escaped a parodying portrayal of their mannerisms. He imitated the tones of their voice and twisted and contorted his face and body to resemble the originals. Nothing was sacred from that mimic any more than from a sapper. He showed us Osman Digna's little ways, and gave ghastly imitations of trials, mutilations and executions by hanging in the Mahdist camps. And these things were for relaxation, though maybe they served as a reminder of the Dervishes' brutal rule. There were vexations and jokes of another sort for Major Girouard and those held tightly responsible for the rapid construction and regular running of the material trains, as indeed all trains were. When the line had been laid beyond Abu Dis, for a time known as Rail-head, the camp and quarters were moved on to the next station. Abu Dis sank in dignity and population until only a corporal and two men were left to guard the place and work the sidings. The desert railway being a single track, frequent sidings are indispensable for the better running of trains. All the control for working the system was vested in the Wady Halfa officials. One night there came to them over the wires an alarmist message to send no more trains to Abu Dis. It was the corporal who urgently rang up his chiefs. What could it mean? Had they deserted, or, more likely, were the Dervishes raiding the district? A demand was made from Wady Halfa for the corporal to explain what had happened. His answer was naive, if not satisfactory: "The wild beasts have come down from the hills, and we really cannot accept any trains from any direction."

"What do you mean?" was again queried back.

So the corporal and his two men responded: "Sir, there are wild beasts all around the hut and tent; what can we do? We dare not stir out."

"Light fires, you *magnoons*," (fools), was the final rejoinder, and the train service went forward as usual. It appeared that the hyenas and wolves, wont to snap up a living around the men's camp, bereft of their pickings were in a state of howling starvation, and had turned up and made an appeal, by no means mute, to the station guard, which the latter failed to understand or appreciate. In a remarkably short space of time the hyenas and pariah dogs had adopted the habit of scavengering around all the camps and sniffing along the track, after the trains, for stray scraps.

DARMALI (BRITISH BRIGADE SUMMER QUARTERS)

I returned to Cairo early in July, where, having paid into the Financial Military Secretary's hands the £50 security required of war correspondents, intended to cover cost of railway fares south of Wady Halfa, and for any forage drawn from the stores, I received the official permit to proceed to the front. All the restrictions as to the number of correspondents allowed up, which were imposed during the Atbara campaign, were singularly enough removed, and the "very open door" policy substituted. In consequence, there was a large number, over sixteen in all, of so-called representatives of the press at the front. As an old correspondent aptly observed, some of them represented anything but journals or journalism, the name of a newspaper being used merely as a cover for notoriety and medal hunting. Having secured my warrant to join the Sirdar's army, I started from Cairo for Assouan and Wady Halfa. The headquarters at that date were still in Wady Halfa. On the 21st of July the first detachments of the reinforcements that were to make up the British force to a division, which Major-General Gatacre was to command, left Cairo for the south. Thereafter, nearly day by day up to the 9th of August inclusive, troops were sent forward. These consisted of artillery, cavalry, the 21st Lancers, baggage animals, Royal Engineers, Army Service Corps, Medical Corps, and the four battalions of infantry which were to form the second British brigade. The brigade in question comprised 1st Battalion of the Grenadier Guards, the 1st Northumberland Fusiliers, the 2nd Lancashire Fusiliers, and the 2nd Battalion Rifle Brigade, together with a battery of Maxims manned by a detachment of the Royal Irish Fusiliers. Brigadier-General the Honourable N. G. Lyttelton, C.B., commanded the second brigade, whilst Major-General Gatacre's former command, the 1st British Brigade, was taken over by Brigadier-General J. Wauchope. The first brigade was made up of the Lincolns, Warwicks, Seaforths, and Camerons, with six Maxims. To prepare for eventualities, and clench the special training he had bestowed upon his men, Major-General Gatacre issued a printed slip of notes, or hints, to his men. I give the salient points of that production:

> 1. As the strength of a European force lies in the occupation of and in movement over open ground, which gives it advantage of fire, so the strength of a Dervish force lies in fighting in depressions of the ground, or in a jungle country out of which they can pour suddenly and quickly their thousands of spear-armed warriors, who, unless checked by a murderous fire, constitute a grave danger, even to a perfectly disciplined force.
> It follows, then, that a force halted for the night must always be protected where possible by a *zereba*, which will check under fire the attacking Dervishes.

2. That a cleared zone be prepared along outer edge of the *zereba*.

3. That a force, when moving, should march at a respectful distance from jungle cover.

4. It should have the ground in its front and on its flanks searched out by cavalry, mounted infantry, or native levies.

5. That when mounted troops have found the enemy, they must invariably clear the front of the infantry to enable the latter to use their rifles.

6. That brigades must be so trained that each battalion and individual soldier must know how to get into the best formation with the least possible delay for meeting the attack of the spearmen, who, it must be remembered, can move at least three times as quickly as a British soldier can double.

To carry out the above, a high standard of training and steadiness is required, and battalions must be provided with a liberal supply of cutting tools, felling axes, hand axes and bill hooks to enable them, the instant the battalion marches into bivouac, to cut down small trees or strong branches of prickly trees with which to construct a thorn fence.

Piquets must be withdrawn at dusk, otherwise they might get surrounded and cut off, or, in falling back, would possibly suffer from the defenders of the *zereba*.

The protection of the *zereba* against surprise must depend on the vigilance of its sentries and piquets which line the fence, and whose strength will naturally depend on the proximity of the Dervishes to the force. With reliable information, and the ground properly reconnoitred, a patrol of ten men per company, patrolling constantly and noiselessly along the inner edge of the *zereba*, is adequate, so long as the enemy's den is say 15 miles distant (a day's march); when nearer than this, the strength of the piquets to remain awake and under arms will depend upon the circumstances of the moment.

All night duties of this nature should be found by companies, so that portions of the line along its whole length shall be on duty. Words of command and orders must be given in a low tone; there must be no shouting and no fires burning till the hour arrives for making the morning tea. Men should always be allowed to smoke, but should be warned of the danger of fire in *zereba* by a cigarette or match-end thrown into dry grass.

Officers must sleep immediately behind their men; a certain number will always be on duty.

All, officers and men, must sleep in their clothes, boots and accoutrements, and each man must have his rifle with him. None but sentries' should be loaded, and bayonets should not be fixed, even by the patrols, except when there is expectancy of attack. Under no circumstances should men sleep with their bayonets fixed, or serious accidents will occur.

And here, one word about 'alarms.' I do not refer to the assembly by bugle sound, but what is ordinarily called a panic, in other words a disgraceful absence of discipline and self-control, which, while ruining the reputation of the corps concerned as a reliable battalion, may be the cause of serious mischief, and must be disastrous to the confidence the General Officer places in its officers and men.

One of the great advantages accruing to an army on service is the close association of the officer with the man; each learns something from the other, and the officer will, in after years, appreciate the value of the habit he gets into of talking to his men and of storing up in his mind all sorts of dodges and hints, which assist troops in the field to make themselves comfortable; more than this, it is in the field only that the officer can get the opportunity of instilling into the men's minds the necessity for deliberation under fire, the high standard of the regiment, its past history, its superiority in everything to all other regiments in the division, and his confidence in his men to maintain such a standard of excellence. In many expeditions it has happened that shots have been fired at nothing, night after night, thus disturbing the whole force; such bad habits must be firmly checked.

Before leaving Cairo I had the opportunity of witnessing a trial of the new siege guns that were to be used in levelling the walls and defences of Omdurman. To the eastward of Abbassieh barracks, near the rifle ranges, 150 feet of stone wall had been erected. It was a replica of part of the structure which the Khalifa had built around the tomb of the Mahdi, his own grounds, that of his body-guard, and the more important buildings situated in the centre of the Dervish capital.

The stout rectangular wall at Omdurman stood with its narrowest side facing the Nile, and its longest sides ran inland from the river for about a mile. It was twelve feet in height, and even more in places, ten feet in thickness at the base, tapering to six feet at the top. It was a well-made structure, laid in mortar and faced on either side with dressed limestone blocks.

Shortly after six a.m. on the morning of 22nd July, a large number of officers assembled at the Abbassieh ranges to watch the result of the experiments of the sham bombardment. Lieutenant-General Sir Francis Grenfell and staff, Major-General Lyttelton, and many others were present. It was arranged that the new 5-inch howitzer battery, with the Lyddite or high explosive shells, was to make the first attempt to breach or throw down the wall. There were six of these new howitzers, and they were worked by the 37th Field Battery, commanded by Major Elmslie. Except that the bore was larger, there was little to distinguish the pieces from the 15-lb. Maxim-Nordenfeldt automatic recoil guns used at the battle of the Atbara. The latter cannon, however, only used cordite, whereas the 5-inch howitzer shells are filled with a picric compound resembling M. Turpin's melinite. For over ten years Russia has had 100-lb. howitzer batteries in the field, firing high explosives. It was the Sirdar who insisted upon the necessity of being supplied with these light and handy cannon. Neither the velocity nor the range of their shell-fire is great, but it is enough—4000 yards or thereby—for all practical purposes, and is fairly accurate. The explosion of the picric shells was very violent, and the danger area about 300 yards from where they burst. It has been found that, with about six or eight mules to draw the guns, the battery was quite mobile. Egyptian drivers were employed, though the men serving the guns were all British artillerymen. Even the drivers of the 32nd Field Battery, commanded by Major Williams, had "gippy" teamsters. Both batteries were drawn by smart Cyprus mules. The howitzers opened fire at 750 yards from the wall. With few exceptions, the Lyddite shells hit the mark. Range is given more by increase or diminution of the charge than elevation or depression of the howitzers. The guns kicked viciously and ran back at each discharge. Bursting violently, the shells threw out big sheets of tawny flame, followed by showers of stones and a cloud of dust and brownish smoke. It was possible to see the missiles in their flight and note where they struck. As each shell rushed through the air it made a noise not unlike an express train passing under a bridge. There were salvoes of two or three guns, and huge chunks were knocked out of the wall. Pieces of flying debris frequently dropped at no great distance from the gunners. It was plain that the shells were bursting upon impact, and only blowing away the face of the wall to the depth of but a foot or two. Had there been thick shells with retarding fuses the structure might have been breached in two or three rounds.

After a preliminary ten rounds had been fired, the wall was closely inspected. It was seen that infantry might have clambered over the debris to the top of the structure and jumped down upon the other side. A strange feature was that wherever the "Lyddite" explosive failed to detonate the stones and ground around had been transformed to a deep chrome colour. The battery was moved closer, to about 350 yards from the wall, and the firing was recommenced at that range. Much better results were obtained, and the upper part of the wall was knocked away, and easy, practicable breaches made. One of the other advantages of these new guns is that with reduced firing charges they become reliable mortars, and the high explosive shells can be dropped over a wall or building, so as to drive the defenders from their works. Not a man would have escaped injury had there been an enemy behind the wall, for blocks of stone were scattered in all directions. When the howitzers had finished their practice, six rounds were fired from two 40-lb. Armstrong guns, which were also ordered to assist in breaching Omdurman's walls. Next to the 7-lb. screw guns the 40-lb. Armstrong is reputed to be the most accurate shooting cannon in the British service. Mounted on lofty carriages, these siege guns were laid to fire at 800 yards range. Oddly enough, one of the 40-lbs. scored as high a percentage of misses as the howitzers. The great velocity of the 40-lb. shells, filled with the slower-bursting gunpowder, carried them well into the part of the wall aimed at, with the result that, in a few seconds, they made a good breach. The morning's experiments were concluded by a detachment of the Royal Irish Fusiliers, under Captain Churches, firing their Maxims against targets representing bands of Dervishes, the dummy enemy being, as usual, riddled with bullets.

From Cairo to Dakhala, evidence was not lacking that the form and movement of preparations for the general advance were growing apace. Every train and boat going south was overloaded with officers, men, and transport animals, together with munitions of war galore for the campaign. The gunboats and deserters brought in reports that the Dervishes were concentrating at Omdurman. The strongly defensible positions of Shabluka, together with the mud forts, had been evacuated by the Dervishes. Very quickly the Sirdar sent small bodies of troops up stream to occupy suitable positions for wood-cutting and forming advance camps. In that way the river pass at the Sixth Cataract was seized without the long anticipated fight for that difficult bit of country. The Nile highway was at length in the Sirdar's undisputed possession up to within thirty miles of Omdurman.

There is no dustier journey by rail, or one of an altogether more uncomfortable nature, than from Cairo to Shellal. It is bad enough in the so-called winter season, for you have to breathe an atmosphere of dust the whole way, and are powdered and almost suffocated before you reach Luxor. The same trip taken in midsummer, in the stuffy, crowded carriages of the Egyptian lines, is real martyrdom, or something akin thereto. High speed or over twenty-five miles an hour is not attempted. Although the journey ordinarily occupies thirty-two hours, I was forty hours *en route*. There are no refreshment-bars or restaurants for the supply of palatable food or drink for the fierce needs of the passengers. I made some provision for the trip, and managed to survive it, as I have done before, but I cannot forget its tortures any more than the newest of new-comers. Not until we reached Assouan could we secure a fair supply of water and get a bath and an enjoyable meal. That same afternoon, I, with three other correspondents, was allowed to take passage on barge No. 9, which, with two *giassas*, was taken in tow up to Wady Halfa by a sternwheeler. Among others proceeding on the craft to join the army were Major-General Wauchope and Surgeon-General Taylor, and a number of other army medicos, fresh in their new dignity as officers of the "Royal Army Medical Corps." Under the instruction of Surgeon-General Taylor, Surgeon-Major Wilson was good enough to present each of us with a packet of first field dressings, a kindness which I appreciated, but of which I hoped not to have need.

GROUP OF STAFF OFFICERS—COLONEL WINGATE IN CENTRE

CHAPTER 3

Mustering for the Overthrow of Mahdism

A hackneyism lacks the picturesqueness of originality, but is as useful in its way as a public road to a desired destination. The quotation which I am at the moment anxious to make use of is, "The mills of the gods grind slowly, but they grind exceedingly small." Time the avenger had all but fulfilled the meed of punishment for the evil day of 26th January 1885, when the streets of Khartoum ran with blood, and the headless body of General Gordon was left to be hacked and hewn by ferocious hordes of Dervishes. Major-General Sir Herbert H. Kitchener had so managed that the decisive blow should be delivered in the most effective manner. Stage by stage he had moved forward and improved his lines of communication. The advanced base, or point of departure for the campaign, was no longer Wady Halfa, or Korti in the province of Dongola, as in 1884, but Dakhala. Nay, with the unassailable power and command of the Nile his flotilla gave him, it might be said the real base of the Sirdar's army was where he chose to fix it, even hard by Omdurman. As for the Khalifa, ruined to some extent by years of successes and easy victories, he was committing the fatal military error of over-confidence. He had drawn around him from all parts of the Sudan the best of his trusty warriors, the pick of the fighting tribes of Africa. The leaders were mostly sheiks who were too far committed to hope for pardon and restoration, in the event of defeat, from the Khedivial Government. Besides, there were still plenty of ignorant fanatics amongst the chosen *Ansar*, or servants of God, to fire the naturally truculent mass of armed men.

To ensure the smashing of the Mahdists, the Sirdar was leading the largest and best equipped expedition ever seen south of Wady Halfa. The river flotilla comprised eleven well-armed steam gunboats. For the transport of troops and stores beyond Dakhala he had numberless native craft, *giassas*, *nuggars*, several steamers, and specially constructed iron barges. What with their crews and detachments of British gunners, engineers, and infantry, each gunboat had a fighting force of about 100 men aboard. These vessels could easily have carried many more hands; indeed, the newest type of Nile men-o'-war, the twin-screw steamers, were built to convey a thousand soldiers. The land forces included over 8000 British troops and fully 15,000 Egyptian and Sudanese soldiery. In artillery the army was exceptionally strong. Lieut.-Colonel C. J. Long, R.A., commanding that arm, had practically eight batteries and ten Maxims at his disposal, not counting the machine guns, Maxims, attached to the British division. The artillery included the 32nd Field Battery R.A. of six 15-pounders under Major Williams; the 37th Field Battery R.A. of six 5-inch howitzers under Major Elmslie, and two 40-pounders R.A. Armstrong guns under Lieut. Weymouth. There were also, No. 1 Egyptian Horse Artillery Battery (Krupps) under Major Young, R.A., of six guns; No. 2 Egyptian Field (mule) Battery under Major Peake, consisting of six 12½-pounder Maxim-Nordenfeldt automatic recoil guns, firing when necessary a double shell, and Egyptian Field Batteries Nos. 3, 4, and 5, each of six of the same type of guns, under Captain C. G. Stewart, R.A., Major Lawrie, R.A., and Major de Rougemont, R.A., and two 6-centimetres Krupps on mules. The ten Maxims, or at least six of them, were mounted upon galloping carriages drawn by horses. On these vehicles or limbers the gunners could remain in position and bring the weapons into action at any moment. Captain Franks had the control of these machine guns, two of which were, nominally, attached to each Egyptian battery. Besides the four brigades of Khedivial infantry, together with artillery, cavalry, and camelry, and minor details, the Egyptian army also included a large transport column of some 2800 camels and about as many men.

A new solar-hat, a poke-bonnet sort of head-gear, was designed and tied on the pates of one thousand transport camels as an experiment to prevent sickness and sunstroke. Although the brutes have the smallest modicum of brains, they are very liable to attacks of illness from heat-exhaustion. That they are born in the tropics confers no immunity. Strange to say, on the march south from Assouan, of a thousand and odd only one animal succumbed to sunstroke, and that was a camel that had no sun-bonnet. If anything could have added to the naturally lugubrious expression of those lumbering freight carriers, it was the jaunty poke-bonnets with the attenuated "Oh, let us be joyful" visages grinning beneath. The transport department was managed by Colonel F. W. Kitchener, brother of the Sirdar. His care it was, when the army actually took the field, to see that the supplies of food, forage, and ammunition advanced with the columns. As a matter of fact, in that respect the campaign, as at the Atbara, was admirably ordered, and the troops lacked for nothing in reason. There were few mules and donkeys employed in the baggage trains, the bulk of the stores being camel-borne. It was the free and full use of water transport, by the Nile, that enabled supplies to be sent on rapidly and regularly with the army when the troops advanced beyond Rail-head. Besides the regular army which was to proceed up the left or west bank and attack Omdurman, there was a column of armed friendlies who were to operate against the Dervishes quartered between Shendy and Khartoum, by the east or right bank of the Nile. Nor were the bands of tribesmen upon that shore the only auxiliaries who had volunteered to assist in overthrowing Mahdism. Jaalin scouts and runners put themselves under the Sirdar's orders to scour the front and flanks of the army, at least up to Kerreri. Colonel Parsons,

R.A., was to lead a mixed force of *fellaheen* soldiers, Abyssinian levies, ex-Italian Ascari, and Arabs from Kassala to attack Gedarif and menace Khartoum from the east.

There was a degree of soreness in several British battalions at not being allowed to bear part in the campaign. The troops forming the Army of Occupation believed that they should have had the first call. Among these were the Royal Irish Fusiliers. It had been anticipated that as they were next on the army list for active foreign service, they would certainly not be passed over. Instead of receiving orders to march, they were left severely alone, another Fusilier battalion being sent in their place. The proceeding gave rise to much bickering and bitterness in certain quarters. An attempt, I believe, was made to send half of the Royal Irish Fusiliers to the front, but that fell through owing to various causes. According to the War Office requirements, the Royal Irish Fusiliers were not in a satisfactory condition. There were serious drawbacks which would have terribly militated against the effective employment of the battalion as a first-class fighting unit. Individually, the men were all right, but the battalion record in certain respects was held to be very faulty. I have no wish to cavil at the War Office authorities' honest desire to serve the public and yet temper their judgment with mercy to individuals. But the case was one where they should not have temporised in any way. As matters turned out, the Royal Irish Fusiliers were very angry at being passed over at the eleventh hour for another regiment. For several generations they have never had a chance of being in action. They were fairly spoiling for a fight, and it was hard, at the last moment, to have the road to glory closed in their faces for the deficiencies of the few.

He whom Arabs and blacks of the whole Sudan call the "Grand Master of the Art of Flight," our old friend Osman Digna, was with the Khalifa in Omdurman. Osman was wily and experienced, and his counsel, had it been listened to by his chief, would have added to the difficulties of carrying the Mahdist stronghold by assault. I have some knowledge of that astute ex-slavedealer and trader's ways in the Eastern Sudan and elsewhere. He, many years ago, even condescended to honour me with his correspondence and an invitation to join the true believers, *i.e.*, the Mahdists. I have no doubt he meant well, but the land and the Dervishes were alike abhorrent to me. Osman had quietly come to the wise conclusion that Mahdism was near its end. With his usual prescience he made his own arrangements without consulting the Khalifa. Early in the year he had all his women and children and such wealth as he could smuggle out of the country sent over to Jeddah. There his family are now living under the protection of some of his old friends and kinsmen. When Omdurman fell he had no intention, the Hadendowas said, of sharing the Khalifa's further fortunes in hiding among the wilds of Kordofan. He would instead try and escape across the Red Sea and rejoin his family. The Arab clansmen are like the Hielan' *caterans*; they may fight and quarrel with one another, but unless there is a blood feud it is unlikely they will help either the English or the Egyptians to bag old Osman Digna. If the Turk gets him for a subject, well, the Sublime Porte is likely to be deeply sorry for it later on. "Fresh troubles in Yemen," or elsewhere in the Arabian Peninsula, will be amongst the headlines of news from that quarter once Osman the plotter finds his feet again after his last flight. After the Atbara he just missed being taken by the skin of his teeth, so to speak. His camp letters and private correspondence were all secured. It was in this way: When the news of the Atbara victory reached Kassala, Captain Benson and a party of about 200 Abyssinian irregulars set out to see whether Osman Digna and his more immediate followers were not trying to make their way back to Omdurman, via Aderamat and Abu Delek. It may be recollected that the fugitive Shiekh had established a camp at the last-named place after he had been driven out of the Eastern Sudan. Sure enough, Captain Benson and the irregulars came up with Osman Digna and 400 of his people encamped near the Atbara. They called on them to surrender, but that they would not do. A running fight began, in the course of which Osman, his nephew Mousa and many more escaped. The Abyssinians, however, killed and captured over 200 of the Dervish leader's followers, and returned in triumph with the captives and spoils. I am told that Mousa Digna, though he watched the fight in question, never fired a shot. The tale goes, that he has never drawn sword or trigger against us since we gave him his life at the battle of Gemaizeh, near Suakin. That morning I found Mousa, shot through the stomach, reclining upon the ground. He was still truculent, and brandishing his spear. The Sudanese were anxious to despatch him forthwith, and fired several shots at him, the aim of which I spoiled by direct interference. I had even then difficulty in getting Mousa to lie down quietly, having to show him my revolver. Finally, he partly realised the situation. He was taken up, carried into Suakin, carefully attended to, fed upon a milk diet, and, in the end, recovered and returned to his Uncle Osman and the Dervishes. It has always been upon my mind that I was therein instrumental in furnishing a Dervish recruit to the cause of furious anarchy, and I am relieved to think Mousa is not without compunction, if not a decent modicum of conscience. But your proper Hadendowa is not a Baggara.

"Three removals are worse than a fire," and it is much the same in campaigning. Constant trudging to and fro, making and breaking camps with the hardships of marches and raw ground for bivouacs, furnish a bigger mortality bill than an ordinary battle. One of the smart things done by the Sirdar, which served to show that he had closely knit all the ends of the new frontier lines together, was to bring troops up from the Dongola province and the Red Sea Littoral, to swell the strength of his army in the field. The 5th Egyptian battalion under Colonel Abd El Borham marched across from Suakin to Berber in eighteen days. It was not by any means sought to make it a forced march. The Fifth was accompanied by a company, 100 men and animals, of the Camel Corps and had 40 baggage camels for ordinary transport. Leisurely, day by day, they tramped along over the 250 odd miles of rock and sand that intervene betwixt the Nile and the sea. Hadendowa and Bishaim tribesmen were friendly, and scouts led them in the best tracks whether they tramped by night or by day. At one place they had to make a long forced march as the water in the wells had been exhausted by a previous caravan. In time to come, with a little outlay, new wells will be dug and an abundant supply of water provided along the whole route. Later on, the 5th Egyptian battalion marched up from Berber to Dakhala camp. The men were tall, muscular *fellaheen*. They were, as has become the custom in Egypt since the army has been officered by the Queen's soldiers, played into quarters on this occasion by a native Sudanese band to the swinging tune of "O, den Golden Slippers."

It is warm enough in Lower Egypt in July to be uncomfortable, and to turn the most obdurate into a melting mood. Assouan has the deserved reputation of being hotter in that month than Aden, the Persian Gulf, or—well, any other hot place. So, as I have said before, the British troops were not required to do more than the minimum of duty at that period. Decidedly "circumstances alter cases," even in matters military. I hope I may be pardoned for these recurring quotations and saws. The intolerably fervent solar heat of the Sudan at that season did not admit of much originality in thought, expression, or act. One of my companions was a veritable modern Sancho Panza, and in one's limp, mental, noontide condition his sapient *instances* were catching. When he left Cairo, as he confided to me, though it was warm enough there, he decided not to buy too thin clothing lest he might catch cold. He therefore purchased articles that even in England would be called woolly and comfortable. Later on, as he reclined upon his couch in a thrice-raised Turkish bath temperature, he lamented that he "could not catch cold" even in a state of nature or next to it. He no longer wondered at Sydney Smith's wish to sit in his bones, and thought that expression would have acquired additional force if the witty divine had added "packed in ice."

CHAPTER 4

By the Way—
From Cairo to Dakhala

Ten days from London to the junction of the Atbara with the Nile: so far from England and yet so near. By-and-by, no doubt, the Brindisi mail, speeding in connection with the Khartoum express, will make the run in seven or eight days. From England to Port Said is now but a matter of four days by the new Peninsular and Oriental service. It took me six days from Cairo to reach Dakhala. The officials prefer to know the place as "Atbara Camp." There is no absolute rule for the bestowal of proper names, or at least no practice one need care about in the Sudan, so I prefer to dub the locality by its native title of Dakhala, or Dakhelha. It saves a word in telegraphing, and there is more fitness in calling that dusty, dirty enclosure by the less euphonious name.

One could not but note what a wondrous change in the military and political situation had been wrought in the land since 1884-85. Railways had solved every difficulty of dealing with the Dervishes. Quite easily nowadays the remote provinces of the whilom great Egyptian equatorial empire can be reached and governed. With ordinary care under the altered conditions millions of Arabs and blacks can be transformed from chronic-rebellious into trusty loyal subjects. There has been blood-guiltiness and to spare in the Sudan since 1883-84, therefore the rehabilitation of the country through the setting up of just government will be in the nature of discharging a duty long incumbent upon Great Britain. From the Atbara southward, the Niles and their tributaries are open to steam navigation the year round. The possession of these noble waterways, which extend over thousands of miles, includes the fee-simple of sovereignty in the fertile lands of the two Nile basins and their commerce. By admirable foresight and indomitable Anglo-Saxon persistence the Sirdar had achieved a unique position in African conquest. He had got together an armed force "fit to go anywhere and to do anything." The heart of Africa was his, to loose or to bind. Of all the terrible railway rides in the world, for dirt and discomfort, none compares with the trip from Cairo to Luxor and Assouan. The carriages are stuffy and unclean, and during the whole journey one stifles in an opaque atmosphere of grit mixed with the sweepings of the ages. The calcined earths quickly cushion the seats, powder you from head to foot, and fill your pockets and every other receptacle with soil enough to make you feel like a landed proprietor—or, at any rate, rich enough in loam to lay out a suburban garden. With all the accessories at hand for the creation of an acrid and measureless thirst, neither the railway authorities nor private enterprise have had the wit as yet to provide travellers with the means of mitigating their sufferings. It is little short of a horror to think of that journey of over forty hours' duration, which had to be endured without the succour to be found in a refreshment-room where, for a consideration, could be got a sparkling cool drink or a mouthful of passable victuals. Were it to take me a month to travel the distance by river, if time permitted I had rather adventure next time upon the Nile than ever go by train over that line again. I confess I have made the journey by rail frequently but it becomes really more unendurable each trip. Of course I laid in stores of liquids and solids for the voyage. I ought to have known better, but one thinks nothing of the toothache when it is past. The mineral waters became too hot to drink, and not quite near enough the boiling-point to make good tea of, whilst, as for the provisions, such as got not too high, were so swathed in layers of questionable dust and grit as to be repulsive. Keeping even passably tidy was impossible, and in personal cleanliness a London scavenger could give a traveller by rail from Cairo to Assouan many points. It was at Wady Halfa that I got booked in the way-bill for Dakhala, or Atbara Camp, 390 miles away. The construction of the Halfa-Atbara line was, as I have said before, a masterpiece of military strategy, the credit for which is due to the Sirdar. By-and-by a railway bridge will span the Atbara at Dakhala, and the iron way will be laid into Khartoum. The 170 miles betwixt the Atbara and Khartoum offer no difficulties, and the line will be laid within a year from the time when the money is granted the Sirdar for its construction.

Since the foregoing was written, the requisite amount has been voted Lord Kitchener of Khartoum, and the contracts for material have been issued and signed. About a quarter of a million sleepers have to be delivered in Egypt before the end of June 1899. The Atbara and forty small *khors* will be bridged, and the work be completed in twelve months. It is intended that the terminus shall be on the east bank opposite Khartoum.

All the trains on the Halfa-Atbara line carried goods, ordinary passengers being incidental. Four of my colleagues, Major Sitwell, of the Egyptian army, and myself got places in a horse-box. In the next truck to us, likewise a horse-box, were five English officers, returning to duty with Gatacre's, or rather Wauchope's, brigade at Darmali. In that same horse-box truck we five contrived to cook, eat, sleep, and dress for two round days, for, as I have stated, there were no restaurants or buffets within 1000 miles of the desert railway. The wayside stations were but sidings or halting-places where the locomotives drew coal and water, of which small supplies were usually stored under an Egyptian corporal's guard. Ours was a long and heavy train, and more than once on the upgrade to No. 6 or Summit station out from Halfa the engine came to a standstill, "to recover its breath," as the negroes said. In the horse-box we got along together for the most part very comfortably, accommodating ourselves to the situation. Such a picnic as we had then made it less of a puzzle to the common understanding how certain creatures are able to do with a tight-fitting shell for their house and home. If Major Girouard, R.E., had not left the direction of the Sudan military railways—which under the Sirdar he built—to join the Board of the Egyptian lines, we should, I believe, have had better provision made for passengers. *Ziehs*, or porous native clay-jars to hold cool drinking water, and various other little accessories to lighten the hardships of the trip would surely have been provided. Later on, the officials took care to have *ziehs* and plenty of cool drinking water in the carriages and trucks of all trains carrying troops, so that the men had at least plenty to drink.

On our way up we passed Wauchope's brigade encamped at Es Selim and Darmali. Colonel Macdonald's 1st and Colonel Maxwell's 2nd Khedivial Brigades started to march from Berber to Dakhala about that time, the end of July. Many of the British soldiers, so as not to sleep upon the ground, had built for themselves benches of mud or sun-dried bricks, whereon they spread their blankets. The plan secured some immunity from such crawling things as scorpions and snakes. Sun-baked mud in the Sudan is a hard and decently clean material for bench or bed. The Theatres Royal, Darmali and Es Selim, were in full swing, though it was very 'dog-days' weather. Officers liberally patronised the men's entertainments and occasionally held jollifications of their own. There were a good many who exercised the cheerful spirit of Mark Tapley under the trials of the Sudan. Lively and original skits and verses were given at these symposiums. Here are a few verses of a topical song on the refractory blacks and *fellaheen* fallen under the condemnation of either the civil or military law and forced to hard labour. It was written and frequently sung by a clever young engineer officer:—

> We're convicts at work in the Noozle,
> We carry great loads on our backs,
> And often our warders bamboozle,
> And sleep 'neath mountains of sacks.

Chorus: *Ri-tooral il looral, &c.*

(The *Noozle* is the commissariat depot.)

We convicts start work at day dawning,
Boilers we mount about noon,
Sleepers we load in the morning,
And rails by the light of the moon.

Our warders are blacks, who cry Masha! (march),
And strike us if we don't obey,
Or else he's a Hamla Ombashi,
Who allows us to fuddle all day.

Hamla Ombashi is a corporal of the transport service, and "fuddle" is to sit down. It was the chorus with spoken words interlarded that caught on astonishingly, and showed that the men's lungs were in magnificent condition. Another howler, but by another author, was "Roll on to Khartoum." Here is a specimen verse and the chorus:—

Come, forward march, and do your duty,
Though poor your grub, no rum, bad 'bacca,
Step out, for fighting and no booty,
To trace a free red line thro' Africa.
No barney, boys, give over mousing,
True Britons are ye from hill and fen,
Now rally lads, and drop all grousing,
And pull together like soldier-men.

Chorus
Then roll on, boys, roll on to Khartoum,
March ye and fight by night or by day,
Hasten the hour of the Dervishes' doom,
Gordon avenge in old England's way.

"Grousing" is Tommy Atkins for grumbling, which is an Englishman's birthright. As for no rum, subsequently the men were allowed two tots a week; Wednesdays and Saturdays were, I think, the days of issue. Less than half a gill was each man's share.

I am inclined to believe had there been a daily issue of the same quantity of rum it had been better, and the young soldiers might have escaped with less fever.

Dakhala had undergone many changes since March. It was bigger in every respect, but no better as a camping-ground. Truth to tell, it was so bad as to be well-nigh intolerable. The correspondents' quarters were exceptionally vile, the location being the worst possible within the lines. We had no option, and so had to pitch our tents behind the *noozle* in a ten-acre waste of dirtiest, lightest loam, which swished around in clouds by day and night, making us grimy as coal-heavers, powdering everything, even our food and drink, with gritty dust and covering us in our blankets inches deep. The river breeze was barred from us, and the green and fresher banks of the Atbara and the Nile, beyond the fort, were for other than correspondents' camps. Many rows of mud huts had been built in the interior. As for the sun-dried brick parapets and ramparts of the fortifications, these were already crumbling to ruin or being cast down for use in newer structures. The lofty wooden lookout staging, called the Eiffel Tower, had been removed, and its timbers converted to other purposes. On the completion of the railway to Dakhala, Abadia had become but a secondary workshop centre. Newer and larger shipbuilding yards and engine works were erected by the Atbara. Under Lieutenant Bond, R.N., and Mr Haig gun-boats, steamers, barges and sailing craft were put in thorough order, native artisans toiling day and night. The clang of hammer-men, riveters, carpenters and caulkers resounded along the river front. The Dakhala *noozle* was an immense depot, stuffed full of grain, provisions, ammunition boxes, ropes, wires, iron, medical stores and other material, like one of the great London docks. As usual the indefatigable Greek trader had adventured upon the scene. North of the fortified lines, with the help of the natives he had run up a mud town. It consisted of a double row of one-storeyed houses, between which ran a street of nearly 300 yards. The place, known as the bazaar, was a hive of stores, wretched cafés, and the like. As the Sirdar had had all the beer and liquor in the place seized and put under seal before the advent of Mr T. Atkins, there was little to be had in Dakhala bazaar besides a not too pure soda-water, coffee, sardines, beans, maccaroni, oil, tobacco and matches.

STREET IN DAKHALA

For six weeks southerly winds blew almost daily. South of 17 degrees, the northerly breeze does not commence to blow before the end of August. It was warm, extremely warm, under the burning tropical sun. The heat bore down like a load upon head and shoulders and enveloped us like a blast from a roaring furnace. About noontide it was ordinarily 120 degrees Fahr. in my tent. Still, I am sure it was by no means so oppressive as at Korti in March 1885. The Atbara and the Nile helped to temper the fiery glow that radiated from the desert rocks and sands. At best, the heat is a sore trial, but to be borne with more patience than the "devils" and sand storms that bother by night as well as by day. Snow-drifts are mild visitations of Providence compared with a dust storm or whirlwind. These latter would smother you, if you would let them, quicker and less respectably than a shroud of snow. Jack Frost bites mildly, preferring to do his serious work by dulling the nerves; but the Dust Devil is a cruel tormentor from first to last. You may bury your head in folds of cloth and mosquito netting, and sweat and stifle in the attempt, but he snuffs you and powders you all the same. He puffs his finest clouds in your face, and round and round you till you find bedding and clothing are no more protection against him than they are against the Roentgen ray. One particular night he came in great strength to Dakhala, heaped waves of sand over us, dug great hollows around our quarters, and completed his diabolical games by completely overturning two of my colleagues' tents. I saw my friends emerge from the ruins of canvas, bedding, and boxes, wild, half-clad, terra-cotta figures, such as may have escaped from the destruction of Pompeii. But the human mind is a curious thing. It does not acknowledge defeat easily, and so a victim said to me he had pulled his tent down to keep it from falling. The Dust Devil had nothing to do with it.

Early in August the situation assumed a peculiar interest to us of the fourth estate. We were told that the troops were shortly going forward to rendezvous at Nasri Island, whereas it was a matter of notoriety that Wad Habeshi, which was further south, had been selected as the advanced camp for the army on leaving Dakhala. Of course, not one word of the true state of matters were we permitted to wire home. Detachments, true enough, had been sent ahead to "cut wood" and set up a camp upon Nasri Island. But that was merely to have a secure secondary depot and hospital station. It had been ascertained after the occupation of Shendy that the Dervishes were in no great strength at Shabluka or the Sixth Cataract. They occasionally sent down about a thousand Baggara horsemen to that place, and their riders scouted around the bluff rocks and hills bordering the Nile on either side of the *bab*, or water-gateway and rapids of Shabluka. As a rule, only about two hundred of them ever crossed to the east bank. The others hung around on the west bank, and built low walls for riflemen and dug a number of trenches and then returned to Omdurman. A few hundred only remained to guard the forts and the narrow fairway. Much labour had been expended and considerable rude skill shown by the enemy in building bastions and other defensive works at various places on the river,—particularly in the Shabluka gorge and before Omdurman. Why the Khalifa committed the blunder of making no adequate preparation for defending the pass at Shabluka it is difficult to understand. Only one conclusion suggests itself. He was probably afraid to trust his followers so far from his sight, lest the negroes should desert. We continually heard from our own blacks that most of Abdullah's *jehadieh* Soudani riflemen would come over to us the first chance they got. Major-Generals Hunter and Gatacre, having learned that the Dervish infantry had been withdrawn from Shabluka, scouted south up to the cataract and selected Wad Habeshi as a suitable camp and rendezvous. That village, or rather district, is on the west bank, south of Nasri Island and but fifteen miles north of Shabluka.

A big *zereba* was made at Wad Habeshi and trenches were dug. The place, in short, long before the British troops stirred south beyond Dakhala, was turned into a fortified post and made the real rendezvous of the Sirdar's army.

TROOPS GOING TO WAD HABESHI

On 2nd August, in the face of a strong south wind, the 1st and 2nd Khedivial brigades, respectively Colonel Macdonald's and Colonel Maxwell's, embarked in very close order on steamers and *giassas* for Wad Habeshi. The distance was about 140 miles by water from Dakhala, but it took the gunboats and their tows over three days to get there, for the craft were deeply ladened with men and stores. The soupy whirling Nile flood washed the decks of the steamers almost from stem to stern. It was little short of the rarest good fortune there was no accident by the way. Everybody turned out to see the brigades off. Merrily stepped the black battalions, their women-folk raising the usual shrill cry of jubilation, whilst the bands played the favourite air, "O, dem Golden Slippers." Regimental bands do droll things occasionally. I remember in the year of the Dongola Campaign and the cholera visitation, 1896, a grim blunder made by a native battalion's band. The serious surroundings of those days led me to say nothing of the matter at that time. Military interments, in cholera cases, were ordinarily made very early in the morning or late in the afternoon, just before sunset. A popular native Egyptian officer fell a victim to the epidemic one afternoon. The sun had but set when the funeral party, headed by the full regimental band, were seen hastening towards the cemetery, for there was no time to lose. The tune actually being played was not the "Dead March in Saul" but "Up I came with my little lot." When the gunboats started up the Nile for Wad Habeshi, towing alongside barges and *giassas*, all the crafts crammed with men and stores, more than one of the *fellaheen* battalions were regaled with the full strains of "'E dunno were 'e are."

By the end of July the Egyptian cavalry—nine squadrons—under Colonel Broadwood, with the camel corps under Major Tudway, the horse artillery and one or two batteries, had been ferried across from Dakhala to the west bank. On the 4th of August the whole of the mounted force named, about 2000 strong, started to march along the bank to Wad Habeshi. Going along the bank means, at high Nile, leading the troops upon a course half to a full mile from the river so as to avoid creeks and overflows and, at same time, secure the advantage of moving upon the more open ground beyond the zone of cultivation, out upon the edge of the bare desert. It was also early in August that the last of the fourteen double-decked iron barges, designed for the conveyance of troops, was finished at Dakhala. Except the surplus and reserve stores everything was put to instant service. As good a march in its way, if not better in some respects than that of the 5th Egyptian battalion from Suakin to Berber, was the tramp of the 17th Egyptian—also a *fellaheen* regiment—from Merawi to Dakhala. They made a record rapid tramp, following the Nile, up to Dakhala.

At Dakhala I frequently saw and conversed with the Sirdar, Generals Rundle and Gatacre, Colonels Wingate and Slatin Pasha. There seemed no reason to doubt but that the Khalifa would remain at Omdurman and give us a fight. Abdullah the Taaisha gave out as widely as he could that he meant actual business and dying if necessary at the Mahdi's tomb. His women-folk had not then been sent away, and that looked promising for battle. We heard that he was building more stout walls and digging numberless trenches for defence. Of ammunition for small arms and his ordinary brass rifled guns we were told he had no lack. For the three or four excellent batteries of Krupps he possessed he had but sixty rounds per cannon—enough, with good common and shrapnel shell, had he made right use of his means, to have made matters unpleasant for us until our gunners and Maxims found the range. It was regarded as doubtful whether he would be able to employ any of the machine guns in the Dervish armoury. Of all Gordon's "penny steamers" only one, it was said, was serviceable, and she was kept under steam night and day at Omdurman.

Though he kept a bold front, blustered, and promised his adherents no end of good things, and told them that, as in 1884-85, it was God's will to turn the English back at the eleventh hour, Khalifa Abdullah was truly in a parlous state. With all the Sirdar's care, we could not keep from the Dervish leader the extent of our preparations or forwardness for the advance. As usual, Sir Herbert Kitchener was well ahead of the time planned for moving on. We learned that, bar unforeseen accidents and delays, the whole of his army would be in front of Omdurman in a little over one month from the 1st of August. Two dates in September were given for the fall of that stronghold. It turned out to be neither. Kordofan had become openly rebellious against the Khalifa. A caravan of over 1140 people, with women, children and cattle marching overland, had arrived from that remote region at Korti in the Dongola province. The multitude, who were accompanied by many influential sheikhs flying from Mahdist misrule, sent a deputation to the Sirdar asking his assistance to take and hold El Obeid. As if that were not enough in the way of shutting the door behind the Khalifa, sheikhs came down from the Blue Nile provinces, seeking protection. Help was given to them, and bodies of friendlies were got together to seize Senaar and other important places. The Nile was running very swift and full in August, the current moving at fully six miles an hour past Dakhala. In July the Atbara, which had again begun slowly to flow, suddenly rose, the muddy water roaring along in a series of terraced wave-walls. Its 300-yards wide bed, where it joined the Nile, was within a few minutes choked with the tawny flood up to nearly the top of the 30-foot banks on either side. Bursting into the Nile the sea of soup seemed to push its way in a well-defined stream nearly across the 1200-yards broad bosom of the Father of Waters.

The first half of the 2nd Battalion of the Rifle Brigade arrived on the 2nd of August at Dakhala, during a blustering dust-storm. For all that, black and travel-stained, they were glad to detrain, and to plod through the sand, and breast the laden atmosphere, in order to get into camp hard by the Atbara. The following day the remainder of the battalion marched in under somewhat pleasanter conditions. Everybody turned out to cheer the smart, soldierlike detachments. On the 6th inst. the first half of the 1st Battalion Grenadier Guards arrived, and later on the remainder. The Sirdar and Generals Rundle and Gatacre, and the staffs went to greet them. A finer and more stalwart body of troops was never seen in the Sudan. Native opinion was more than favourable respecting them, and I heard observations on all sides that the Khalifa had no men he could set against them. The Sirdar and General Gatacre also expressed themselves much pleased with the appearance of the Grenadiers, who looked like seasoned soldiers and came in without a sick man in their ranks.

CHAPTER 5

Dakhala Camp: Gossip and Duty

Dirt is the essence of savagery, and there is a superfluity of both in the Sudan. I have no desperate wish so to describe the vileness of the surroundings of the correspondents' camp at Dakhala that even casual thinkers will sniff at it. The place was bad enough in all conscience, and, mayhap, therein I have said all that is necessary. As for the worry of our lives, squatted as we were in the least agreeable quarter of the big rectangular fort, long will the memory of those days and nights burden our existence. What a time I had on those sand and dust heaps, where every puff of wind and every footfall raised clouds of pulverised cosmos. For two weeks, amid the wretched scene, hideous by night as by day, I persisted in existing. It was a huge pen with men, horses, camels, donkeys, dogs and poultry hobnobbing amid a daily wreckage of old provision tins, garbage of soiled forage and stable-sweepings and whatnot. All that, with a temperature of 116 degrees to 120 degrees Fahr. in the shade, wore the temper and added amazingly to the consumption of wet things. At the Grenadier Guards' mess one sultry evening they consumed twenty-eight dozen of sodas, and it was not a record night. Without giving anybody's secret away, I may say I know a gentleman who could polish off three dozen at a sitting, and unblushingly call for more. These are details of more interest to teetotallers than to the general public. Yet, not to let the subject pass without a word of caution to afflicted future travellers in the Sudan, the inordinate use of undiluted mineral waters of native manufacture is most dangerous to health.

We correspondents had to wink both eyes in much of our telegraphic news from the front, for military reasons. The press censor was Colonel Wingate, chief of the Intelligence Department. In his absence, Major-General Rundle, chief of staff, usually acted. Personally, either gentleman was all that could be desired. Both were alike ready and courteous in the discharge of their at all times rather onerous duty, giving frequent audience to the numerous contingent of eager newsmen, garrulous and prodigal with pencil and pen. Some of the new-comers to the business felt sorely hit, because they were precluded from writing at large upon all subjects connected with the campaign. The excision of their copy grieved and hurt them as much as if they had been subjected to a real surgical amputation. Yet those two officers but obeyed orders, for after all, and under every circumstance, the Sirdar, as I am well aware, was the real censor. It is perhaps fairly open to argument whether the course adopted in dealing with correspondents' copy was wise or necessary in a war against an ignorant and savage foe. There was, at least, one official blunder which gave occasion for much annoyance, and ought to have been promptly remedied, or better still, never committed. It was expected of Colonel Wingate, the censor, that amid multifarious important responsibilities as chief of the Intelligence branch he should find time daily to peruse and correct tens of thousands of words, often crabbedly written, in press messages. With the approach of the day of battle, his own department taxed more and more his entire attention, and side by side the correspondents' telegrams grew in length and importance. The task of proper censorship under such conditions was impossible for any human being to discharge adequately. On that account the public interest suffered, for press matters were often neither promptly nor fully despatched. As a rule, the correspondents were left in blissful ignorance of what had been cut out of their copy, as well as of the exact nature of the residuum transmitted. Besides these grievances there was one of favouritism alleged, but of that there is always more or less in every phase of life and association. All told, it may be thought that the correspondents' complaints were of no very serious character. That depends on how they are looked at. I have no taste for cavilling or grumbling over events that are past. Surely, however, there is a middle way somewhere to be found between the absolutism of a general in the field, who may gag the correspondents or treat them as camp followers, and the clear right of the British public under our free institutions to have news dealing with the progress of their arms rapidly transmitted home. I am well aware of the grave responsibilities that hedge a commander-in-chief, and the cruel injury that an unrestrained non-combatant may do him by recklessly writing on subjects calculated to jeopardise the success of a campaign and hazard countless lives and fortunes. The latter is an remote possibility. A commander-in-chief has to consider that any enemy worth his salt is usually kept informed by spies and deserters, and press-men who are known and cognisant of their duty are no more likely to betray secrets to their country's enemies than any officer or soldier in the Queen's service. And nowadays the private correspondence from troops in the field cannot be suppressed, and it is often published. Commanders of armies will either have to accept the presence of recognised writers, over whom they can exercise some control, or instead stand powerless before a dangerous flood of random army letters poured into the public press. The case can be met with judgment and care—plus penalties where deserved. I am bringing no charges here, but discussing a vexed and withal important question. I am glad to say that during the Omdurman Campaign there was no attempt, within my knowledge, of muzzling the press. This does not bear upon the Fashoda incident, but that came later.

Nasri Island as a base of concentration was, as I have intimated, a blind. Although we correspondents were not permitted to go up the river, or indeed move beyond the Atbara, until the Sirdar and headquarters had started, yet we kept ourselves fully informed of all that was happening at the front. There had been one or two little skirmishes between bands of mounted Dervishes and our wood-cutting parties of Khedivial infantry. In these encounters our men had generally the best of the fighting, and the Baggara horsemen invariably retreated with a few empty saddles. In July Major-Generals Hunter and Gatacre had, during a small reconnaissance, proceeded as far up as Shabluka Cataract or Rapid on one of the gunboats. The enemy, it was seen, were in no great strength there, and the seven well-planned, thick-walled mud forts blocking the passage were weakly held. Those two officers landed with a small body of troops and surveyed a suitable camping site, at what they called Wad Hamid, but which, in reality, was north of that place and close to Wad Habeshi. The object was to find a spot easily accessible by river and land, and with not too much bush about. At that season, the Nile having in many places overflowed its lower borders, marshes extended for miles along the ordinarily solid river banks. Wad Habeshi was merely a native wood-cutting station at first, but little by little troops appeared on the scene, and a large entrenched camp, with lines extending for several miles, was duly formed. At the end of July two steamers, which had made the perilous voyage up the Nile from the province of Dongola, came in and made fast alongside the mud bars at Dakhala.

It was still early in August when all the four battalions of Major-General Hon. N. G. Lyttelton's Second British Brigade reached Dakhala. They were quartered in a cool and cleanly camp by the Atbara, to the south-east of the fortified lines. The 21st Lancers also arrived at Dakhala in due course. Major Williams' Field Battery, the 32nd R.A. of 15-pounders; Major Elmslie's 37th R.A., with the new 50-pounder Howitzers firing Lyddite shells; and Lieut. Weymouth's two 40-pounder Armstrong guns, besides other cannon and Maxims, were likewise on time. Very smartly the batteries and Maxims were stowed aboard native craft, which were taken in tow by gunboats to Wad Hamid. Detachments of gunners accompanied the pieces and carriages, but the majority of the artillerymen were ferried to the west bank, whence they marched overland to the new camp. It was at Wad Habeshi that the army was first actually marshalled as a concrete force, and forthwith took the field. Not a moment was lost by day or night in moving men and supplies onward. The little paddle steamer captured from the Dervishes during the 1896 Dongola Expedition, which had been repaired and sent to Dakhala, was continually carrying troops and stores from the east to the west bank. As the Nile was running at the rate of six miles an hour in its wide bed, the *El Tahara*, as the craft was called, had to make a big circuit to effect a passage. The *El Tahara* was one of the boats General Gordon built at Khartoum but never lived to launch. As she was a new craft, the Mahdi changed her name, calling her "The Maid," instead of "Khartoum," as it had been intended to dub her. She was an excellent vessel, with fine engines much too powerful for her frame.

WOOD STATION (*EN ROUTE* TO OMDURMAN)

Both Surgeon-General Taylor, on behalf of the British division, and Surgeon-Colonel Gallwey, for the Egyptian troops, completed their arrangements for succouring the sick and wounded upon the march from Shabluka to the attack upon Omdurman. Adequate provision was made for field hospitals, floating hospitals and relief stations, for medical officers, and attendants, with cradlets and stretchers, to follow each military unit into action. For the British infantry it meant, substantially, that behind each battalion a medical officer and two non-commissioned officers should march, accompanied by six camels bearing *cacolets*, and men with nine stretchers. A somewhat modified scheme was got out for the cavalry and artillery, as well as for the other Khedivial troops. In the anticipated action before Omdurman, temporary operating stations were to be set up, out of ordinary rifle-range, and native craft, which had been fitted up with cots, were to be brought as near the scene as practicable to receive the wounded.

An attempt made to lay a cable from Dakhala to the west bank was not over successful. It was found that the great sag, caused by the current, carried the cable downstream, so the whole length ran out before the opposite bank was reached. The steamer *Melik* was the telegraph ship, and paid the cable out from a wooden reel placed on her stern quarter. A few days after the failure she was employed picking up the wire, most of which was recovered by Captain Manifold, R.E., who was the director of military telegraphs in the last as in the three previous expeditions against the Dervishes. The recovered line was relaid across the Atbara, which is barely a third of the width of the Nile. From the south bank of the Atbara two land lines pass up the east shore of the Nile. Upon a lofty corresponding pair of trestles an overhead wire was also hung across the smaller river. A few miles south of Dakhala a cable had been laid to an island and thence to the west bank. From the latter point an ordinary land wire ran along the desert to Metemmeh. Later on it was laid to Omdurman. The line was put down step by step as the troops advanced. Thus an alternative system of telegraphic communication with Khartoum was early provided for.

It stirred the blood of everybody in our dull camp to see detachment after detachment of the second British brigade detrain. Most of us turned out and like schoolboys followed the drums and fifes as they played the troops to their camping-ground. A half-battalion of the Grenadier Guards, led by Colonel Villiers-Hatton, arrived at Dakhala on the 6th of August. Hale and strong the big fellows looked in their campaigning khaki. "First-class fighting material," as Arabs and negroes, who are by no means poor judges, were openly heard to confess in their interchange of confidences. There is always much camp chaff and yarning amongst Tommies—and their officers, too, for that matter—at the expense of England's picked battalions. "Have you seen the 'Queen's Company,' my man," asked a subaltern of the Grenadiers one day of a private in the Northumberland Fusiliers. Now the "Queen's Company" are all over six feet in stature, and there was a friendly rivalry in grenadiership between them and certain Fusilier regiments. The question was asked when the troops were marching over undulating but rather bare ground where the tufted grass was little over knee high. It happened the officer had been detached on other duty, and was anxious to rejoin his command. "I think, sir," said the Northumbrian, saluting respectfully, "that they have got lost in the long grass." The subaltern looked unutterable things, but the "Tommy" held a stoical face and said not a word more till the officer went off to hunt anew for his men. For all the chaff, everyone was glad to see the Guards, and to speak of them as the Queen's soldiers. Of the second brigade General Gatacre said that a better body of troops could not be wished for by any general.

I rode out to several of the brigade field-days, or rather, mornings, for there was plenty of drilling and field exercises for Lyttelton's men. The brigade was repeatedly practised in attack formation against imaginary bodies of Dervishes, as well as at assaulting supposed works. On more than one of these occasions the gallant Colonel of the Guards, not having his charger up at that date, led his Grenadiers afoot, and once, at any rate, was mounted on donkey-back. Particularism gets lost in the desert. In the manoeuvres the troops were usually led in line, the flanks being supported by two or three companies in quarter column, and the centre having in rear a few sections of companies ready to fill gaps. Save for a little noise in passing orders, the result of a fast-becoming obsolete school of training, even captious criticism could find no actual fault with their work. Advancing across *wadies* and scaling knolls upon the desert, the troops were instructed to open fire with ball cartridge. The range given was

500 yards, and the ammunition used was the tip-filed Lee-Metford bullets. As at the Atbara, without halting, the line moved slowly on, the front rank firing as at a *battue*, each man independently. There were a few section volleys tried, the soldiers pausing for an instant to deliver their fire. Once or twice also, the rear rank was closed up, and joined in the fusillade. One effect was to paralyse the deer and birds within range. I noticed that the tip-filed bullets did not usually spread, and that their man-stopping quality was something of a myth. Even the dumdum does not invariably "set up" on striking an object. For the Omdurman Campaign a new hollow-nosed bullet was issued for the Lee-Metfords. So far as I was able to judge, it generally spread on hitting, and made a deadly wound, tearing away bone and flesh at the point of exit.

On the 12th of August the 21st Lancers, together with camel and mule transport animals, were crossed to the west bank in readiness for marching to Wad Hamid. Saturday, the 13th August, was a very busy day at Dakhala. On that date the Sirdar went by steamer to the front, direct to Wad Habeshi. It was given out he was merely going on a flying visit for inspection. There was renewed active drilling of troops. Eight steamers that came down were reloaded and sent back with troops and stores in the course of twenty-four hours. General Gatacre went to Darmali, and there assisted in the embarkation of his old brigade, Major-General A. Wauchope's. The task was effected within the course of twelve hours, the Camerons, Seaforths, Lincolns and Warwicks, with their kits and supplies, being densely packed upon the steamers *Zafir, Nazir, Fatah*, and the barges and *giassas*, which these craft towed. Had the Thames Conservancy writs run on the Nile there would have been terrible fines exacted for unlawful overcrowding. On the 14th August these stern-wheelers, heavily laden with Wauchope's men, steamed at a fast rate past the Atbara camp, on their way south. These craft, the first of which took part in the 1896 Dongola Expedition, turned out to be really the most useful and dependable of the whole Nile flotilla. They steamed remarkably well, towed splendidly, and were, besides, good fighting craft. The three Admiralty-designed twin-screw steamers, *Sheikh, Sultan* and *Melik*, were not as fast as had been expected; they could not tow any reasonably big load, and, though they were stuffed with many novelties, few of the innovations were of the least practical value. They needed all their engine power to steam and when under weigh had none to spare for driving the circular saws to cut firewood for fuel, or to start the dynamos to work the search lights with which they were fitted. Major Collinson, commanding the 4th Khedivial Brigade, left Atbara camp for the front with the 17th and 18th Battalions, or half his force, the 1st and 5th Battalions having preceded him some time previously.

CHAPTER 6

From Dakhala to Wad Habeshi

What a land the Sudan is! As a sorely-tried friend said to me, after passing a succession of sleepless nights owing to the dust and rain storms, and overburdened days because of the heat, "What do the British want in this country? Is it the intention of the Government to do away with capital punishment and send all felons here? I am not surprised the camel has the hump. I would develop one here myself. What an accursed country!" Yes, it is not an *elysium*; and when one allows the dirt, heat, and discomfort to wither all power of endurance, the Sudan becomes a horror and anathema, particularly in the summer time. Now, the camel is to me the personification of animal wretchedness, a fit creature for the wilderness. The Arabs have a legend that the Archangel Michael, anxious to try his skill at creative work, received permission to make an attempt, and the camel was the issue of his bungling handiwork. Poor brute, his capacity for enjoyment is, perhaps, the most restricted of the whole animal kingdom. Ferocious of aspect, with a terrible voice, he is nevertheless the most timid of beasts, and his fine air of haughty superciliousness is, like the rest, but a sham. It might be fancied that he is forever nursing some secret grief, for he takes you unawares by lying down and suddenly dying. Yet that is ordinarily but his method of proclaiming an attack of indigestion.

I struck my tent at Dakhala on the 15th of August, packed my gear, and during the course of the day crossed over to the west bank with my servants, horses, camels and other belong-

LOADING UP—BREAKING CAMP

ings. Having obtained permission from headquarters to go up to the front, I decided to go by land, marching with the cavalry and guns, for I was not free to travel except in their company, at least until we reached Metemmeh but of that anon. The column in question was under Colonel Martin of the 21st Lancers, and comprised three squadrons of that regiment, or about 300 men mounted upon Arab horses; three batteries, the 32nd R.A., the 37th R.A. (howitzers), and the Egyptian Horse Artillery; two Maxims with division and transport trains, and a number of officers' led horses. As I have already explained, the guns of the 32nd and 37th field batteries, together with the limbers and ammunition, were sent on to Wad Habeshi by water. There was much merrymaking as usual that evening, for we were to start on the morrow. I squatted like many more in the low rough scrub by the river's brink with my caravan around me. During the evening I went out to dine with some officer friends. As I had over a mile to walk to their pitch, the poor glare of the camp fires made the darkness more inky, and I had sundry narrow escapes from tumbling into ditches and water holes. Our bivouac was an ill-omened beginning to the route march of the column under Colonel Martin. One of the periodical summer gales came on, raising whirlwinds of dust and sand. To complete our discomfiture a thunderstorm followed, and there was a heavy sprinkling of rain for herbage, but too much for men. Truly, misfortunes rarely befall singly. It was a big Nile year, not a flood, but enough and to spare. A blessing, no doubt, for Lower Egypt, but a calamity for us, for during the night the river rose 2 feet, and overflowed its low, level banks. The water overran part of the camping ground, compelling many a drenched soldier to shift his quarters hurriedly. We got through the dark and troublous night somehow, though keenly vexed by the muttered discontent of the camels, and the persistent, blatant, variegated amorous braying of 500 donkeys. A cat upon the tiles, a Romeo, was to this as a tin whistle to a trombone. Sleep was a nightmare. It was after six a.m. before the head of the column moved out towards the desert track. The rear did not get away before eight o'clock, much too late an hour for marching in the Sudan. The weather was hot, the sun scorching despite a brisk southerly breeze. Lieutenant H. M. Grenfell had charge of the fine Cyprus mule train for carrying the British divisional baggage. There was with the column a great following of native servants mounted upon sturdy Sudan donkeys. The gawky camel shuffles along, a picture of woe with a load of 2 cwt. to 4 cwt., whilst the little moke trips smartly with almost an equal weight upon his back. Two Jaalin guides were supposed to show us the shortest and best track. Major Mahan, of the Egyptian Cavalry, had been told off to keep an eye on them and to assist us generally during the march. Two squadrons of Lancers rode in front, whilst the rest of the troopers were supposed to protect the flanks and act as "whippers-in" to the column. Fortunately, there was no enemy nearer than Kerreri or Omdurman, for our line was usually stretched out for a great distance; two, three, and four miles often intervened between the head and rear of the column.

 After a few days of such marching as we had, straggling became the normal condition of affairs, except so far as the leading squadrons of Lancers were concerned. The last three days of the journey, in fact, became a sort of "go-as-you-please" tramp. To inexperience and want of wise forethought may be set down most of the difficulties, hardships, and losses that befell that column on its 140-mile march south, whereof later.

During the earlier portion of our first day's march (16th August) the track lay along the edge of a pebbly desert, which left but a skirting of one to three miles of loam and rank vegetation between its measureless sterility and the tawny Nile waters. The small rounded pebbles and the fine sand of the Nubian wilderness were surely fashioned in some great lake or sea of a prehistoric past. Far as we were from the Dervishes, a childish terror of them was entertained by the servants. At the last moment several domestics decamped, my cook among them. I rode back three miles to catch the rascal. With unwonted alacrity and prescience he had recrossed to the opposite bank before I arrived at the place of bivouac, and, having no time, I had to retrace my steps without his enforced attendance. It had been arranged that the column should only go fifteen miles the first day. What with winding and twisting to avoid flooded *khors* or shallow gullies we marched over twenty miles I fancy. At any rate, with no protracted halting for meals or for baiting the animals, we trudged on throughout the heat and worry of the day until sunset. It was putting both men and animals to the severest possible strain, and few of the soldiers, at least, had had any preliminary hardening, for they had been travelling for days by boat and train and were out of condition. As a rule, the Lancers trotted a few miles ahead, halted, dismounted, and waited for the convoy to come up. Then they would ride on again, halt, and so on, repeating the proceeding many times during each day's march. From start to finish the column was ever a loosely-jointed body. The pace was slow, little more than 2¼ miles an hour, though Sir Herbert Stewart's Bayuda desert column managed to average upon a longer and almost waterless route, from Korti to Metemmeh, 2¾ miles an hour. In that campaign, however, most of our marching was done during the cooler hours of very early morning and late eventide.

The head of the column turned in towards the river about three p.m. on the 16th, at Makaberab, or, as the natives call it,

Omdabiya—*i.e.*, the place of hyenas. For over a mile, men and animals had to make their way through *halfa*-grass scrub, and then over bare alluvial land, deeply sun-cracked and scored in all directions. The ground was criss-crossed like a chessboard, the lines being a foot to two feet apart, and four to six inches wide, and several feet in depth. There were numberless spills through these pitfalls. One camel snapped his leg, and many mules and horses were strained and lamed. It was indeed fat land, and had formerly grown cotton. The cracks, as we found later, were full of scorpions. During that night's bivouac, and in the early morning, very many men and animals were stung by these venomous pests. Only one soldier succumbed from a scorpion sting during the campaign. The pain of the wound is as an intense burning or wounding, and continues troublesome for hours. Ammonia was freely used by the doctors when the stings were severe, but where whisky could be got, that was preferred.

21st Lancers—Advance Guard

We were early astir on the 17th inst., but it was not until daylight or 5.30 a.m. that it was safe for the column to pick its way out of the field of cracks. Why the spot was selected, except as an earthly trial, I am unable to state, officially or otherwise. Hard by, on either hand, there was solid and most passable ground for bivouacking. We had a good many stragglers on the 16th inst., most of whom came rather late tumbling and grumbling to supper and bed on the rough dank ground. Others lost their way and wandered to the Nile, where they were guided by natives, and later were lucky to get a lift to the front upon gunboats. Two men of the 21st Lancers left upon the desert with a sick comrade down with sunstroke, watched him die, and, scraping a grave, buried him where he expired. Lieutenant Winston Churchill, who was detained until late at Dakhala, in trying to follow us, lost his way, and had to pass the night alone upon the desert. He sat holding his horse till daybreak, and then, burning with thirst, made his way to the Nile. Subsequently he hired a native guide and was enabled to come up with the column on the afternoon of the 17th. Spending the night alone upon the desert has been many times my lot in Sudan campaigns.

During Wednesday's march, 17th August, we crossed the low shoulders of many rocky ridges. They are called *jebels* (hills), but most of them, including Jebel Egeda, which we passed, are little, if any, higher than Primrose-Hill, London, though it is not a conical, but a long, barn-roofed range. Near there I saw an enormous native cemetery. It extended to perhaps fifty acres, the pebble-covered mounds over the graves dotting the bare desert and the sides of the hills. I have an impression that there are ancient funeral mounds near there, and that the burying-place of Aliab is older than the invasion of the Arab Jaalin. There were fragments of sculptured stones, granite, and blocks of sandstone, and I noticed one broken memorial slab covered with Greek characters. Farther on we had to turn aside to avoid *wadies* and *khors*, up which the Nile had flowed. We were able to water the animals at some of those places. The mules and horses buried their noses in the flood and drank greedily, and the camels also had a fine, long-necked thirst. We were ourselves too parched to care about the impurities of the Nile, and soldiers and officers swallowed great draughts of the soupy stuff.

Late in the afternoon of the 17th the column turned to the river to bivouac at Kitaib, a twenty-two miles journey for the day. Too late it was found that the ration depot there, from which the column was to draw fresh supplies, was upon the farther side of a newly-made inlet. The column had to repack, and turn west to round the creek. We reached Kitaib No. 2 about six p.m. Part of the battery mules and transport, however, got leave to remain at the first halting-place, as they stood in no need of supplies, and I unpacked by myself, bivouacking under a clump of tall mimosa trees hard by a vast deserted village and a long grove of date palms. I believe that over a score of men lost the road that night and ultimately wandered to the river and got to the front by steamer. There were several cases of heat exhaustion and sun-stroke, but happily few of a serious nature. Two troopers, who floundered through the marshy land, got taken aboard a gunboat when they were utterly prostrate. Others, whose horses went lame or had to be killed, were ordered down to the Nile to secure passage on as best they could. In the darkness, as I was eating my evening meal by candle-light, two Lancers shouted and rode up. They had the too common but true story to tell of having missed the track. I found supper and breakfast for them, and started them off with their troop at eight o'clock next morning, the 18th August, for the column left Kitaib at a late hour. My servants were glad of the soldiers' arrival, for they were terribly afraid of robbers, the district being infested with marauding natives. During the night several fugitives from Omdurman passed us going north. Eighteen Shaggieh, who had escaped in a sail-boat, were but four days out from Khartoum. They professed to be delighted to get away. The Khalifa, they said, had ordered every sail-boat to go south of Khartoum. Taking advantage of a thunderstorm, they headed down stream and got away. According to them, the Dervishes were killing all the Jaalin who were suspected of trying to escape north, and the Shaggieh and other northern tribesmen stood in little better plight. All natives, other than blacks and Baggara, who could get away from Omdurman were running off, as they believed the fall of the Dervish rule was assured. The Khalifa's son, Osman, whose title was Sheikh Ed-Din, wanted to make terms. For months the youth had been in disgrace, but his father had reinstated him in the position of Commander-in-Chief of the Forces. Osman openly declared that fighting against the Sirdar and the English was hopeless, and that it was wiser to try and treat with us. Khalifa Abdullah and his brother Yacoub, however, would not hear of treating for peace, urging that their own people in that event would kill them. The only possible course was war to the death. From an excellent source I learned that the Dervishes were well supplied with guns and ammunition, and that the Khalifa had about five millions sterling of treasure laid by.

From Kitaib can be seen the dozen pyramids of Meroe, part of the kingdom of the famous Queen of Sheba. To right and left upon the opposite bank are catacombs, ruins of old temples, towns and forts of a bygone civilisation. The country on both sides of the Nile in that region has spacious alluvial belts, big as the Fayoum and as susceptible to the arts of the cultivator. Such hills as there are rise for the most part abruptly from flat land capable of limitless irrigation. To anticipate somewhat: the region, south of Abu Hamed, up to and even beyond Khartoum, has all the natural advantages of Lower Egypt and something more. Berber is but 245 miles from Suakin. The Nubian kingdom of antiquity, or that of the Queen of Sheba, must have been of enormous extent, marvellous fertility and great richness. Ethiopia may yet fulfil the prophecy. From Kitaib we marched about eighteen miles to Maguia, passing through a forest of mimosa bush, the track but rarely branching out amongst the *halfa*-grass upon the more open country. About three p.m. the column turned in towards a side stream and settled down near the village of Maguia. The wind rose as usual at night, yet for all that the bivouac was fairly good, and there was plenty of grazing. Next day, the 19th, we managed to make an early start, getting away about 5.30 a.m. The distance to be traversed was but fourteen or sixteen miles, and the column reached the halting-place, Magawiya, about two p.m. We made our way over broken, cracked ground to the river's edge, and there bivouacked under the shade of a magnificent forest of stately date palms. The ripening fruit had been extensively plucked by thieving natives, but there was enough left for our men. It was a most picturesque scene for a camp, but an unwholesome place for all that. It was given out that the column was to rest a day at Magawiya, as the place was a wood and food supply depot. During the course of the evening the sternwheeler *Kaibur* came in, and a sick officer, Lieutenant Russell, and about a score or more of men were sent back upon her to Dakhala, or Atbara camp. It merits record that a party of Egyptian gunners carried upon a native bed or *angreeb* a sick British artilleryman from Maguia to Magawiya, from bivouac to bivouac. That was something like good comradeship and *esprit de corps*.

HALT BY THE WAY

At nightfall the column was formed up so that the men slept upon the ground within supporting distance of each other. Sentries and patrols also were set, but the force was not one, I fancy, that would have been able to offer a stubborn resistance to a surprise party of Dervishes. On Saturday, the 20th of August, as was anticipated, the troops remained in camp and enjoyed much needed rest and opportunities for washing. Several gunboats and steamers passed us during the day going south, including one upon which were a number of correspondents who were enjoying their *dolce far niente* under awnings in a breezy draught with inexhaustible supplies of filtered and mineral waters. We saw the Grenadier Guards, the Lincolns, and other battalions pass us, and steam slowly up stream towards Wady Hamed. On Sunday, the 21st, a really early start for the first time was effected. We were to march as far as Abu Kru that day, and encamp near the spot held by Stewart's handful of men in 1885. Major Williams, R.A., went off with his battery, the 32nd, at 3.30 a.m., and the 37th battery accompanied him. Lieutenant H. Grenfell got away at four a.m., and the Lancers at 5.20 a.m. I pushed ahead of the troops in order to have time to revisit some of the old ground I had been over with the Desert Column in 1884-85. It was odd, that though hundreds still survived who marched with Sir Herbert Stewart, there were but fifteen persons in the whole of the Sirdar's army who got through to Metemmeh. Of those still less went in and left with the force that fought at Abu Klea and Abu Kru. Of the very numerous body of correspondents there were but two. I regretted that there were not several score or more of old officers and men who went through the terrible Bayuda Desert campaign. Most of them would have sacrificed much to have been in at the death of Mahdism.

SLATIN PASHA (ON FOOT)

Metemmeh had been made a slaughter-pen by the Dervishes under Mahmoud. It was truly an awful Golgotha. Dead animals lay about in all directions in thousands, without and within the long, straggling, deserted town. I rode up and looked at the remains of the little fort and the loopholed walls on the south end of Metemmeh, close to which I had ridden on 21st January 1885, and got hotly fired at for my pains. Then I walked over the ruins of the Guards' triangular fort at Gubat. The place was still capable of defence, and the trenches and rifle-pits were much as we left them on 13th February with General Buller. As for the graves, they were intact. The big earthwork we all helped to raise near the river was covered with water, except a corner of the western parapet. It was, however, partly thrown down, and the ditch and slopes were overgrown with grass and bushes. Then I rode away to Abu Kru battle-field and had a look at what remained of the *zereba*, the little detached fort I had asked might be built, and the graves of our dead. Some of these had been rifled. Heaps of dead animal bones lay about, for we lost many camels that 19th January 1885. The enemy had gathered up and buried all their own dead. So overgrown was the place that it was barely recognisable. I stood, however, again where Stewart received his fatal wound, where Cameron, of the *Standard*, and St Leger Herbert lay with soldier comrades, and I wandered round to where Lord Charles Beresford worked the Gardners against the Dervishes outside Metemmeh, whilst I found the range for him through my glasses, by watching the spatter of the bullets upon the sand. That night my thoughts were full of bygone scenes and doings in the most heroic campaign of modern history, Stewart's magnificent ride from Korti to Metemmeh. There came back to me the pain felt on the receipt of the evil news of Gordon's death, brought to us by Stuart Wortley, and of the slaughter at Khartoum, all of which might so easily have been averted but for——

On Monday, 22nd August, the batteries again got away before the Lancers, starting at 3.30 and four a.m. The day's march was to Agaba, about twenty-six miles, and the next day's about nineteen to Wad Habeshi. Wady Hamed, which is nearer Jebel Atshan, was where one of Gordon's steamers, the *Tal Howeiya*, returning with Sir Charles Wilson's party, was wrecked on 29th January 1885. Making a detour into the desert on quitting Abu Kru, I left Colonel Martin's column, and rode on with one native servant to Wady Hamed. As a matter of fact, the camp was neither at Wad Habeshi nor Wady Hamed, but between the two. The latter, however, was the official name. But that my man was very apprehensive of meeting patrolling Dervishes, I would have ridden direct across country, starting from a point opposite Nasri Island, where the depot of supplies was. On the pretext of watering the horses he got me back to the river. The consequence was that I rode over fifty miles on Monday. However, I managed to reach Wady Hamed before sunset. On my way in I met the Sirdar, out, as usual, on an inspecting tour. He was good enough to greet me kindly and direct me to the correspondents' camp; those of my comrades of the Press who voyaged by steamer had just arrived. The new camp was an immense place over three miles long. It was a *zerebaed* enclosure lying along the margin of the Nile in a field of *halfa*-grass broken up with clumps of palms and mimosa. The country all around was as a vast prairie. Beyond the reach of the Nile's overflow the sand and loam was bare of vegetation. The river was studded with scores of verdant islands, and to the south we could see the peaks and ridges of Shabluka, through which the Nile, when in flood, surges like a mill race between narrow rocky barriers.

CHAPTER 7

Wad Hamid to El Hejir

Wad Hamid was a camp of magnificent distances, restful to the eyes but distressful to the feet. The soil was rich loam, and at no remote date had been mostly under cultivation. There were several pretty clumps of *dhoum* palms, and a few scraggy mimosa by the river's margin. Of tree-shade for the troops there was practically none. Much of the thorny bush had been cut to form a *zereba*. In fact, there were two *zerebas*, the British division having a dividing line between their quarters and those of the Khedivial force. There was also a semblance of cleared roadways about the camp, but the ground was too spacious to be easily made snug and tidy. Wad Hamid camp was quite five miles nearer to Omdurman than Wad Habeshi. We were within the long stretch known as the Shabluka or Sixth Cataract. For 15 miles or thereabouts the Nile pours in deep, strong flood through a narrow valley, which in places contracts to a gorge or canyon. The channel is studded with islets and rocks, and at one point the river races through a wedge-shaped cleft, apparently little more than 100 yards in width.

After my long ride in from Metemmeh I had to let my horse rest for two days. So until my servants arrived with my spare led horses I had to go about afoot. My camels and baggage were with the column. It was more of a hardship tramping from place to place in the hot dusty camp than roughing it upon the bare ground and living upon scratch and scrappy meals of biscuit, "bully beef," and sardines, till my men came in, put up my tent, and cooked my food. The British division was at the south end of the long rectangular encampment. An interval of a mile or more separated the divisional headquarters, whilst some of the battalions had their lines 2 miles apart. Beyond all, another 2 miles off, was the camel corps bivouacking by the rocks and foothills of the Shabluka range. Their only shade from the noonday glare was such as they could get behind detached black granitic boulders and blocks. Wad Hamid camp, viewed not too closely, was a pleasing picture set in a background of dark hills with a bordering of wide tawny river flowing in front. There were a good many tents in the British lines, but relatively few in the Khedivial, for there *fellaheen* and Soudani had sheltered themselves as usual under palm leaf and grass huts, or beneath their brown soldier blankets. It was one of the clever campaigning dodges recently taught the native soldiers by our officers, to attach loops of twine or tape along the edges of their spare blankets, so that these coverings could be quickly laced together and spread over light bamboos or sticks, forming very comfortable quarters. The Sirdar's headquarters tents were always distinguishable by the big waving Egyptian flag, a crescent and star on a red ground, and near it a bigger *drapeau rouge* flaunted the talismanic lettering—"Intelligence Headquarters." Before Major-General Gatacre's divisional headquarters flapped Britain's emblem, a full-sized Union Jack. Major-General A. Hunter's tent had an Egyptian flag dangling from a native spear, and the Brigade-Commanders all had their respective colours planted before their quarters. Colonel H. A. Macdonald, "Fighting Mac," had a characteristic brigade banner, readily distinguishable. It was an ensign made up of four squares or blocks of different colours, the colours of the respective battalions of the command. To descend to particulars, besides the Sirdar's and the Generals' flags, there were battalion and company colours, and hospital, artillery, engineer, and various other flags. In the Khedivial army the battalions were known by numerals from 1 to 18. The Arabic numeral of each native battalion was worn by the men on their tall *fezes* and the khaki covers for the head-gear. It was found necessary to devise a head-covering to shield the men from sunstroke. That worn over the fez could be so adjusted as to afford shade for the nape of the neck, and in front a scoop for the eyes, so that the article became transmogrified into something between a kepi and a helmet. The British Tommies' khaki helmet-covers were ornamented with coloured cotton patches and regimental badges. Of course the object of the patches was to enable officers and men to identify easily their respective commands. The Rifles wore a square dark green patch, which the Sudan sun bleached to a pea green. The Lancashire Fusiliers wore a yellow square patch, and the Northumberland Fusiliers a red diagonal band round the helmet. As for the Grenadier Guards their insignia was a jaunty red and blue rosette. In Wauchope's brigade the Lincolns sported a plain square white patch, the Warwicks a red square, the Seaforths a white plume, nicknamed the "duck's tuft," and the Camerons a "true blue" square patch.

The rapid thrusting forward of his whole army from Darmali and Dakhala within a period of ten days was not the least astonishing and brilliant strategical feat achieved by the Sirdar. In that space of time troops, stores, and all the impedimenta for an army of 25,000 men had been moved forward about 150 miles in an enemy's country. No doubt he knew his foe; he certainly always had them under the closest observation. For that reason the Sirdar was able to do things, and did do them, that other Generals would have blundered over. The great river before the camp, with its flotilla of gunboats, looking like American river-steamers, the forest of masts, the lofty poles of the lateen-rigged *giassas*, and the abundance of commodious barges gave a broad hint how the transport of so many men and so much material had been so smartly effected. Provisions, forage, ammunition, all on the most liberal scale, he had got together. With the troops there were to be carried supplies for fifteen days, and enough to last as long again were to be accumulated upon Royan Island at the south end of the Sixth Cataract. Placing the reserve supplies and base hospitals upon islands meant that both would be safe from any raiding Dervishes. Beyond Wad Hamid everybody was to move in the lightest possible order. Officers had to limit their baggage, so that it should not weigh more than 60 lbs., and the men were to march in the lightest of kits. Camel transport was cut down, and all animals not absolutely necessary were to be left behind. For the conveyance of the baggage of each British battalion 32 camels were allowed. All the men's heavy baggage, overcoats, knapsacks, kit bags were sent on by river transport in native craft. A blanket a-piece was what the men had, and that was carried for them by the baggage camels. Quite enough for any European to carry in the Sudan in August were his clothes, rifle, accoutrements, and 100 rounds of ball cartridge. The native battalions had assigned to each command 39 to 42 camels, as well as two *giassas* or *nuggars*. These carried all the regimental belongings, and also most of the men's things, for the Khedivial troops never marched with kits, blankets, or any encumbrances upon them. Clad in comfortable knitted jerseys, with breeches, putties, and good serviceable high-lows, the men of the native regiments stride freely along, each bearing only rifle, bayonet, and ammunition.

The massing of the forces at Wad Hamid was all but complete. Part of the Rifle Brigade, detained on the river by storms and contrary head winds, were the only absentees. On the opposite bank of the Nile had been mustered the mixed body of friendly natives, who, accompanied and supported by a gunboat, were to clear that side of the Dervishes when the Sirdar advanced. It was known that they would have to deal with, probably, 1000 Mahdists under Zeki Osman. Our allies included Ababdeh, Bisharin, Jaalin, Shaggieh, Shukrieh, Aburin, and other tribesmen led nominally by Abdul Azim, the brave Ababdeh Sheikh. They were armed with Remington rifles, but carried in addition their own swords and spears. That they might be better led and prove to be of real value, Major Stuart-Wortley, with Lieut. Charles Wood as his A.D.C., was sent across to take the command. Wortley was received with every demonstration of heartiness by the Sheikhs, who placed themselves and their followers entirely under that able officer's orders. The friendlies were most enthusiastic and eagerly asked to be led against their Dervish enemies. As these allies and the Sirdar's forces were to march by the river's margin when possible, signalling would be nearly always practicable between them. Telegraphic communication was opened to Wad Hamid from Dakhala by Captain Manifold, R.E., and his sappers almost as soon as the troops got into camp. With much hard work the line had been put upon poles as far south as Nasri. When the army subsequently advanced, as poles were not readily procurable the bare iron telegraphic wire was laid upon the ground. In the crisp, hot atmosphere of the Sudan, as there is little leakage, long distances can be worked through an unprotected wire laid upon the desert. When there were rain-storms of course telegraphic communication over such lines became impossible.

On 23rd August, the day following my arrival at Wad Hamid, the Sirdar held a great review of his army. At 6 o'clock in the morning the force was paraded upon the open desert a mile and half inland from the Nile. Reveille had been at an hour before sunrise. It was a pleasant morning, for a fresh breeze was blowing, and the air was agreeably cool. Several of the younger soldiers, however, succumbed to the effects of the tropical sun during the few hours the troops were kept employed, and they had to be carried back to camp. Although the cavalry, with part of the artillery and Maxims, did not parade, there was a big enough force upon the ground to make an imposing display. The army was drawn up in line with a front over a mile in length. Major-General Gatacre's division was upon the left, with the Grenadier Guards forming his right. The Queen's soldiers were ranged in mass of companies, column of fours right, whilst the native soldiery were brigaded in line, Macdonald upon the extreme right, with Collinson's brigade in reserve. The troops wheeled into column, deployed, changed front, and engaged in firing exercise. As might have been expected, there was more celerity and accuracy in changing formation displayed by the British than in the native brigades. All the men were very keen at their work, the expectation of being about to engage the enemy doubtless lending special interest to their field-day. The camp, as all camps ever were, was full of strange yarns—"shaves" about what was going on at Omdurman, and the Khalifa's intentions. "Abdullah would fight? No, he would run away; he was laying down mines in the Nile to blow up our gunboats. A Tunisian had devised a torpedo, but as it was being lowered from a Dervish boat, the machine exploded, and the engineer was hoisted with his own petard." Then there were stories of extraordinary discoveries of precious minerals—gold mines by the score. Two young officers, who wished some fun with a distinguished military gentleman not unconnected with South Africa, persisted in finding diamonds, pieces of rock-crystal, which, with an air of mystery and importance, they submitted to his contemptuous inspection. But a Major had the better of the expert on one occasion. He vowed he had found diamonds, genuine diamonds, upon the open desert, as good as any in South Africa or anywhere else; that he would be sworn to forfeit £50 if the expert did not endorse his judgment. He had picked up in one small spot no less than five. Burning with impatience to see these precious jewels, the expert begged for just one peep at them. The Major gratified him with some feigned reluctance; produced a "five of diamonds," a castaway from some "Tommy's" pack of cards.

On the night of the 23rd of August Wad Hamid camp was swept by a fierce storm of wind and rain. The temperature dropped 22°, and it became positively chilly. As we were within the rainy belt, which extends up to 17° North, visitations of that sort during the summer were to be expected. The troops bore the discomfort of cold and wet clothes uncomplainingly, waiting for daybreak, and the tardy sun, to get dry and warm. Bugle calls were a work of supererogation on the morning of Wednesday, 24th August, everybody having been astir long before reveille. It had been given out in general orders—one of those gracious niceties of military courtesy never exhibited to the correspondents in these later Sudan campaigns—that the Khedivial troops were to proceed that day to the south of Shabluka Cataract. The journey thither was to be made by the army in two stages, and the British division was to follow on Thursday. Wad Bishari, about half-way, was the first portion, and there the men were to bivouac one night. Next day they were to complete the distance, making a detour to avoid the rough hills of Shabluka, and going into a new camp laid out at El Hejir. At 5 a.m. Macdonald's and Lewis's brigades paraded, and under the command of Major-General Hunter, stepped off. So the end at last began to loom in sight. Major-General Gatacre wished to go part of the way the same day, in order to reduce the distance to be marched, but the Sirdar put his veto thereon, observing that if the Tommies could not do a little march of 13 miles, they could not walk any distance. In the afternoon, at 4 o'clock, the remainder of the Khedivial division—Maxwell's and Collinson's brigades—set out for Wad Bishari to join their comrades. The men were in fine spirits as they left, cheering and singing to the strains of their bands as they gaily marched away. Some of the Egyptian soldiers were told off to remain at the worst places of the Cataract to assist in towing the native craft through the rapids.

The bugles called the men of Lyttelton's brigade to duty at 3 a.m. on Thursday, the 25th of August. I cannot say that the call awoke them from slumber, for all night there had been most disturbing noises coming from the riverside, where native soldiers were reloading *giassas* with stores going forward to Royan Island, for that new depot. Royan occupies a position at the south gateway of Shabluka. It is a finely conspicuous island, for upon the north end there is a lofty barn-roofed *jebel* or hill. From the summit of Jebel Royan, at an altitude of 600 feet, can be seen 40 miles away the outlines of Omdurman and Khartoum—that is in the morning or evening, when the distorting freaks of the mirage are not in evidence. The steamboat skippers who had ten-horse power steam sirens, used them, after the manner of their kind, and made night doubly hideous. At 3 a.m. began our orchestra in the 2nd British brigade lines. All the camels, horses and mules had to be watered and fed. The cheerful camels then had to be loaded, that operation being carried on as usual with a terrible grunting chorus, all the brutes taking part. The gunboats got off before daylight. At five o'clock sharp, ere it was full daylight, Lyttelton's men started, marching off in three parallel columns, each battalion having its own advance guard. Four Maxims were with the brigade. Behind the infantry was part of the Egyptian transport train. The Sirdar inspected the column, and saw them started fairly on the way to Wad Bishari. Major-General Gatacre, as usual, rode out with them to the bivouac, and then galloped back to camp. The troops were in great glee at setting off. The men marched briskly, their officers tramping beside them. On the whole, the track was tolerable, mostly compact sand and gravel. In some places, however, it was rough and full of loose stones, and the sand lay deep and soft in several *khors* and *wadies* that had to be crossed. The worst bit was in the second day's march into El Hejir, where a detour had to be made to avoid the Shabluka Hills.

At 5 in the afternoon of the 25th of August the 1st British brigade, Major-General Wauchope's men, also left for El Hejir *via* Bishari. The "Rifles" or, rather, half the battalion, marched with them. Owing to various causes, the "Rifles" were not all assembled with the British division until the army reached El Hejir. In the end, the second half of the battalion of that crack corps was transported by water direct to El Hejir. They had quite a grievous mishap at Wad Hamid. The upper part of a barge, on which many of the men's kits and coats were stored, collapsed, and most of the articles fell into the river and were lost. Wauchope's brigade marched forward in five parallel columns, with intervals for deploying between each. The men turned towards the west to get clear of the cultivable belt, for the track afforded easier going along the margin of the desert. Behind the brigade, protected by the usual rear-guard, were six Maxims, the medical corps, a transport column, and a numerous following of native servants riding on heavily laden donkeys. The battalion bands played favourite regimental tunes as the men marched away. The pipers of the Camerons gave the "Earl of Mansfield," whilst, with fifes and drums, the Seaforths' pipers skirled *Black Donald of Balloch*. News was heliographed into Wad Hamid headquarters before we left that the gunboats had seized Royan Island and established a post there, the natives not disputing possession.

By the end of that week, 27th August, Wad Hamid camp was evacuated. Nasri Island, however, was retained as a depot, and a small force was left there. On Friday, the 26th of August, after a great fantasia and war-dance, Stuart Wortley's column of armed friendlies moved south. That evening they encountered and drove back a small body of Dervish horsemen. On our side of the Nile, part of the cavalry had been scouting up to 10 miles south of El Hejir. Captain Haig, with a squadron of Egyptian horse, fell in with a small body of Baggara under Sheikh Yunis, and had a brush with them, one or two being wounded on either side. The Sirdar and headquarters embarked at 9 a.m., 27th August, on the gunboat "*Fatah*," to steam through Shabluka. I left Wad Hamid the same day with one servant, rode through to El Hejir, 22 miles, and arrived in the afternoon, having ridden out of my way to see the narrower gorges of the Cataract. The spaciousness of the previous camp was conspicuously absent at El Hejir. In rather thick bush and on partly overflowed alluvial ground, the lines were drawn closely together. As the river kept rising, it soon became difficult, without making a considerable detour, to pass from one part to another of the ground by the water's margin.

Chapter 8
El Hejir to Um Terif

Your Arab is picturesque but poisonous: a fine specimen of a man, though his usefulness in the economy of things is not apparent, at least upon the surface. He dislikes steady, hard work, is a dreamer with a deeply religious tinge, but all the same cruel and remorseless in the pursuit of any object. We were well into the region that he had ruled and ruined: a country capable of easily producing wealth, charred and laid waste. The indigenous negro, on the other hand, is not averse to toil,—nay, generally delights in it under normal conditions,—is simple in his tastes, true in his conduct according to his lights, and readily turned to better things. Your Arab seems to be the reverse of all that, and yet he is a delightful person in his way, though a belated savage. Burned villages, blackened hearths, destruction on every hand, these were the telltale evidences before our eyes of what the Khalifa and his hordes had achieved. Behind all that there were the ruins of a great and long departed civilisation that the early flood of Arab invasion doubtless did something to destroy. Once again, as in the Atbara campaign, was the army closely followed by bands of the faithful wives of the black soldiers. These women as aforetime pitched their camp ordinarily half a mile or so in rear of the men's, choosing broken ground and thick bush through which they could escape if attacked by Dervish raiders. In rude huts and shelters built with their own hands amid the thorny mimosa and *dhoum* palms, they washed, ground corn, made bread, cooked food, patched and mended, and waited upon their uxorious soldier lords. "If handsome were what handsome does," these negresses would have been beautiful, but they were very far from it, poor creatures, except as I hope in the eyes of their husbands. Talk of the cares of a young family, not even that vexed their stout hearts and merry natures nor made them lag in marching to war with their spouses. Alas! even the pains and toils of maternity were fought down by young negro mothers, and I had my attention called more than once to women with almost new-born babies in their arms trudging along to keep up with the army. In such cases the women and men generously did all in their power to lighten the burden of the new mothers. Their household goods were borne upon other already overloaded backs, and if a donkey was procurable the mother and child were set to ride upon its back.

El Hejir camp was fenced about with a stout hedge of cut mimosa. Besides that there were several smaller *zerebas* enclosing different commands and several of the headquarters. There was plenty of *halfa* grass for grazing and an abundance of mimosa for firewood for the men's cooking pots and the steamers' boilers. Roads had been laid out, and troughs of mud were built, at which the horses and camels were watered, for the river's bank was unsafe. The site of the camp was not unattractive. In front the great river was dotted with luxuriant islands. On the left hand rose Jebel Royan, a Bass-rock-like hill rising from Royan island around which the Nile flowed like a sea. Again the Khedivial division had sheltered itself in straw huts, *tukals* and under blanket shelters. The British soldier had a few tents and much uncovered ground at his disposal for bivouac. It may be added that the health and general spirits of the army were splendid.

At El Hejir the press correspondents, or at any rate those representing the big dailies, except the *Times*, discovered they had a grievance. The news agencies shared that feeling with their colleagues. Even into war the affairs of business life obtrude. It is not an unmixed evil to have a grievance; trouble and ridicule come of having too many at the same time. I drafted a letter to Colonel Wingate on the subject—a sort of "Round Robin" which the majority of the correspondents signed, after which it was given to that gentleman, who stood in a sort of god-fatherly position to us. A form of telegram was also written and handed him for his *visé*, that it might be forwarded, though in somewhat slightly altered phraseology, to each of our journals. These papers explain themselves, and as they have never seen the light and the incident is as yet one of the unrecorded events of the campaign, I append them:

(Cablegram)
Daily Telegraph
London
Matter-Notoriety, *Times* has two correspondents here although one, Howard, ostensibly represents *New York Herald*, but all his messages are addressed *Times*, London, where read. I suggest your getting *World* or other American newspaper, which would give advantage additional correspondent. Recollect all telegrams are despatched in sections of 200 words. *Times* therefore gets 400 words messages. Correspondents have lodged formal complaint.
Burleigh
El Hejir

The following is a copy of the letter handed in:—

28th August, 1898
El Hejir Camp
Sir,—It has been a matter of notoriety for some days that the *London Times* has two correspondents with the Sirdar's army, Colonel F. Rhodes and the Hon. Hubert Howard. No doubt it may be said that the latter represents the *New York Herald* to which he is nominally accredited. We are, however, well aware that his dispatches are forwarded directly to the *Times* Office where it is not over-straining the question to say that they are there read and used. Under the rules, all telegraphic messages must be delivered

in sections of 200 words, each correspondent being only permitted to send in rotation that number of words and no more.

The fact that the *Times* has practically two representatives to other newspapers' one gives them a manifestly unfair advantage.

We need scarcely state, that in a campaign of this importance the British public are most keenly interested. Our Editors would have sent out, had not the military regulations precluded their doing so, more than one representative from each newspaper or agency to accompany the army. We respectfully submit that it is our duty to claim equal facilities with the *Times*, and we ask you to take such action as may be necessary, that our employers shall not be placed at any disadvantage.—Yours respectfully,

To Colonel Wingate
Chief Intelligence Department

It was a fine way of spending the Sunday, but really we were all too busy to bear the troops company at any of the services that day. Colonel Wingate laid the matter before the Sirdar, who struck with the justice of our plea summoned us all before him, when we stated our case anew. He gave his decision, that the *Times* correspondents twain should only have the right to send 100 words each by telegram. We disclaimed having any desire to curtail their letter-writing. That did not matter. The affair I am glad to say was conducted throughout with much good feeling, both Colonel Frank Rhodes and Mr Hubert Howard acknowledging the right of our contention, and the affair gave rise to no break in friendship. Colonel F. Rhodes acted very promptly and generously, for before the Sirdar gave his decision he came to us and offered his individual undertaking, that he would decline to send a line by telegraph, leaving to Mr Howard the sole right to wire.

On Saturday the 27th August, whilst the deeply laden stern gunboat *Zafir* with *giassas* in tow alongside was coming up the river, she suddenly commenced to sink. The water rushed over her fore-deck, and the officers, soldiers and crew were unable to beach her on the east bank before she went down. Indeed there was a scurry to get into the *giassas* and cut them loose lest they also should be lost. The vessel went down about ten miles north of Shendy, subsiding in water 30 feet deep, and only part of her funnel and upper structure remained visible. With her there was temporarily lost over 70 tons of stores, including much ammunition and many bales of clothing. She had been chosen by Commander Keppel, R.N., as the flag-ship of the flotilla and was rightly regarded by the Admiral as a fine vessel. It appeared that through over-loading and rough weather water got into the hold, and within two minutes, or before anything could be done to save her, she sank. Captain Prince Christian Victor was aboard, he having been assigned to duty with the Admiral, for the craft carried a number of soldiers as well as an ordinary crew. Both the Prince and Commander Keppel had narrow escapes. Providentially, no lives were lost, everybody being picked up by the *giassas* or managing to scramble ashore. As soon as possible afterwards operations were commenced to recover part of the cargo. The ship was secured from drifting by a hawser being passed around her standing gear, and made fast to stout trees ashore. Then some of the natives dived and several of the Maxims and boxes of ammunition were salved. As for the craft there was nothing to be done under the circumstances but to place a guard and wait until the fall of the Nile enabled her to be unloaded and refloated. Whilst Commander Keppel and his officers and crew were making the best of it, the little ex-Dervish steamer *El Tahara* hove in sight with Major-General Rundle and several officers on board. She lent all the assistance possible and then taking in tow the *giassas* with Prince Christian Victor, Commander Keppel and the rest of the shipwrecked crew, except the guard left behind, the *Tahara* with an extra head of steam, churned up to El Hejir.

I think there had been an intention at headquarters to make a few days' stay at El Hejir, and get the army well in hand before going closer to the enemy. The gunboats began embarking all their ammunition and commenced putting up their extra bullet proof protecting shields. But the Nile persisted in rising and again flooding part of our camp, interposing once more between the British and Egyptian lines a broad arm of water. So again the army was ordered to "move on." Drills and sundry other plans for exercises fell through and special precautions were taken to guard camps and convoys from surprise as the army drew nearer to Omdurman.

On Sunday, 28th August, at 3.40 a.m., the bugles were sounding in the Egyptian portion of El Hejir camp. It was nearly an hour later before reveille went in the British lines and the Lincolns made us think of our sins and forswear all sleep by playing their awakening air, "Old Man Barry." By 5 a.m., Major-General Hunter's division of four brigades, with bands playing, were streaming out of their *zereba* openings and taking the broad, well-worn tracks across the sand and gravel ridges towards Um Terif. Macdonald's brigade was in the van, and was followed in order by Lewis's, Maxwell's, and Collinson's, with the baggage of each brigade behind the command. The guns were upon the right of the division, the steamers covering the left. As for the cavalry and camelry, spread over a wide front, their duty was to search for the enemy and make sure the troops should have ample warning of the approach of any Dervishes. The two military attachés, Major Calderari, Italian, and Captain Von Tiedmann, German, rode on with the native troops. It was a cool morning and the battalions headed by their bands playing all the while marched as if going to a review. The Sudan soldiers' wives turned out again and mustered along the line of route just beyond the camp confines. As the battalions passed them, they shouted and gesticulated to their husbands, calling on them to behave like men and not turn back in battle. Yet probably over half of these same doughty black soldiers had been Dervishes before they came over to us. "Victory or death," was the cry of these fiery Amazons to their warrior lovers. He would have been recreant indeed or a marvellously brave man that would have returned to one of them a confessed runaway from battle. It was not surprising that the Sirdar did not object to their presence in the field, and occasionally saw that they were helped with rations when food was not otherwise procurable.

The desertion of El Hejir proceeded apace. In the afternoon of Sunday at four o'clock, when the fierce heat of day had declined, Major-General Gatacre's division in its turn marched off to Um Terif. The brigades moved onward in parallel columns, with the artillery in the interval and the 21st Lancers covering the front, flanks and rear of the infantry. Tommy was jubilant and carolled, as he tramped, topical songs and patriotic ditties. He heeded not the boisterous south wind that ladened the atmosphere with dust till there was darkness as of a city fog. Battle-day and settling of old scores was near, and withal the end of the campaign, so he pounded along. It was a rough tramp by the light of a growing moon. About 9 p.m. they reached their camping and were assigned their usual position, facing south, the side nearest the enemy. There was necessarily some delay as the battalions were being told off to their assigned limits where each had to pass the night ready to spring to arms. Detachments were detailed to cut bush and form a *zereba*, whilst others attended to the indispensable culinary department.

Each day our cavalry had seen slowly retiring before them a few of the mounted Dervish patrols. Nearing Um Terif, the enemy's scouts became more numerous and inquisitive. Whilst a company of the Lancashire Fusiliers stood on guard during the making of the *zereba* the infantry had their first encounter with a Dervish. From the desert there came a rush and rattling over the gravel and loose stones, as from a stampeded horse or mule. It was coming in their direction but neither sentry nor main body thought of challenging. In an instant a mounted Baggara dashed past the sentries and ran plump against a corner of the company bowling over two or three men. Whether it was a deliberate madcap charge, or the fellow was bolting from the other battalions and lost his way is never likely to be known. Possibly he did not anticipate finding British troops three-quarters of a mile from the river. At any rate he dropped or threw his spear wildly, then, wheeling about, galloped back into darkness almost before the fact that he was an enemy had been realised. The men's rifles were unloaded, so the Dervish was not fired upon. And had they been loaded, under the circumstances even then the officer, as he informed me, would have hesitated to shoot, lest he should unnecessarily alarm the whole camp. The spear left behind by the Dervish horseman was one of the lighter barbed-edge kind.

Um Terif camp was not a pleasant location. There was overflowed land between the troops and the river, and the ground we had to bivouac upon was rough. On Monday morning, the 29th August, before full dawn, four squadrons of Egyptian horse and four companies of Tudway's Camel Corps proceeded on a reconnaissance towards the Kerreri. The twin-screw gunboat *Melik* also steamed up the river a few miles, but neither quest resulted in adding much to the information already possessed as to the Khalifa's intentions and exact whereabouts. Whether or not we were to have our first battle at Kerreri none knew. The fact was that during the night there had been a violent thunderstorm accompanied by wind and rain. Daylight came with a cessation of rain but the gale blew steadily from the south, raising quite a sea on the Nile and a fog of sand and dust on land. It was impossible to see or move any distance with security, and that was no doubt the cause why the reconnaissances in both instances drew blank.

Formal councils of war were rare events during the campaign. A chat with his officers, the eliciting of their opinions off-hand and a watchful pair of eyes in every direction early and late, was enough for the Sirdar. The delays caused by the storms however were becoming embarrassing, and it was certain the men's health would suffer if they were compelled to linger much longer *en route*. Still it was well to be quite ready before pushing in to attack the Khalifa whose large army, it was reported, would fight desperately. At a council of war held on Monday, August 29th, at which all the Generals, including the Brigadiers, were present, it was decided to remain until the next day in Um Terif. The flotilla had been unable to concentrate in time, the strong current and head wind making most of the vessels unduly late in arriving from El Hejir. A piece of good news came to us from the friendlies over the river. They were wont to march abreast with us, moving up the east bank. We could usually see them across the half mile or more of water that intervened, streaming along in their conspicuous garments under the mimosa and palms, or treading through the bush and long grass. On their way to their encampment opposite they had fallen in with a small band of Dervishes who were busily looting a village. The natives of the place had offended the Khalifa by absenting themselves from Omdurman, and so were being cruelly maltreated. Major Stuart-Wortley's Arabs ran forward and opened a sharp rifle fire upon the raiders, who replied with a few shots and then bolted. A hot pursuit was instituted and five of the Dervish footmen were caught. The friendlies also had the luck to capture a Dervish sailing boat laden with grain. That evening at sunset, a few Baggara horsemen and footmen were seen upon the nearest hills watching the Sirdar's camp.

It was at Um Terif that the army, with all its equipment, was for the first time got together within the confines of the same encampment. From there also it set out next day in battle array, ready to encounter the Khalifa's full strength. In the clear atmosphere of the early morning and in the late afternoon when the bewildering mirage and dancing haze had vanished, from any knoll could be seen the large village of Kerreri. There the Mahdists had built a strong mud-walled fort by the bank of the Nile. They had besides blocked the road with a military camp big enough to shelter in huts and *tukals* several thousand men. Information brought us by natives, spies and deserters, was to the effect, that only a small body of Dervishes had been left at Kerreri under Emir Yunis for the purpose of observing the movements of our army. Kerreri, which the Arabs pronounce with a prolonged Doric or Northumbrian roll of the r's, as though there were at least a dozen of them in the word, is upon the margin of a belt of rough gravel, stone, and low detached hills that extend to the southward, to Omdurman and beyond. The alluvial strip by the Nile, along which we had marched so many days, gave place to ridges and hummocks of sand, gravel, and rock.

So we waited impatiently at Um Terif for the flotilla with the fifteen days' supplies on board. Meanwhile the axes of an army of soldier wood-choppers were clanging upon the hard timber, which was being felled for firewood. The ruin of agriculture had meant the growth of bush, and there was an abundance of useful mimosa and *sunt* growing on the alluvial lands by the river.

I ought to reproach myself, but I don't, for not having written of the aggravating southern gale with its accompaniment of drifts of horrid dust and sand as the terrible *khamseen* or sirocco. Travellers' tales about having to bury yourself in the sand, or at least swathe head and body in folds of cloth, in order to avoid being choked with grit, I know. The real thing is bad enough without resorting to poetic or journalistic licence, though some will do that anyhow. It is sufficiently trying to grow hot and perspire so freely that the driving dust, the scavenger drift of chaos and the ages, caught by the moisture, courses down the features and trickles from the hands in so many miniature turbid streamlets. During a dust-storm everybody has the appearance of a toiling hodman. Feminine relations would have wept had they seen and recognised their soldier lads in that sorry state. Even the dashing officers and men of the Grenadier Guards ceased to be objects of admiration, and the War Office would have howled with exquisite torture at sight of their hair and clothes. Speak of wrapping clothes around head or body to keep out the dust? It is sheer nonsense to prate so. Why it is hard enough to gape and gasp and catch a mouthful of sanded breath, without that added worry. There is nothing for it, but to grin and bear it and get through with the swallowing of that proverbial speck of dust in a life-time, as quickly and quietly as possible.

The fighting gunboats or armed flotilla consisted of the *Sul-*

tan, Lieutenant Cowan, R.N.; *Sheik*, Lieutenant Sparks, R.N.; *Melik*, Major Gordon, R.E.; *Fatah*, Lieutenant Beatty, R.N.; *Nazir*, Lieutenant Hon. Hood, R.N.; *El Hafir* (*El Teb*), Lieutenant Stavely, R.N.; *Tamai*, Lieutenant Talbot, R.N.; *Metemmeh*, Lieutenant Stevenson, R.E.; and *Abu Klea*, Captain Newcombe, R.E. On the loss of the *Zafir*, Commander Keppel, R.N., transferred his flag to the *Sultan*, one of the new twin-screw gunboats.

Chapter 9

Skirmishing With the Enemy

"Death and his brother sleep" can only be staved off; they overcome in the end. The tired soldiers dropped into profound slumber, although the night of the 29th August at Um Terif was boisterous and the cruel enemy near. It was one of the real surprises of the campaign, that the Mahdists never really harassed us, or ventured to rush our lines under cover of night, or in the fog of a dust storm. It has often been too hastily assumed that the Dervishes never attacked by night. By the Nile and in the Eastern Sudan they repeatedly pushed attacks under cover of darkness, or worried their opponents by persistent sniping,—as for instance at Tamai, before Suakin and Abu Klea. Then again, their final and successful assault upon Khartoum was delivered at dawn. Hicks Pasha's force was hammered early and late. It is all the more strange, therefore, that they left the Sirdar's army severely alone, never practising their familiar harassing tactics and seeking to secure an advantage. Numerous, swift of foot, with spears and swords, the odds would have been much more in their favour had they come down like wolves in the night. It is difficult to say exactly what would have happened, and it is not pleasant to contemplate what might have befallen. In such a conflict the Sirdar's losses would have been great. Could it have been that the Khalifa believed some of the stories set about that our army intended paying him a surprise visit by night, as we did Mahmoud, and so he kept his men in camp quietly waiting for us. The utmost precautions were taken by the Sirdar and his generals to protect the lines. A strong *zereba* surrounded the camp; sentries were doubled, and active patrols were on the alert all night. The gale continued until after sunset, when heavy rain clouds gathered, obscuring the moonlight. By and by there came on a violent and protracted thunderstorm, accompanied by an almost continuous deluge. There was nothing to be done but to lie fast wrapped in great coat or blanket and await the passing of the hours, wet, chilled, ruminating on all sorts of queer subjects. I managed to undo a corner of my packed tent and under it obtained relative warmth, and dryness in spots.

The persistence of that storm bred despair. It was nearly 8 a.m. on Tuesday the 30th August, when, having drenched us all to the marrow, the rain ceased. The sun, although two hours high, was battling with a fine mist. It was in a perfect downpour of rain at four o'clock in the morning, that reveille had been sounded. And it was in sludge and slush camels and mules were fed and loaded, and horses baited and saddled. By 5.20 a.m. the army was at length on the march out of camp, our faces set towards a village called Merreh, best indicated upon the maps as Seg or Sheikh el Taib, the latter being the name of a low hill. The distance the force was expected to trudge was about eight miles, but the overflowed land put two miles more on. When daylight came we could see Abdul Azim's friendlies upon the opposite side of the Nile. Led by Major Stuart-Wortley, with whom were Lieutenant R. Wood and Captain Buckle, the camels of their column kept pace with ours. Closely skirting the east bank that day, Abdul Azim's warriors had their right supported by one of the gunboats.

With the Sirdar and staff riding at the head of the infantry columns, the army advanced in the formation in which it had been determined to attack the enemy at Kerreri. Once more our mounted troops pushed far ahead, covering a wide stretch of country, the 21st Lancers under Colonel Martin on the left, the Egyptian cavalry under Colonel Broadwood and eight companies of the Camel Corps under Major Tudway on the extreme right. The infantry presented a front of three brigades marching in echelon. A battery of artillery was attached to each infantry brigade except Collinson's brigade. Three battalions were detached from the whole force to guard the baggage and transport which followed in the rear. In front on the left, or nearest the Nile, was Wauchope's brigade. The four British battalions thereof marched side by side in column, the Lincolns upon the right, the Warwicks on the left, with the Seaforths and Camerons between them. To the right of Wauchope's brigade was Maxwell's, and next it Lewis's Khedivial brigades. Behind each of the three leading brigades above named (reading from left to right) were Lyttelton's, Collinson's, and Macdonald's commands. Seen upon the desert the army had the appearance of a huge square with front a mile broad. The day being cloudy, and cooler than usual for the season, General Gatacre and his brigadiers voted at a council to extend the march. That course was adopted, the army keeping on, but with very many brief halts for the brigades to regain their formation. By the extra tramp the troops were enabled to pass beyond the broad margin of thick bush out upon the comparatively open, pebbly, and rocky ground, which sloped to a narrow strip of soft, wet loam fringing the river. About 1 p.m., when still fully one mile north of the hill of Sheikh el Taib, the army halted and a camp was made. Access to the Nile was very difficult, for overflowed, boggy land interposed. Roads, however, were made with cut bush, and the animals were led over them to be watered. During the army's march the Lancers scoured the country far in front. They managed to get into touch with some Dervish patrols whilst scouting. The opposing troopers looked at each other from relatively open ground, and standing separated by only a few hundred yards. One Baggara horseman came within 150 yards of our men. The Lancers, keen to engage with steel, did not attempt to fire upon their intrusive foemen, but innocently tried instead to bag them. Several times our troopers advanced to the charge, but the enemy, when the Lancers sought to put hands upon them, were gone. That day the Baggara horsemen were met with in far greater numbers than previously. By instructions, the Lancers rushed one of the many small villages, or groups of native mud-dwellings and beehive straw huts that dotted the sparse bush-land a mile or more inland from the river beyond Sheikh el Taib. Several of the enemy hastened away, and in one of the huts a man in Dervish dress was found awaiting the troops. He turned out to be a secret agent of Colonel Wingate's Intelligence Department. The spy in question was a Shaggieh, named Eshanni, and but thirty hours out from Omdurman. I was led to understand that he gave much valuable information as to the position and strength of the Khalifa's force and the state of affairs in Omdurman. We were told that the Khalifa meant to attack us at or near Kerreri. There was an old-time prophecy of the Persian Sheikh Morghani, whose tomb is near Kassala, that the English soldiers would one day fight at Kerreri. Mahomed Achmed and Abdullah had further added to the prediction that there they were to be attacked and defeated by the Dervishes under the Khalifa. Kerreri plain, therefore, had become a sort of holy place of pilgrimage to the Mahdists. It was called the "death place of all the infidels," and thither at least once a year repaired the Khalifa and his following to look over the coming battle-ground and render thanks in anticipation for the wholesale slaughter of the unbelievers and the triumph of the true Moslems.

All except those on duty were abed by last post on 30th August at Sheikh el Taib camp. Lights were ordered out, and the camp for a time relapsed into darkness and silence. Headquarters and all other tents had been struck and packed. During the night there was shooting, the crack of the musketry sounding relatively near, but occasioning little annoyance. The bullets were badly aimed if directed against the British quarters. Whether the firing was really meant for "sniping" by the Dervishes, or was only a note of warning to their friends of our presence, was not easy to decide with any degree of certainty. There was no big roll of wounded to test the enemy's intent by, and a later incipient alarm caused in another part of the camp in the small hours was possibly all a mistake. One

ARTILLERY GOING TOWARDS OMDURMAN

thing the Dervishes did do. After the manner of hill-men, they lit beacon fires on the rocky ridges around us to warn the Khalifa of our whereabouts.

That night the camp lines had been drawn still closer than ever, only 260 yards' front being given to each battalion. On the morning of 31st the troops were early astir. By 5.30 a.m. the main body, following the mounted troops, had faced to the right, and were marching to the westward so as to clear the bush and get out upon the open desert tracks leading to Omdurman. The ground the army passed over was broken, and there was scrub with several small *khors* to cross, so the force proceeded slowly and cautiously. Four of the gunboats steamed up the river, keeping abreast of our widely spread out cavalry. About six o'clock the Lancers had again ascended to the top of El Taib, a hill from which at that hour I was enabled to get a view of the Dervish camp. It appeared to be about ten miles due south. The Mahdists were disposed in three long dense lines, at almost right angle to the river. They were partly hidden among the low scrub west of Kerreri town or village, their right being quite 2000 yards from the Nile, which showed they had a wholesome respect for the gunboats. Flags and helios were speedily busy in the hands of our signalmen sending back information to the Sirdar. Seeing groups of Dervishes within range, as well as bands of Baggara horsemen, the gunboats opened fire from their 15-pounders and Maxims shortly after 7 a.m., driving the enemy's nearest patrols into hiding or out of range.

In one of the numberless villages passed, there were several mutilated and charred human bodies, victims of Dervish suspicion, greed and cruelty. Pushing well ahead on our right the Khedivial mounted force got a chance to send a few volleys into groups of Abd el Baki's scouts. That Emir commanded the Dervish outlying forces. It was still quite early when after an easy journey of eight miles the infantry turned aside towards the river. The army was halted at a place called Sururab, a few miles north of Kerreri. Why it was called Sururab I know not, nor have I found the name on any map; but that was the official designation given to the place where the force subsequently bivouacked. The only reasonable fault to be found with Sururab was that the river banks were exceedingly difficult of access. Our camps were getting from bad to worse. That day flocks of huge vultures were to be seen circling overhead as the army advanced. It may have been our approach that disturbed them from their carrion feasts in the devastated villages and the abandoned Dervish camps. Omdurman itself must also have long been a choice feeding place for them.

Once more the Sirdar's army had to spend an uncomfortable night. The few tents that had been carried so far afield belonged to headquarters, generals, commanding officers, and correspondents. They were more of a burden than a comfort, for all canvas had to be struck by last post, and thereafter neither lights nor loud talking were permitted. The native troops' low shelter tents made out of their spare rough blankets were allowed to pass unchallenged. It was another night to be remembered which the army passed at Sururab. Early in the evening the clouds gathered, and a series of violent thunderstorms, accompanied by heavy rain, continued almost without cessation through the weary, lagging hours. Rolled in their blankets, the soldiers, wetted through, lay upon the sodden ground. Such of us as could crawled under sheets of canvas or waterproofs, but these afforded little protection from the driving sheets of falling water. From Sirdar to private none escaped a thorough wetting. The enemy, had he chosen, might have advanced from Kerreri or Omdurman, and been upon us ere an alarm could have been given. Shortly after sunset everybody had to be within the *zereba*. All openings in the hedge were thereafter stopped up, and no one was allowed outside before reveille. Officers and men of Gatacre's division had as usual to sleep in their places lying down in the ranks fully dressed, with their arms beside them, ready to spring to attention. Sentinels and patrols, watchful and observant, moved noiselessly about throughout the whole night. True, there were outside a few of Slatin's most trusted native friends, chiefly Jaalin, set to listen and raise an outcry if the Khalifa's Dervishes came down upon us under cover of the inky night. But I had grave doubts whether these native allies would have been of any service, as the likelihood was that they were huddled under some rock or tree, shivering in their wraps and sheepskins. Had the Khalifa been astute or a tactician he would have attacked our camp at Sururab that night or early next morning. He must have succeeded, at any rate, in getting close enough to us without our hearing a note of warning to have placed his army upon a practical equality with ours in point of value of rifle fire. The Remington at 300 yards is as good as the Lee-Metford for killing or wounding. His superiority in numbers and mobility would have been all in his favour. Luckily, it was not to be. We were again allowed to sleep in such peace as the elements would permit. The fact remains that the Dervishes lost another of the several excellent chances they had to do us signal hurt.

Reveille went at 3.45 a.m. on 1st September. Little need of it there was, for the men were astir, trying to keep warm by stamping about. In the driving rain and slush the army got ready to march forward. The boats, as usual, were sent on with the surplus stores, whilst the men carried one day's emergency rations in their haversacks, and two days' ordinary food was taken upon the camels of each battalion. Once more the brigades marched in echelon. Gatacre's division was leading as before on the left, with Wauchope's brigade in front, and Lyttelton's behind. Steadily, deliberately, the armed tide of men flowed over the undulating plain, down into shallow *khors*, swelling through the scrub, their serried ranks always plainly to be seen. I went forward again with the cavalry, accompanying the 21st Lancers, who were upon the left front. The Egyptian troopers and the camelry went to their usual place upon the right. In a short time we found that the Dervish advanced camp west of Kerreri had been abandoned, the enemy having fallen back and joined their main force under the Khalifa nearer Omdurman. Word was sent back to the Sirdar that the track was clear of the enemy, and so the skirmish before getting into camp, which all the infantry expected with some degree of confidence and elation, did not happen. By 10 a.m. the army had wheeled into the lines assigned it in the southward portion of the scattered village of Kerreri. Once more both wings rested upon the Nile, Gatacre's division in front (south), Macdonald's brigade at the north, with Collinson's brigade within and in reserve. The army encamped in an irregular triangular enclosure, on one side being the river, our flanks and face being protected by the gunboats. Our *zereba* outline was something like a broken-backed pyramid.

Whilst the infantry were settling down in camp at Kerreri the cavalry were pushing in the enemy's outposts. The British division cut and built around their front a good stout thorny *zereba*. Lyttelton's brigade and three batteries were placed nearest the river. Upon their right was Wauchope's brigade, next to it was Maxwell's and Lewis's brigades, and then to the right, Macdonald's crack command. Collinson's brigade was held in reserve within the *zereba*; Colonels Maxwell, Lewis and Macdonald had their front protected by a double line of ordinary shelter-trenches dug in the loose sand and gravel. The British Tommies had no trench. Going forward a mile or so to rejoin the cavalry I climbed the rugged granitic slopes of Surgham Hill. Like most of the "*jebels*," or mounts, in this region, compared with the spacious wilderness about them they are but toy hills. Few of them are much over 150 feet high, large as they often loom in the deceiving light of the Sudan. Many are but 50 feet in height, and there are regular, peaky, and prettily-shaped little mountain ranges, the summits of which overtop the plain but five to ten yards. Such hills children might build in play by the sea-shore. Surgham was quite a big one, and the signallers soon took possession of it, flagging and helioing back to camp. From its top I was enabled to see Omdurman, with Khartoum in the distance. The Mahdi's white, cone-shaped tomb, its dome girt with rings, and ornamented with brazen finials, globe and crescent, shone not six miles away in the midst of miles of mud and straw huts. Four arabesque finials rose, one from each corner of the supporting wall. Before the town was a wall of white tents, the original camping ground of the Khalifa's levies and reinforcements drawn from distant garrisons. Midway to Omdurman, or within three miles of where I stood, was the whole Dervish army. Clearly they had moved out from the city, and were organised as a force prepared for instant battle. Their tents, camels, and impedimenta had been left behind. Only a few low shelter-tents marked the lines in which the Khalifa's army lay in the sparse bush. There were flags and banners by hundreds, indicating the position of the leaders, chiefs and lesser emirs. The Khalifa's great black banner, with its Arabic lettering sewn in the same material, was displayed from a lofty bamboo pole, planted in the dense central part of the force. To the left of it, our right, were green and blue flags of the Shereef, or second Khalifa, and Osman or Sheikh Ed Din, the Khalifa's son and generalissimo of his army. Osman, we heard, had been reinstated in parental favour, for he had fallen from grace for advising his father to make peace with the Sirdar. As in a daisy-pied field, there were Dervish battle flags everywhere among the thick, swart lines that in rows barred our way to Omdurman. The banners were in all colours and shades, shapes, and sizes, but only the Khalifa's was black. The force was apparently drawn up in five bodies or divisions. Abdullah's, in the centre, must have numbered fully

10,000 men. Counting as carefully as I could, I estimated the enemy who were to be seen as at least numbering 30,000, and, perhaps, 35,000 men. Horsemen and camelmen could be seen moving about their lines, and here and there others riding, native fashion, on donkey-back. It seemed to be a well-organised, intelligently-handled enemy we had in front.

Thereafter I rode onward and joined the farthest Lancers' outposts. Small parties of Dervishes, mostly Jaalin and blacks, who were caught by the troopers, but had perhaps purposely given the Khalifa the slip, were rounded up and sent back under escort as prisoners. Meanwhile both the British and Khedivial mounted troops kept pushing on, driving in the enemy's scouts. By noon there had been a series of attempts on our side to charge, but the foemen always gave way. The Egyptian cavalry under Colonel Broadwood and the camelry under Major Tudway, making a wide detour, got close to the Dervish left, and engaged the enemy occasionally with rifles and Maxims. But the enemy's horse came out in strength, supported by footmen, and threatened them, so Broadwood's men had to fall back.

Four of the Sirdar's gunboats, which had meanwhile steamed ahead, were briskly battering the Mahdist riverside forts. These works, like those abandoned to us at Shabluka Cataract and Kerreri, were strong, well-built earthen bastions, with flanking curtains. The central semicircular portion was pierced with three embrasures for ordnance, but so badly made as to admit of but a limited area of fire. Each curtain was loopholed for musketry. There was a deep, wide trench before the works, the parapet of which was about ten feet high, whilst the walls of earth were about three yards in thickness. Despite the skill shown in the construction and placing of the forts, the gunboats, by bringing their Maxims and quick-firing guns to bear, passed them unscathed. There were Krupp guns mounted in most of these works, but not a steamer was hit. Another event of even greater importance was meanwhile happening. From the first it had been planned that the Lyddite guns and the 40-pounder Armstrong cannon should be employed to batter down or breach the

Khalifa's walls. The howitzers were sent on by one of the gunboats to be landed on Tuti Island, which is opposite Khartoum, for that purpose. But it was found the maps were wrong, and a better position was selected within suitable range on the solid land of the east bank. As for the 40-pounders it was found too inconvenient to tranship such heavy ordnance.

The battery firing the 50-lb. Lyddite shells having found the range, about 3000 yards, opened fire upon Omdurman. In quick succession rapid splashes of lurid flame burst in the town, followed by great clouds of dust and whirling stones. I watched them training the howitzers on the great wall and the whited sepulchre of the false prophet. With the third shot they struck the base and anon the top of the Mahdi's tomb, smashing the structure, and bringing down the uppermost cap of it. The nature of the bombardment and its success was galling to the Dervish force, as could be seen by the commotion it excited in the city and their camp. Our cavalry on the left got to skirmishing again with the enemy's outposts, on which we had closed to within 800 yards. Bodies of their horsemen came out and drove our advanced scouts in. Then, three squadrons of the Lancers were led forward by Colonel Martin, and the enemy once more retired. This, seemingly, was too much for the Khalifa, so his whole army was set in motion against us. They came on deliberately, but smartly, their infantry trying to surround and cut our troopers off. Dismounting part of his men, Colonel Martin materially delayed the enemy's advance, for the Dervishes sent out lines of black riflemen to deal with the Lancers. A rattling skirmish at 500 to 800 yards ranges was in a few minutes in full progress. News was sent back to the Sirdar that the enemy's army were coming on *en masse*, and step by step Colonel Martin's troops were retired towards Mount Surgham and the river. Our retreat was pressed, and the regiment had to mount and trot off behind the shelter of Surgham to avoid the vigorous advance of the Dervishes. Among our mounted troops there were relatively few losses, although the enemy must have suffered considerably. I noticed many of them being knocked over by the Lancers' fire.

Before 3 p.m. the Sirdar had all his infantry and guns in position, awaiting the expected attack within his lines at Kerreri. A few mud-huts on the south face of the *zereba* materially added to the strength of the position. Our cavalry had all to continue retiring, and ultimately the Lancers went down to the river so as to clear the front of the army. Surgham Hill was occupied by a few of the Dervishes. From there they must have had an excellent view of our camp; indeed, they had as good a panoramic peep at us as we had at them. For some reason the Khalifa thought better of attacking us that day, and so halted with his main body quite out of range. Towards sunset his men gradually retired, going back to their former position. They had left their camp-fires burning, and their chunks of meat and cakes of rough grain cooking under the supervision of slaves and followers when they came out against the Lancers. So it happened on the eve of the coming battle both armies rested quietly in their respective camps, eating, sleeping, and the devout praying, within a five miles' march of each other. For supper our men had stringy bully beef and biscuit or bread. The Dervishes had hunks of freshly roasted mutton, goat and cattle, done on the embers, and bannocks of *dhura* meal. Extra precautions were again observed to secure the Sirdar's army from any night attack.

CHAPTER 10

The Battle of Omdurman
—First Phase

In this and the succeeding chapter, the account given of the victory of Omdurman is substantially the same as that which appeared in the columns of various issues of the *Daily Telegraph*. The narrative, although hastily prepared, gives an accurate description of the fight, and copies of it not being now procurable, I venture to make use of it, adding only here and there lines of new matter. I have reserved to a later chapter the personal narratives of officers who were in the action, and who have kindly supplied me with particulars of the part borne by the gunboats, the cavalry, and Major Stuart-Wortley's friendlies. With these I have coupled various details drawn from my own observation. I found that through errors in transmission of the messages, or mistakes in dealing with them, part of my copy had got credited to other sources.

Omdurman, 2nd September 1898

The supreme and greatest victory ever achieved by British arms in the Sudan has been won by the Sirdar's ever-victorious forces, after one of the most picturesque battles of the century. At last! After fifteen vexatious years spent in trying to get here, an Anglo-Egyptian army has recovered Khartoum and occupied Omdurman. Gordon has been avenged and justified. The Dervishes have been overwhelmingly routed, Mahdism has been "smashed," whilst the Khalifa's capital of Omdurman has been stripped of its barbaric halo of sanctity and invulnerability. Striking and dramatic as has been the manner in which the ending of the curse of the Sudan has come about, the tale need lose none of its force by being simply told. The grandeur of the plain story requires no straining after catchwords. Of those who with Sir Herbert Stewart's desert column toiled and fought to reach Metemmeh in January 1885, less than a dozen are with the Sirdar's army, and of these but three, including the writer, were correspondents. But to the narrative of the battle which, at a stroke, has broken down the potent savage barriers of blood and cruelty, and re-opened the heart of the great African continent to the sweetening influences of civilised government.

Storm and cloud had passed. The moon rose early on the night of 1st September. It shone brightly over and around our bivouac, south of Kerreri village, or near Um Mutragan, according to the cartographers. The north end of our camp lines approached the river just 500 yards south of the ruined Dervish redoubt of Kerreri. Sentinels were posted along the irregular-shaped triangle, or, shall I call it, broken semi-circle, within which the army lay. The sentries had a fair range of view to their front. Men on the lookout also occupied the roofs of the few native mud-huts at the south-western corner of the camp. Four Jaalin scouts were sent forward to Surgham Hill to listen, and to apprise the troops of any movement on the part of the Khalifa's army. Other friendlies lay about outside, hearkening and watching, to warn us of any attempt of the enemy to surprise the *zereba*. The sentries were bid to shoot at any man rushing singly upon him, and to fire upon large bodies advancing at the double. Men running in, however, in pairs, were either to be challenged or allowed to come in without being fired on. Such was the simple yet ample arrangement. To anticipate somewhat, it so happened that about midnight there was some firing, and the four Jaalin "smellers of danger and Dervishes" upon Jebel Surgham came sprinting in, a four-in-hand, and cleared the broad cut mimosa hedge that was piled before the lines of Gatacre's division, at a bound. The time they made broke all records.

From the north to the south end along the river the camp was about one mile in length, and its greatest width about 1200 yards. There were a few mud-huts within the space enclosed by mimosa and the double line of shallow shelter-trenches. The cut bushes were piled in front of the British troops, who were facing Omdurman and the south; the trenches covered the approach from the west and north where the Khedivial troops stood on guard. Neither extremity of the lines of defence, *zereba* or trench, quite extended to the river. Openings of about thirty to fifty yards were left. Besides these there were other small passage-ways left open during daylight, but closed at night. Near the river facing south the ground was rough, and there were several huts, so that the security of the camp was not imperilled by the failure to carry the hedge or trenches to the Nile's brink. Lyttelton's brigade were placed upon the left south front. Wauchope's men continued the line to the right. In the south gap were three companies of the 2nd Battalion Rifle Brigade, their left resting on the river. On their immediate right were three batteries—the 32nd Field Battery of English 15-pounders, under Major Williams; two Maxim-Nordenfeldt mountain batteries, 12½-pounders, respectively under Captains Stewart and de Rougemont; and six Maxims under Captain Smeaton. Later on these guns and Maxims during the first stage of the battle—for the action resolved itself into a double event ere the combat ceased—were wheeled out until they were firing almost at right angles to the *zereba* line. On the right of the guns, in succession, were the remainder of the Rifles, the Lancashire Fusiliers, the Northumberland Fusiliers, and the Grenadier Guards. In the interval between General Lyttelton's brigade and General Wauchope's, which stood next to it, were two Maxims. Then came the Warwicks, Camerons, Seaforths, and Lincolns. To the Lincolns' right, where the trenches began and the line faced nearly west, was Colonel Maxwell's brigade. Between Wauchope's and Maxwell's brigades were two Maxims, and, I think, for a time during the first attack made by the Dervishes, the two-gun mule battery of six-centimetre Krupp guns. To complete the tale of the guns placed for defending the camp, there was Major Lawrie's battery of Maxim-Nordenfeldts on the right of Maxwell's brigade next Macdonald's, and on the north side, near the right of the position facing west, Major Peake's battery of Maxim-Nordenfeldts. These guns had done so well at the Atbara, that the Sirdar promptly increased his artillery by adding three batteries of that class. Maxwell's brigade was composed of three Sudanese and one Egyptian battalion, *viz*., 8th Egyptian, and 12th, 13th, and 14th Sudanese. Farther north, to the right of Colonel Maxwell's men, was Lewis Bey's brigade of Egyptian troops— the 3rd, 4th, 7th, and 15th Battalions. The 15th Battalion was a fine lot, mostly reservists. Upon the farthest west and northern face of the protected camp was. Colonel Macdonald's oft-tried and famous fighting brigade, made up of the 9th, 10th, and 11th Sudanese, with the true-as-steel 2nd Egyptians. Within the wall of hedge, trenches, and armed infantry, in reserve, was another brigade, the 4th Khedivial, commanded by Major Collinson. It was made up of the 1st, 5th, 17th, and 18th Egyptian battalions. The two last-named were relatively newly-raised regiments, but were composed of fine soldierly-looking *fellaheen*. The divisional brigade and battalion commanders and staff were:—British division, Major-General Gatacre commanding; staff: Major Robb, D.A.G.; Captain R. Brooke, A.D.C.; Lieuts. Cox and Ingle, orderly officers; Surgeon-Colonel MacNamara, P.M.O. First British Infantry brigade, Brigadier-General A. Wauchope; staff: Major Doyle Snow, brigade-major; Captain Rennie, A.D.C.; Surgeon-Lieut.-Colonel Sloggett, P.M.O. Second brigade, Brigadier-General, Hon. N. G. Lyttelton; staff: Major A Court, brigade-major; Captain Henderson, A.D.C. Surgeon-General W. Taylor was the principal medical officer of the British division. Lieut.-Colonel C. J. Long, R.A., commanded all the artillery. Khedivial troops—Infantry division, Major-General A. Hunter, commanding; staff: Surgeon-Colonel Gallwey, P.M.O.; Captain Kincaid, D.A.G.; Lieut. Smythe, A.D.C. 1st brigade, Brigadier H. A. Macdonald; Major C. Keith

Falconer, brigade-major. 2nd brigade, Brigadier Lewis; 3rd brigade, Brigadier Maxwell; 4th brigade, Brigadier Collinson.

The battalion commanders of British troops were:—Grenadier Guards, Lieut.-Colonel Villiers-Hatton; Lancashire Fusiliers, Lieut.-Colonel Collingwood; Northumberland Fusiliers, Lieut.-Colonel C. G. C. Money; Rifle Brigade, Colonel Howard; Warwickshires, Lieut.-Colonel Forbes; Lincolns, Lieut.-Colonel Louth; Camerons, Lieut.-Colonel G. L. C. Money; Seaforths, Lieut.-Colonel Murray. Those of the Khedivial battalions were:—Macdonald's brigade, Majors Pink, 2nd Egyptian; Walter, 9th Sudanese; Nason, 10th Sudanese; Jackson, 11th Sudanese. Lewis's brigade, Majors Sellem, 3rd Egyptian; Sparkes, 4th Egyptian; Fatby Bey, 7th Egyptian; and Major Hickman, 15th Egyptian. Maxwell's brigade, Majors Kalousie, 8th Egyptian; Townsend, 12th Sudanese; Smith-Dorian, 13th Sudanese; Shekleton, 14th Sudanese. Collinson's brigade, Captains (O.C.'s) Bainbridge, 1st Egyptian; Abd El Gervad Borham, 5th Egyptian; Bunbury, 17th Egyptian; and Matchell, 18th Egyptian.

The troops were ranged two deep in front with a partial second double line or supports placed twenty yards or so behind them. These assisted in the fight to pass ammunition to the firing line and carry back the dead and wounded. Somewhat removed from the *zereba* and trenches, and nearer the Nile were the hospitals, the transport, the stores, nearly 3000 camels, and about 500 mules. The Egyptian cavalry and camelry were picketed at the north of the camp, and the 21st Lancers at the south end, both being within the lines. All along the river's bank beside the camp were moored the gunboats, steamers and barges, with a fleet of a hundred or more native sailing boats, at once a means of defence and a supply column. The gunboat *Melik* was moored a few hundred yards south of where the Rifles were posted. Occasionally the flotilla flashed their search-lights upon Jebel Surgham, and swept the scrub and desert in front of the troops. The enemy's scouts, however, were never disclosed in the radii of the electric beams. In fact, the first notice we had that the Dervishes were about to inspect our environment was the impetuous incoming of our friendlies from Jebel Surgham and the cracking of snipers' guns in the bush mingled with the buzzing of bullets overhead. A battalion rose quietly from the ground, for the troops slept clear of the hedge, and went forward a few paces to man the *zereba*. On learning what was actually taking place they returned to their blankets and to sleep.

For all the row the Dervish spies, snipers and others made, the army was not really disturbed. Once more we had to thank fortune that the enemy made no vigorous attempt to assail the camp during the night. True, earlier in the evening a few badly-directed rifle-shots had come whistling across the *zereba*. Prowling Dervish scouts had even occasionally crept close enough to draw upon themselves the attention of our double sentries and alert patrols. A small section volley at one period of the night was fired at a knot of the enemy's would-be bush-whackers. The unusual rattle of musketry caused an incipient alarm in one of the battalions. Tommy, however, behaved well, collectively, never stirring, but waiting "for orders." The peace of the night hours was, I repeat, never seriously broken, the Anglo-Egyptian army enjoying their needed sleep. After midnight things quieted down and from the Dervish camp no sound was carried to us by the soft south wind. All was absolutely still in that direction. The *noggara* or war-drum was a dead thing, beating not to quarters, as we had heard it during the day when out with the cavalry. Nor was the deep-bayed booming of the *ombeyas*, or elephant horns, re-echoing to rally the tribesmen under their leaders' banners.

It was 3.40 a.m. on 2nd September when the bugles called the 22,000 men of the Sirdar's army from slumber. Quickly the troops were astir, and the camp full of bustling preparation. It was given out that we were not to move forward quite as early as usual. But circumstances alter cases, and very soon loads and saddles were adjusted with extra care. Everything was made as trim as possible, and belts were buckled tightly for action. There was a sense and expectancy of coming battle abroad, and an eager desire permeating all ranks to have it out with the Dervishes then or never. It had come at length to be generally accepted that the enemy would not bolt nor slip through our fingers, but would accept the gage of battle which the Sirdar meant shortly to give him. We were going to march out, attack, and storm the Khalifa and his great army in their chosen lines and trenches. In a way we felt half-heartedly grateful to our sportsmanlike enemy for not having harassed our marches or bivouacs. We were, within the next hour or so, to have yet more to thank the Dervishes and their Khalifa for. Truly Abdullah was amazingly ignorant of war tactics, or astoundingly confident in the prowess of his arms. From the reckless, magnificent manner in which the Dervishes comported themselves in the earlier stages of the fight that ensued, I incline to the belief that the Khalifa and his men, true to their crass, credulous notions, were overweeningly confident in themselves. A fatal fault, they underrated their opponents. His Emirs, Jehadieh, and Baggara had so often proved themselves invincible in their combats against natives of the Sudan, that they had come to hold that none would face their battle shock. There was pride of countless triumphs, and the long enjoyment of despotic lordship that hardened their wills and thews to win victory or perish. I failed later to see the old fanaticism that once made them, though pierced through and through with bayonet or sword, fight till the last heart-throb ceased. Let me not be misunderstood. Despite their possible doubts about the Khalifa's divine mission, the Dervish army fought with courage and dash until they were absolutely broken. Their personal hardihood bravely compared with the days of Tamai and Abu Klea. It was when the fight was nearly over that there were evidences of that of which there was so little in the old days, *viz.*, that a large remnant would accept life at our hands. Again, as the sequel showed, the Sirdar's star was in the ascendant.

Everything was in readiness in our camp by 5 a.m. Camels, horses, mules, and donkeys had been watered and fed, and the men had disposed of an early breakfast of cocoa or tea, coarse biscuit, and tinned meat. Infantry and artillery had made sure of their full supply of ammunition, and the reserve was handy to draw more from. Tommy Atkins carried 100 rounds of the new hollow-nosed Lee-Metford cartridges. Behind him were mules loaded with a further twenty rounds for him. The Khedivial soldiers had 120 rounds of Martini-Henry cartridges. To hark back: at 4.30 a.m., ere dawn had tinged the east, the Sirdar bade Colonel Broadwood, commanding the Egyptian cavalry, send out two squadrons to ascertain what the enemy was about. Thereupon one squadron rode off to the hills on the west—known locally as South Kerreri *jebels*, but marked on most maps as Um Mutragan. Besides being misnamed, they are plotted in out of place and as if the range trended east and west. It runs nearly north and south. Kerreri hills were low and black, like most of the *jebels* thereabout. They stand fully two miles west of the Nile. Another squadron, under Captain Hon. E. Baring, proceeded south to Jebel Surgham, the low hill, about one mile in front of the British division. I have written about it before. Surgham was used for heliograph and flag signalling on the 1st, the previous day, and is the last of the detached hills or ranges lying near the river on the north towards Omdurman. The squadron going west soon reached South Kerreri hill, and reported that the enemy were still in camp. It was early, and not clear daylight, and the distance to the Khalifa's encampment was greater from South Kerreri hill than that from Jebel Surgham to where the Dervishes lay in the bush and hollows around Wady Shamba. Captain Baring's party, on the other hand, met with small patrols of the enemy near Jebel Surgham. Turning the hill at a few minutes past five o'clock, in the yet slanting daylight, he at once detected that the Khalifa's army, which had apparently been largely reinforced during the night, was marching forward to attack us. Gallopers and orderlies came riding back furiously with the news for the Sirdar. Sir Herbert Kitchener, Major-General Rundle, and the whole headquarters staff were already mounted. Colonel Broadwood was despatched to verify the startling report, and to bring in further particulars. Meantime the preparations on our side for an advance were suspended, and guns, Maxims, and infantry moved up and wheeled into positions upon the firing line. Ominous was that silent march of six paces to their front made by the British infantry to get close to the *zereba* and the clearing for action of Maxims and cannon, and the examining of the breeches of the Lee-Metfords. For the first time the magazines were to be used. The Khedivial soldiers swarmed into their trenches. Anon, the Tommy Atkinses were ordered to lie down behind their hedge of cut mimosa to rest and wait. From a little distance, no doubt, our camp looked silent, deserted, and as void of danger as any other part of the plain. Standing a few yards behind each command were placed in reserve sometimes two, sometimes three companies, which had been withdrawn from the battalion on their immediate front. These reserves were to fill gaps or stiffen the firing line, should it be too closely pressed. With the companies in reserve were the stretchers and bearers. A little farther back was the British divisional field hospital, planted in a congeries of native dirt-huts. The scattered mud-huts within the lines afforded excellent cover to the sick and wounded, as well as a degree of protection for the camels, horses, mules, and donkeys picketed near the middle ground of the camp.

Colonel Broadwood returned swiftly with the news that the whole Dervish army was really in motion, and that if it held upon its apparent course its right wing would pass about 500 yards to the west of Jebel Surgham. That hill was within easy shelling distance from the gunboats, and the solitary instance of prudence that the Dervishes had so far shown was to keep far enough inland to render the assistance of the flotilla of as little help as possible to us. Some there were who thought that Jebel Surgham should have been made the central stronghold of our camp, and that the army ought to have slept behind it on the previous night. The wisdom of that suggestion was most doubtful. Where we were the gunboats could more easily cover the whole position.

It was about 5 a.m. when the 21st Lancers started forward to undertake their daily task of scouting and covering the left flank of the Sirdar's army. They reached Jebel Surgham a few minutes later and relieved Captain Baring's squadron, which at once rode away and joined the remaining squadrons of Egyptian cavalry on South Kerreri hill, whither Colonel Broadwood had by that time gone with his troopers. Every inch of Surgham hill and the yellow sand ridges, gravel mounds, and shallow *khors* to the south and west of it had been explored by the Lancers the day before. Riding straight out from the *zereba* ere the faintly-glowing dawn had come, I joined the Lancers on Surgham. A dismounted squadron occupied part of the southern slopes, a troop or more were on the higher points and summit keeping sharp eyes on the enemy. Flag-signallers were preparing for work at the place where the day before helios had been busy flashing news from gunboats and cavalry to the headquarters. As I climbed the rugged slopes of Jebel Surgham leading my horse, I heard a mighty rumbling as of tempestuous rollers and surf bearing down upon a rock-bound shore. When I had gone but a few strides farther there burst upon my sight a moving, undulating plain of men, flecked with banners and glistening steel. Who should count them? They were compact, not to be numbered. Their front from east to west extended over three miles, a dense mass flowing towards us. It was a great, deep-bodied flood, rather than an avalanche, advancing without flurry, solidly, with presage of power. The sound of their coming grew each instant louder, and became articulate. It was not alone the reverberation of the tread of horses and men's feet I heard and seemed to feel as well as hear, but a voiced continuous shouting and chanting—the Dervish invocation and battle challenge, *"Allah el Allah! Rasool Allah el Mahdi!"* they reiterated in vociferous rhymed rising measure, as they swept over the intervening ground. Their ranks were well kept, the serried lines marching with military regularity, with swaying of flags and brandishing of big-bladed, cruel spears and two-edged swords. Emirs and chiefs on horseback rode in front and along the lines, gesticulating and marshalling their commands. Mounted Baggara trotted about along the inner lines of footmen. There were apparently as before five great divisions in the Dervish army. The Khalifa's corps was near the right centre, with his son, Sheikh Ed Din's division on his left. The relative positions of the great chiefs were readily recognisable by their banners, which were carried in the midst of their chosen body-guards. Khalifa Abdullah's great black banner, black-lettered with texts from the Koran and the Mahdi's sayings, was upheld by his Mulazimin. It flew, spread out, flaunting in the wind, acclaimed by his followers. The flag was about two yards square, and was supported on a 20-feet bamboo pole, ornamented at top with a silver bowl and spandrel, as well as a tassel. The force marching with it must have numbered 20,000 armed men, besides servants and followers. His son, Osman, known as Sheikh Ed Din, and the nominal commander-in-chief of the Dervish armies, led into battle a division of the *Jehadieh* (riflemen) and spearmen, together 15,000 strong. His force was ranged under blue, green, yellow, and white banners. With him was Khalil, the second Khalifa, Osman Azrak, Emir Yunis, Abdel Baki, and other noted chiefs of the Baggara. Yacoub, the notorious brother of the Khalifa Abdullah, commanded the big column upon his relative's right hand. Still farther to their right were the divisions led by Wad Helu and Wad Melik. The joint forces of these twain probably numbered 12,000 or 14,000 men. Besides the main army there was a second line, possibly made up from the Omdurman populace, with a baggage train of camels and donkeys. I found out subsequently that the enemy were amply provisioned. Camels and donkeys carried water and grain, mostly *dhura*, for the Khalifa's army. The Dervishes, as a rule, had their goatskin wallets filled with grain, onions, and a piece of roasted meat.

The battle of Omdurman began at 5.30 a.m. with a salvo of six guns from Major Elmslie's battery on the east Nile bank. They were fired from the 5-inch howitzers, which sent a half-dozen of 50-lb. Lyddite shells hurtling around the tomb and the Khalifa's quarters. Like a spouting volcano, clouds of flame, stones, and dust burst from out the city. The line of strong forts before the town and upon Tuti island had been silenced by them and the gunboats the previous day. Although the Dervishes had built stout works, and had plenty of cannon and ammunition, they made a wretchedly bad stand against the gunboats, injuring none of them. The overpowering weight as well as the accuracy of our steamers' fire ended the naval part of the battle almost as soon as it was begun. Quick-firers and Maxims were trained to bear into the embrasures of the Khalifa's forts. As a consequence, the enemy's gunners were only able to fire a few wild rounds at the vessels. Jealous and suspicious of everyone, Abdullah left his arsenal full of unemployed batteries, Krupps, and machine guns, and only took three of either of the latter weapons with him into the field against us. After the labour too of taking them there, he made but little use of them. As I learned, the Greeks, some thirty-five, and all able-bodied men, had to march out of Omdurman and follow the Khalifa to battle. I by no means, I think, over-estimate the enemy's numbers when I state that there were 50,000 Dervishes of sorts who advanced against us, sworn to leave not a single soul alive in the

BATTLE OF OMDURMAN—*ZEREBA* ACTION

Sirdar's army. Abdullah, professedly sanguine of success, had bade the *mollahs* and others attend him at noon prayers in the mosque and Mahdi's tomb, where he would go to worship immediately after his victory. He had returned into town, and spent part of the night of 1st and 2nd September in his own house.

The gunboats, which had gone on that morning, joined in the renewed bombardment of Omdurman, begun by Major Elmslie. But it was only for a short space, for the Sirdar recalled the steamers by signal to assist in repelling the attack when it was seen the Khalifa meant giving battle. Three squadrons of Lancers halted on the northern side of Jebel Surgham. A troop of them pushed on to the sandy ridges south-west of Surgham hill. Part of them dismounted, and with much hardihood began firing at about 1000 yards' range at the oncoming Dervishes. It was as if a few men afoot were seeking to interpose to hold back the invading ocean. Instantly Dervish riflemen and horsemen shot out from the Khalifa's lines and came streaming to engage the handful of troopers. The skirmishing Lancers desisted, mounted, and rode back to their main body. Of those of the Lancers who stood it out longest were the groups upon the top of Surgham and upon its eastern side. Colonel Martin got his four squadrons together as the Dervishes drew in towards him. The enemy's right was now thrown forward, facing straight for the angle of the camp where the British division stood. At a swinging gait came the vast army of Mahdism. I was still near Surgham and believed that I could discern the Khalifa himself in the centre of a jostling, excited throng of footmen and horsemen. He was seated upon a richly caparisoned Arab steed, guarded on all sides by stalwart natives armed with rifles and swords. A troop of mounted Emirs in front and a big retinue of Baggara and other chiefs on horseback riding behind surely proclaimed him to be Abdullah, the Mahdi's successor. Far before him was borne his terrible black banner. Around him religious Dervishes screamed, gesticulated, and shouted "Allah's" name, confident that they had come out to see the annihilation of the invading infidels. Had it not been long foretold that the victorious battle would be fought at Kerreri, which ever after should be known among the faithful as "the death-field of the infidels"? Were not the white stones there already to mark our graves? I was fortunate to be able to scan the nearest of the Dervish columns, from a distance of but 800 yards. The battle was about to open in fierce earnest. Away went the Lancers at the gallop, back to the *zereba*, but, edging towards the river, to clear our infantry's front and line of fire. It was around the left of the 2nd battalion of the Rifle Brigade that the troopers passed in. I took a somewhat shorter, hasty cut, entering the *zereba* near where the three batteries stood, on the British left. Away off upon and under Um Mutragan, the Egyptian mounted troops, the nine squadrons of cavalry, eight companies of the Camel Corps, and the horse artillery, all under Colonel Broadwood, were pluckily endeavouring to tackle the left wing of the Khalifa's forces. They held on, perhaps, too long; at any rate, until most of them were in a position of serious danger. As their fight and the more important general action happened at the same time, I must defer further description of it for the moment.

It was a magnificent spectacle that rose before the Sirdar's army as the Dervish columns came sweeping into view, filling the landscape between Surgham and Um Mutragan. In that great multitude were gathered the fiercest, most sanguinary body of savage warriors the world has ever held or known. Arabs and blacks, chosen by Abdullah himself, picked out because of their tried courage, strength, and devotion—the flower of the fighting Sudan tribes. Under other conditions Abdullah's army might have matched itself to win against double their number of any men similarly armed. Fearless of danger, agile yet strong, each man carried with him into the fight the conviction that the Khalifa would conquer. A great shout of exultation went up from the Dervish legions when they saw, ranged in the low ground before them, the Sirdar's, small army, their imagined prey. There was a mighty waving of banners and flashing of steel when, breaking into a run, they bent forward to close upon us. The British division rose to their feet to be ready, and the Khedivial troops closed up their ranks. There was a murmur of satisfaction from Gatacre's division and real cries of delight from the black troops on seeing the enemy were coming to attack. Never was there a grander, more imposing militant display seen than when the great Dervish army rushed to engage, heedless of life or death. In an instant the Sirdar, who stood near the right of Wauchope's brigade, passed an order for the three batteries on the left—Major Williams', Stewart's, de Rougemont's—to open fire. The guns were laid at 2800 yards, a range the delight of gunners, and sighted to the west of Surgham, where the black flag and the largest mass of the enemy were. The hour was 6.35 a.m. Almost at the first shot the true range was found. Quick as thought thereafter the eighteen guns on our left began raining fire, iron, and lead upon the leading and main columns of the enemy. Two batteries to the right and many of the Maxims added to the fury of the fearful death-dealing storm bursting over and amongst the Dervish ranks. The long 15-pounder English field cannon hit with the precision of match rifles, and were discharged as though they had been quick-firing guns. As for the stinging Maxim-Nordenfeldts, with their big single and bigger double shells, they bucked and jumped like kicking horses, yet were fired so fast that the barrels must have been well-nigh red-hot. The air was torn with hurtling shell at the first awful salvo, when shrapnel burst in all directions, smiting the Dervishes as with Heaven's thunderbolts, and strewing the ground with maimed and dead. The leading columns paused as if they had received a shock, or had stopped to catch breath. Hundreds had been slain in that one discharge, and the fire was rapidly increasing, not slackening. Disregarding their dead and wounded, the Dervishes closed their ranks as with one accord, and came on with fresh energy. Their banner-bearers and the Baggara horsemen pushed to the front, doubtless to further encourage the still dauntless footmen. Surely there never was wilder courage displayed. In the face of a fire that mowed down battalions and smashed great gaps into their columns they flinched not nor turned. Noticing the enemy's persistency, the Sirdar sent bidding General Lyttelton try them with long-range volleys from the Lee-Metfords. Major Lord Edward Cecil took the message, and Lieutenant H. M. Grenfell got the range from the gunners. The Grenadier Guards, who had the honour of being the first of our infantry to engage, were ordered to fire section volleys to their right at the Khalifa's division; the range 2700 yards. Standing up and pointing their rifles over the hedge they blazed away very steadily at the Dervishes. Occasionally they caught and slew a group, but at that period it was difficult to make out, even through good field-glasses, whether the infantry fire was really effective. There was no doubt about what the gunners were doing, for horses and riders and footmen were bowled over or sank to the ground as shrapnel and common shell struck their ranks. The artillerymen invariably trained their weapons to bear upon the front of the densest of the Dervish columns, seeking to pulverise them. As for the Maxims—and I closely watched the effect of their fire through my glasses—I am compelled to say that they often failed to settle upon the swarming foe. At any rate, their effectiveness was not equal to what might have been expected. Would the Khalifa succeed, in the face of such an awful cannonade, in reaching the *zereba* with a corporal's guard? But after all, it usually takes tons of iron and lead to kill a man. There was marvellous vitality in the Dervish masses. Thousands were knocked over by the screaming, bursting shells, which made hills and plain ring with thunderous uproar. But numbers of the apparently killed were merely wounded, and they speedily rose and truculently hastened forward anew with their fellow-tribesmen. A diversion that told momentarily in the enemy's favour occurred. The extreme Dervish right at that moment appeared climbing the slopes of Jebel Surgham. Emir Melik's wing, hidden from view by that intervening high ground, had, as it came on, been reinforced by a part of Yacoub's division. By other accounts Osman Digna, as well, had united forces with Melik. There suddenly sprang into threatening proximity before us, a force of at least fifteen odd thousand men, with a wide surf-line of white, red, and gold lettered banners, less than a mile away. Brandishing their weapons and shouting "Allah!" down the slopes they ran towards the *zereba*. Emirs rode in front, and gaunt, black riflemen sped like hounds, keeping pace with the horses. The guns of one battery, then another, and finally all three, upon General Lyttelton's left, were turned upon them. Maxims also were swung round, and the long-distance volleys were dropped for shorter ranges. The Dervish main columns which had got shelter in low *khors* re-appeared, and without pause joined in the hot rush for our *zereba*. Our elated foemen evidently thought they would at last be able to close with us. In their ignorance they reckoned not with the accuracy and discipline of the British infantry fire. Nor had they then learned to dread the terrible bullets of our men's Lee-Metford rifles. Later in the day, as well as on the following one, I heard many expressions of regret from wounded and unwounded Dervishes that they were so mad as to charge the white soldiers, whose bullets rarely missed. The light was good, the hour about 7 a.m., and the ranges shifted rapidly from 1700 yards to 1500 yards, 1200 yards down to 1000 yards. Guns, Maxims, and rifles were blazing in fullest fury at the enemy, as, in their heroic effort, they sought to charge home upon us. From wing to wing Gatacre's division was firing sharply, a blaze of flame, section volleys and independently. The Grenadier Guardsmen's shooting was noted as conspicuously steady and deadly effective. Except the two companies of the Rifles on the left, who, owing to the nature of the ground on their front, could do little, the British infantry were hotly occupied. Rifles became too warm to be held, and were in some cases changed for those of rear-rank men's. In one or two instances the reserves closed up, to give every soldier an opportunity of being actually engaged. They took the place of sections in the firing lines, whilst their comrades fell back and refilled their cartridge pouches. The Lancers sent forward a dismounted squadron or two which filled the gap between the *zereba* and the Nile, whilst the gunboats *Melik* and *Sultan* moved in and took part in that stage of the battle. And still the Dervishes got nearer, swinging up their left, for their right was now fairly held by the British fire. Colonels Maxwell's and Lewis's brigades had to address themselves to the task of checking the Khalifa's attack. Colonel Long had so disposed the cannon and Maxims that the guns rendered invaluable help. At that period the main body of the Dervishes moved forward more carefully, taking cover and evidently watching the issue of Yacoub's and Wad Melik's assaulting columns.

The army of white flags, led by Yacoub and Wad Melik, exhibited dash, courage, and persistence. Never was a column of men so hammered and mutilated and probably so surprised. They were torn and thrown about as puppets before the hurricane of shell fire, and laid in windrows like cut grain before the hail of the Lee-Metfords. Twelve hundred short yards away, Surgham's bare slopes were being literally covered with corpses and writhing wounded. In sheer blundering brutishness, the ferocious Dervishes tried to stem the storm. Wave followed wave of men, they surged together, inviting greater disaster, but always striving to get nearer us. Their front had covered the whole slopes of Jebel Surgham and their left overlapped part of the Khalifa's right. Death was reaping a gigantic harvest. Hecatombs of slain were being spread everywhere in front. The fight was terrible, the slaughter dreadful. So far we had scarcely suffered loss, only a few of the enemy's riflemen having paused and thought of firing at us. Muskets they had discharged in the air, after their manner, when advancing from their encampment. But that is one of their customs, employed to work up a proper warlike ardour. Viewed from our side, it had been so far the least dangerous battle ever soldier bore part in. For five, ten minutes, less or more—the drama being enacted was too fearful and fascinating for one to take note of time—Yacoub and his legions still strove to breast the whirlwind of destruction involving them. Battered, torn, rent into groups, the survivors at length began to move off rapidly across our front, to their left. As yet there was no running away, they were but changing direction and massing at another point. With, if possible, swifter, deadlier fire they were followed and driven. Maxims, Lee-Metfords, and Martini-Henrys from Maxwell's brigade shattered the loose and weakened Dervish columns. The few rounds fired back at us by the enemy from their Krupp gun and rifled cannon, which were stationed near the Khalifa's banner during the first part of the action, did no harm. In fact, their shells burst two or three hundred yards short of the *zereba*. At first they were mistaken for badly-aimed shells fired by the gunboats, from which a few pitched near us, or by the batteries upon our left. For a moment the Sirdar was wrath at what was fancied to be our gunners' blundering practice. It was quickly discovered, however, that the particular shells in question were aimed by the Dervishes. Very soon,—whether settled by our guns, our Maxims, or by infantry volleys, I know not,—the Dervish cannon and their foolish efforts to shell our lines troubled us no more. We knew afterwards that they had also got one of their 5-barrelled Nordenfeldts to work for a while. Nobody in our ranks, I think, was actually aware of the fact at the time, so indifferent was the aiming and so bad the handling of the gun.

Still, the crucial stage of the first action was not over. The Sheikh Ed Din had driven the Egyptian cavalry and Camel Corps from Um Mutragan, inflicting loss upon them and getting temporary possession of several guns of the horse battery. He was following them up vigorously, and the Camel Corps, protected by the gunboats' fire, was seeking shelter near the river and close to the north end of the *zereba*, where it luckily succeeded in getting. It was after seven a.m., and Colonel Broadwood's troopers were trying to shake off flanking parties of the enemy as they rode to the north, towards our previous camp. Our batteries were still pounding the Khalifa's main body, which had got to within 1400 yards of the south-western angle of the *zereba*. Wavering, and driven before the murderous tornado of exploding bombs and pitiless lead, they too swung round and made for cover beyond range, flying towards the west and slightly to the rear. Yacoub and Melik followed the black flag in the same direction, and the Dervish left wing edged off to Um Mutragan. They had come, first of all, direct, as if intending to assault the western angles of the *zereba*. Then Yacoub and Melik had led them to the right, so that they covered Surgham and came on in front of the British division. Blindly they had stumbled into the impassable fire from the south face of our lines and ultimately relinquishing the task had hastened, as I have stated, across our front towards their main body. The guns and Maxims withal of Wauchope's and Maxwell's infantry, must have weakened the hope in the Khalifa's breast of closing with us. Although the range was longer, the central columns had been subjected to almost as destructive a cannonading as the Dervishes on Surgham's slopes got. So far it had been a gunner's day, and to the artillery in the preliminary stages, if not—with one exception—in the later, belonged the full honours of the fight. At length with one mind, banner-bearers and all, swiftly the Dervish columns, remaining intact, faced to the left, and moved behind the western hills. There was a pause, a respite for some minutes, which their *jehadieh* and others left upon the field of battle profited by to crawl upon their stomachs to within 800 yards less or more of the *zereba*, and open a sharp rifle fire upon us. Volley firing and shell firing dislodged many of them, but others kept potting away, increasing our casualty returns, particularly in the 1st, or Wauchope's brigade. Just then the battle broke out with greater fury than ever. What happened in the Dervish army may be guessed. Out of immediate danger and re-formed, the Khalifa and Yacoub determined upon a second attack. With a rush like a mountain torrent three columns spouted from shallow ravines, and at a break-neck run came forward. Part of Wad Melik's men uprose from the west sides of Surgham, the Khalifa and Yacoub came upon us from the south-west, and a smaller body from the west. In half delirium and full frenzy on rushed the Dervishes. Our guns, knowing the range to a nicety—for they were able to see landmarks put down the day before—hurled at them avalanches of shell. The vivid air blazed and shook, and the hail of Lee-Metfords cut, like mighty scythes, lanes in the columns massed ten-deep. Greater resolution and bravery no men ever possessed. In face of destruction and death they continued their wild race. But they were thinning or being thinned as they drew nearer. When about 1100 yards away a body of horsemen, two hundred or so, the Khalifa's own tribesmen, Taaisha Baggara, chiefs and Emirs, setting spurs to their horses charged direct for the *zereba*. Cannon and Maxims smashed them, infantry bullets beat against and pierced through them. At every stride their numbers diminished, horses and riders being literally blown over or cut and thrown down. Undaunted a remnant held on to within two or three hundred yards of Colonel Maxwell's line, where the last of the gallant foemen tumbled and bit the dust. Partly encouraged by the self-sacrificing devotion of the horsemen, the footmen followed. The black flag was carried to within 900 yards of Colonel Maxwell's left. Learning from their earlier failure, the Khalifa's men directed their attack upon the Egyptian troops. But the British division's cross-fire smote them, and the guns and Maxims knocked all cohesion out of their ranks. Still defiantly they set their standards and died around them. Then I noted there were again signs of wavering amongst the main body, who were hanging back. The big black flag was stuck in a heap of stones, and the more devoted sought to rally there. Abdullah himself and his chiefs endeavoured to collect the broken columns. It was attempted in the face of a bombardment that would have shaken a city, and a fusillade that ought to have mown down every blade of *halfa*-grass near. But Maxwell's men seemed not quite to get the range. The flag and flagstaff were riddled with bullet holes, and the dead were being piled around. Still, Dervish after Dervish sprang to uphold the black banner of Mahdism. A herculean black grasped the staff in one hand, and leaned negligently against it for what appeared to be the space of five or ten minutes,—probably less than one minute,—ere the soldiers managed to give him his final quietus. Then it was that the remnant of the army of the Khalifa began to melt away. It was more than human nature could bear. The dense columns had shrunk to companies, the companies to driblets, which finally fled westward to the hills, leaving the field white with *jibbeh*-clad corpses like a landscape dotted with snowdrifts.

It was about eight o'clock, and the first action was virtually over and won. Good fortune, as the Sirdar admitted, had in many respects attended him. With a trifling loss of a few hundred men he had discomfited and slain 10,000 of the great Dervish army.

Presumably, Abdullah had lost the flower of his brave and devoted troops. There were yet a thousand or more of *Jehadieh* lying about under cover potting at the *zereba*. Many of them shammed being wounded to get closer to us. Sharp volleys and more shell-fire duly disposed of those determined snipers. It was from that source, during the critical stages of the battle when the infantry were stopping the Khalifa's columns, that our chief casualties occurred. Some of these sharpshooters crept to within 800 yards of the British lines, and up to 400 yards from Maxwell's. It was from them that Captain Caldecott received his death-wound and the Cameron losses came. I could not but observe the fact, as I walked and rode about behind the firing lines during the action. Still, the battle of Omdurman has the right to be considered from the victor's point of view the safest action ever fought. The Warwick loss in the first action was one officer killed and two men wounded; the Camerons, one man killed and two officers and eighteen men wounded—Colonel Money had two horses shot under him, as at the Atbara; the Seaforths had eighteen men wounded; and the Lincolns ten men wounded. In General Lyttelton's brigade the Grenadier Guards had one officer, Captain Bagshot, and four men wounded; the Northumberland Fusiliers had but one man wounded; the Lancashire Fusiliers four men wounded; and the Rifles six men wounded.

CHAPTER 11

The Battle of Omdurman
—*Continued*

Before I deal with the second phase of the battle, there is something more to be said of the first. So far I have but written of the infantry and the artillery. It is no easy task to give a succinct account of a whole catalogue of events happening at the same time over so widespread a field. The battle of Omdurman was full of incident and of Homeric combats. Whilst we in the *zereba* were awaiting, ready and confident of the issue, the oncoming of the enemy, the two regiments of Egyptian cavalry and the Camel Corps, which had advanced on the right to Um Mutragan hills,—South Kerreri *jebels*,—like the 21st Lancers at El Surgham on the left were opposing the Dervish advance. Their orders were to check the Dervish left. The nine squadrons of troopers with Colonel Broadwood remained on the plain, but the Camel Corps, seven companies, with four Maxims, and the horse battery went up the west shoulder of one of the Um Mutragan hills. As the Dervishes were advancing very rapidly, the four Maxims under Captain Franks were recalled into the *zereba* before they had fired a shot, or ere the mounted troops got into action. Three dismounted squadrons of Egyptian troopers thereupon went forward and temporarily occupied the position which had been assigned to the Maxims. The Camel Corps were already afoot, and had lined the crest and slopes of the hill, waiting to fire as soon as the Mahdists came within range.

When the big columns of the Dervishes, led by the Sheikh Ed Din, Khalifa Khalil and Ali Wad Helu, approached nearer, Major Young's horse battery of six guns began shelling them at 1500 yards range. The Camel Corps then opened a sharp fusillade, and within a few minutes a brisk fight was going on. But the enemy neither halted nor stayed in face of the fire. It only served to quicken their pace, and they ran forward shooting rapidly the while. An order was sent to the Camel Corps to retire at once, as the Dervishes were seen to be trying to cut them off by advancing on both sides of the hill. Before the order carried by Lieutenant Lord Tullibardine actually reached them, they had suffered severely and were falling back. A large number of men and camels had been hit. The cavalry endeavoured to relieve the pressure. Ultimately, though hotly pressed by the Dervishes who got to within a few hundred yards, the Horse Artillery and the Camel Corps took up a second position upon a ridge fully half a mile to the rear. From the *zereba* we could see that the mounted troops were being hurried, and that the action taking place was an exceedingly sharp one. In fact, before the guns and the Camel Corps got into position upon the second ridge, the Dervishes were firing at them from the summit and slopes of Um Mutragan. Major Young had only fired a round or two from his guns when the enemy were but 600 yards off. The Dervishes were swarming along the eastern sides of Um Mutragan, running direct for the guns and the Camel Corps. Colonel Broadwood formed his cavalry up to charge, and Major Mahan led his regiment of "Gippy" troopers forward. But a detachment of the Camel Corps under Captain Hopkinson pluckily stood their ground, covering the retirement of their comrades and the batteries down the very rough slope. Unfortunately, Captain Hopkinson was severely wounded, and a native officer and a number of men were killed. Falling back along the east and north sides of the hill the force was sorely pressed by the enemy, and a series of brave and bristling hand-to-hand encounters took place. Near the crest of a hill, one of the "wheelers" of the horse battery was shot. The traces could not be cut in time, so the gun had to be abandoned. At the critical moment another gun collided with it, and was upset beside the first, so both pieces, with, later on, a third, fell temporarily into the Dervishes' hands. They did nothing with them. Colonel Broadwood, on finding the enemy pushing so determinedly, as though they had struck the whole of the Sirdar's army, directed the Camel Corps to retire to the *zereba*. Luckily, two of the gunboats, getting sight and range of the eager Dervishes who were hunting the camelmen, began firing with every piece of armament they could bring to bear. I assume they saved the situation, for the Camel Corps were hard pressed, and lost eighty men before they got to the river and into a safe position under the shelter of the gunboats and Macdonald's brigade, which was at the north end of the *zereba*. The myth of a Camel Corps as a useful fighting unit had been exploded. Meantime, Colonel Broadwood's troopers rode away to the north, trying to shake off outflanking parties of Dervishes. The Sheikh Ed Din and Khalil continued to pursue the cavalry with great eagerness and venom. Several times bodies of 200 and 300 Baggara horsemen threatened to charge, but Majors Mahan and Le Gallias turning upon these riders sent them flying back helter-skelter. For five miles the cavalry was, so to speak, driven from pillar to post by the Dervish infantry. When the pursuit had been pressed four miles, and more, north of the *zereba*, Major Mahan succeeded in clearing the flanks, whereupon the Dervishes gave up the chase and sat down to rest. One advantage came of the hot-headed pursuit; it led two columns of the enemy away, and only a portion of those Dervish commands got back in time to engage in the assault upon the *zereba*.

When the Khalifa Abdullah, who escaped being killed, retired with his shattered army after their futile attack behind the western hills a little south of Um Mutragan, it was thought that the fighting spirit had been knocked out of the enemy. There was no assurance that if the Sirdar and his men followed after the Khalifa the Dervishes would risk a second battle. They had the legs of us, and would presumably use them to run away, or to harass us if we went after them into the wilderness. Discreetly and shrewdly the Sirdar decided to march his army straight into Omdurman, but six miles distant. We were able to move upon inside lines and over open ground, so that if the Khalifa meant to race us for the place he would have to fight at a disadvantage. The command was issued about 8.30 to prepare to march out of camp for Omdurman. Our wounded, who had been borne from the field on stretchers, were put upon the floating hospitals. Colonel Collinson's brigade was told off to guard stores and material to be left behind for a time. Ammunition was drawn from the reserve stores afloat, and the supply columns' boxes were refilled, as well as the battery limbers and the men's pouches. The army was again equipped for action as though it had not fired a shot. Camels were reloaded, and all was in readiness for a start. We could see bodies of the enemy still flaunting their banners, and watching our every movement from the western hills. Wounded Dervishes were crawling and dragging wearily back from their fated field towards Omdurman. There was the occasional crack of a rifle as some Dervish sniped us, or invited a shot from the Egyptian battalions. Many of our black soldiers actually wept with vexation on being withdrawn from the firing line to make room for guns and Maxims. One man, who declared he had not fired a shot, was only comforted on being assured that the battle was not altogether over, that his chance would come later.

I think it was about 9 a.m. when the Sirdar's army, re-formed for marching, stepped clear of the *zereba* and the trenches. The order of advance for the infantry was as before, in echelon of brigades, the British being on the left and in front. Lyttelton's 2nd brigade was leading, Wauchope's was behind it. On the right were Maxwell's and Lewis's brigades. Macdonald was to look after our extreme right rear flank, whilst Collinson followed in the gap nearer the river. Lyttelton's brigade was directed to pass to the left, east of Jebel Surgham, Maxwell's left was to extend to and pass over the hill, whilst Lewis and Macdonald would sweep part of the valley between Surgham and South Kerreri. Such was the general direction to be taken, exposing a front

MACDONALD'S FIGHT AND 21ST LANCERS' CHARGE

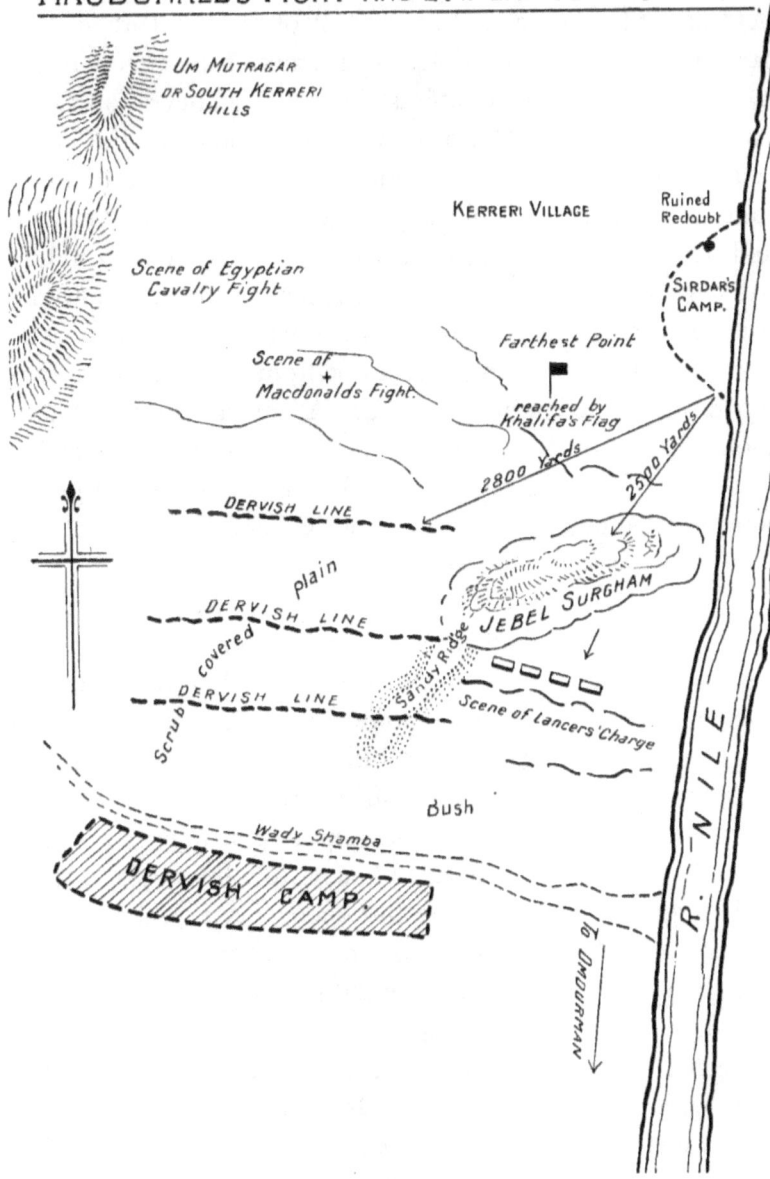

measured on the bias, of fully one mile. Once more the 21st Lancers trotted out towards Jebel Surgham to make sure there were no large bodies of the enemy in hiding. Keeping somewhat closer to the river than previously, and avoiding the main field of battle, they passed to the east of the hill. Part of their duty was to check, if possible, any attempt of the enemy to fall back into Omdurman, or at least delay such an operation. Great numbers of scattered Dervishes were seen, some of whom fired at the troopers. Keeping on until about half a mile or more south of Surgham, a small party of Dervish cavalry, about thirty, and what was thought to be a few footmen, were seen hiding in a depression or *khor*. Colonel Martin determined to push the party back and interpose his regiment between them and Omdurman. A few spattering shots came from the *khor*, as the four squadrons formed in line to charge. "A" squadron, under Major Finn, was on the right, next it was "B" squadron, commanded by Major Fowle. On the left of "B" was "D," or the made-up squadron, led by Captain Eadon, and "C" squadron, under Captain Doyne, was on the extreme left.

Leading the regiment forward at a gallop from a point 300 yards away, the Lancers dashed at the enemy, who at once opened a sharp musketry fire upon our troopers. A few casualties occurred before the Dervishes were reached, but the squadrons closed in and setting the spurs into their horses rushed headlong for the enemy. In an instant it was seen that, instead of 200 men, the 21st had been called upon to charge nearly 1500 fierce Mahdists lying concealed in a narrow, but in places deep and rugged, *khor*. In corners the enemy were packed nearly fifteen deep. Down a three-foot drop went the Lancers. There was a moment or so of wild work, thrusting of steel, lance, and sword, and rapid revolver shooting. Somehow the regiment struggled through, and up the bank on the south side. Nigh a score of lances had been left in Dervish bodies, some broken, others intact. Lieutenant Wormwald made a point at a fleeing Baggara, but his sabre bent and had to be laid aside. Captain Fair's sword snapped over Dervish steel, and he flung the hilt in his opponent's face. Major Finn used his revolver, missing but two out of six shots. Colonel Martin rode clean through without a weapon in his hand. Then the regiment rallied 200 yards beyond the slope. Probably 80 Dervishes had been cut or knocked down by the shock. But the few seconds' bloody work had been almost equally disastrous for the Lancers. Lieutenant R. Grenfell and fifteen men had been left dead in the *khor*. It so happened that the squadrons on the two wings had comparatively easy going and did not strike the densest groups of the enemy. Squadrons "D" and "B" fared badly, and particularly Lieutenant Grenfell's troop, of whom ten men fell with that officer. In their front was a high rough bank of boulders, almost impassable for a horse. They were cut down and hacked by the enemy. His brother, Lieutenant H. M. Grenfell, subsequently recovered his watch, which had been thrust through by a Dervish lance point and had stopped at 8.40 a.m. Young Robert Grenfell was probably struck from behind with a Mahdist sword blade, and killed instantly as his charger was endeavouring to scramble up the wall of loose stones and rock. Melees were taking place to right and left, every trooper having any difficulty in getting out of the *khor* being instantly surrounded by mounted Dervishes and footmen. Lieutenant Nesham in leading his troop was savagely attacked. His helmet was cut off his head, and he was wounded severely upon the left forearm and right leg. The bridle reins of his charger were cut, but he piloted the animal safely through. "B" and "D" squadrons lost respectively nine killed and eleven wounded, and seven killed and eight wounded. Lieutenant Molyneux, R.H.G., had his horse knocked over. He called to a trooper not to leave him, and the man replied, "All right, sir, I won't leave you." Together they had a busy time. Two Dervishes attacked the lieutenant; he shot one, but the other cut him over the right arm, causing him to drop his revolver. He then ran for it and got away. Lieutenants Brinton and Pirie received wounds. Private Ives of "A" squadron picked up a wounded comrade in the *nullah*, and got chased and separated from his regiment. He reached the infantry covered with his comrade's blood. The latter was killed, but Ives was not seriously hurt.

Lieutenant Montmorency, having got through safely, turned back to look for his troop-sergeant Carter. Captain Kenna went with him. At the moment they were not aware that young Grenfell had fallen. Lieutenants T. Connally and Winston Churchill also turned about to rescue two non-commissioned officers of their respective troops. They succeeded in their laudable task. Surgeon-Captain Pinches, whose horse had been shot under him on the north side of the *khor*, was saved by the pluck of his orderly, Private Peddar, who brought him out on his horse. Meanwhile, Captain Kenna and Lieutenant Montmorency, who were accompanied by Corporal Swarbrick, saw Lieutenant Grenfell's body and tried to recover it. They fired at the Dervishes with their revolvers, and drove them back. Dismounting, Montmorency and Kenna tried to lift the body upon the lieutenant's horse. Unluckily, the animal took fright and bolted. Swarbrick went after it. Major Wyndham, the second in command of the Lancers, had his horse shot in the *khor*. He was one of the few who escaped after such a calamity. The animal fortunately carried him across, up, and beyond the slope ere it dropped down dead. Lieutenant Smith, who was near, offered him a seat, and the Major grasped the stirrup to mount. Just then—for these events have taken longer in telling than in happening—Montmorency and Kenna found the Dervishes pressing them hard, both being in instant danger of being killed. Swarbrick had brought back the horse, and Kenna turned to Major Wyndham and gave him a seat behind, then leaving Grenfell's body they rejoined their command. Proceeding about 300 yards to the south-east from the scene of the charge, Colonel Martin dismounted his whole regiment, and opened fire upon the Dervishes. Getting into position where his men could fire down the *khor*, a detachment of troopers soon drove away the last of the enemy. Thereupon a party advanced and recovered the bodies of Lieutenant Grenfell and the others who had fallen in the *khor*.

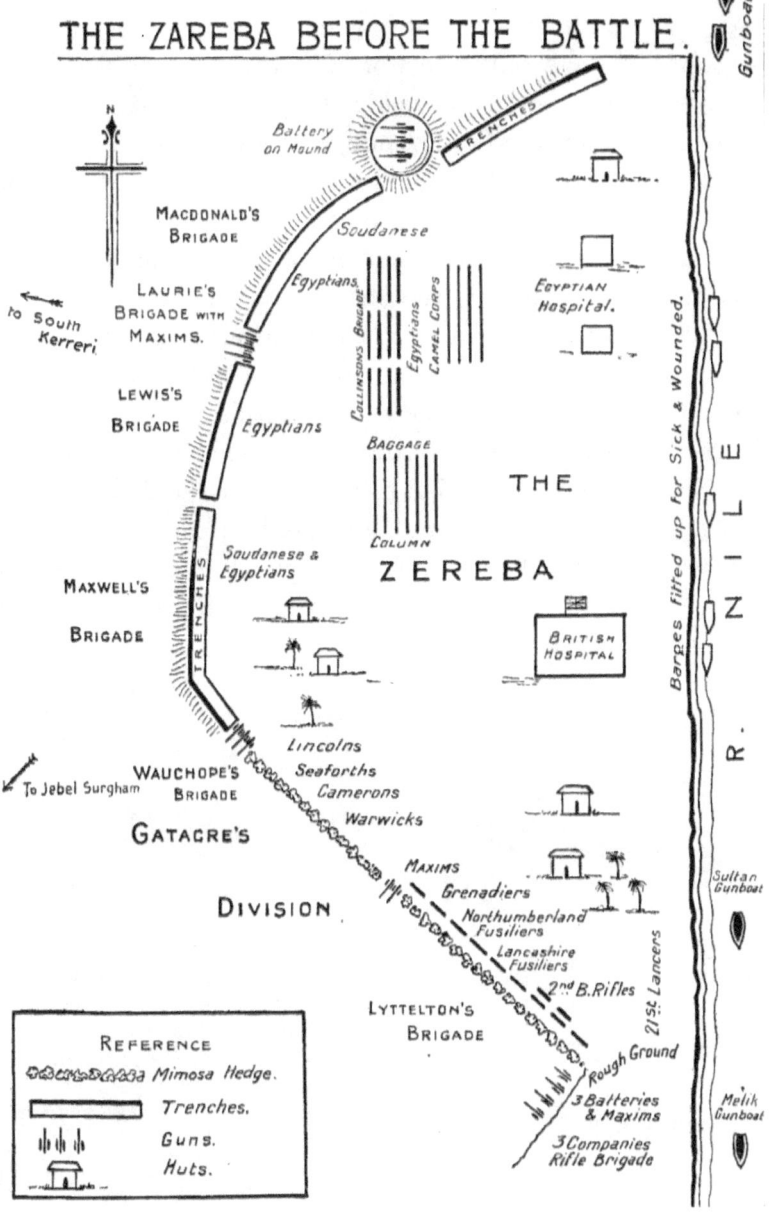

It was a daring, a great feat of arms for a weakened regiment of 320 men to charge in line through a compact body of 1500 Dervish footmen, packed in a natural earthwork. Perhaps it is even a more remarkable feat that they were able to cut their way through with only a loss of 22 killed and 50 officers and men wounded and 119 casualties in horseflesh. Many of the poor beasts only lived long enough to carry their riders out of the jaws of death. One cannot refuse to admire the gallant deed, which probably had as good an effect upon the enemy as a bigger victory of our arms; but the obvious comment will be that made about the Balaclava charge—equally heroic, and not, I honestly think, less useful—"*C'est magnifique, mais ce n'est pas la guerre.*" On searching the ground inside the *khor* sixty dead Dervishes were found where the central squadrons passed over. A small heap lay around Lieutenant Grenfell and his troop. Four of our men were found alive, but died before they could be moved. A sword-cut had cleft young Grenfell's head and given him a painless death. The bodies were, as usual, full of sword-cuts and spear-thrusts inflicted by the enemy before and after the victims had breathed their last.

MACDONALD'S BRIGADE ADVANCING

Egyptian Heroism

It is a long tale I am telling, but yet the most brilliant and heroic episode of a day so full of glowing incident remains to be told. About 9.20 a.m. the Sirdar led his troops slowly forward towards Omdurman. Great as the slaughter had been, thousands of Dervishes could be seen still watching us from the western hills. Behind them they had re-formed again into compact divisions. The Sirdar's direction, I have said, was that his troops were to swing clear of the *zereba* and march in echelon with the 2nd British brigade leading Moving out a few hundred yards, Lyttelton's brigade, which, as before, marched in four parallel columns of battalions, the Guards on the right, swung to the left. They were making to pass Surgham, leaving it upon their right. The 1st British brigade, Major-General Wauchope's, was behind, and had turned to the left to follow the 2nd brigade. Behind, in succession, were Maxwell's, Lewis's, and Macdonald's Egyptian or Khedivial brigades. The nature of the ground forced some of them out of their true relative positions. Macdonald had marched out due west. The Dervishes, like wolves upon the scent for prey, suddenly sprang from unexpected lairs. With swifter feet and fiercer courage than ever they dashed for the comparatively isolated brigade of Colonel Macdonald. Although I was far away at the moment with the 1st or Lyttelton's brigade, the shouts, the noise of the descending tornado reached me there. From behind the southern slope of Um Mutragan hills the Khalifa was charging Macdonald with an intact column of 12,000 men, the banner-bearers and mounted Emirs again in the forefront. A broad stream, running from the south and the east, of Dervishes who had lain hidden sprang up and ran to strike in upon the southeast corner of Macdonald's brigade. Worse still, Sheikhs Ed Din and Khalifa Khalil, returned from chasing the Egyptian cavalry, were hastening with their division at full speed to attack him in rear. Scarcely a soul in the Sirdar's army, from the leader down, but saw the unexpected singular peril of the situation.

I turned to a friend and said, "Macdonald is in for a terrible time. Will any get out of it?"

Then I rode at a gallop, disregarding the venomous Dervishes hanging about, up the slopes of Surgham, where, spread like a picture, the scene lay before me. Prompt in execution, the Sirdar rapidly issued orders for the artillery and Maxims to open fire upon the Khalifa's big column. Eagerly he watched the batteries coming into action. At the same moment the remaining brigades were wheeled to face west, and Major-General Wauchope's was sent back at the double to help the staunch battalions of Colonel Macdonald, now beset on all sides. Fortunately Macdonald knew his men thoroughly, for he had had the training of all of them, the 9th, 10th, 11th Sudanese, and the 2nd Egyptians under Major Pink. No force could have been in time to save them had they not fought and saved themselves. Lewis's brigade was nearest, but it was almost a mile away, and the Dervishes were wont to move so that ordinary troops seemed to stand still. And Lewis, for reasons of his own, determined to remain where he was.

Indecision or flurry would have totally wrecked Macdonald's brigade, but happily their brigadier well knew his busi-

SIRDAR DIRECTING ADVANCE ON OMDURMAN

ness. An order was sent him which, had it been obeyed, would have ensured inevitable disaster to the brigade, if not a catastrophe to the army. He was bade to retire by, possibly, his division commander. Macdonald knew better than attempt a retrograde movement in the face of so fleet and daring a foe. It would have spelled annihilation.

The sturdy Highlandman said, "I'll no do it. I'll see them d——d first. We maun just fight."

And meanwhile Major-General A. Hunter was scurrying to hurry up reinforcements—a wise measure. Other messages which could not reach Macdonald in time were being sent to him by the Sirdar to try and hold on, that help was coming. Yes; but the surging Dervish columns were converging upon the brigade upon three sides. Surely it would be engulfed and swept away was the fear in most minds. And what other wreck would follow? Ah! that could wait for answer. It was a crucial moment. A single Khedivial brigade was going to be tested in a way from which only British squares had emerged victorious. Most fortunately, Colonel Long, R.A., had sent three batteries to accompany Colonel Macdonald's brigade, namely, Peake's, Lawrie's, and de Rougemont's. The guns were the handy and deadly Maxim-Nordenfeldt (12½-pounders). Macdonald had marched out with the 11th Sudanese on his left, the 2nd Egyptian, under Major Pink, in the centre, and the 10th Sudanese on the right, all being in line. Behind the 10th, in column, were the 9th Sudanese. Major Walter commanded the 9th, Major Nason the 10th, and Major Jackson the 11th Sudanese battalions. Going forward to meet the Khalifa's force Colonel Macdonald threw his whole brigade practically into line, disregarding for the moment the assaulting columns of Sheikh Ed Din, which providentially were a little behind in the attack. The batteries went to the front in openings between the battalions and smote the faces of the Dervish columns. Steadily the infantry fired, the blacks in their own pet fashion independently, the 2nd Egyptians in careful, well-aimed volleys. Afar we could see and rejoice that the brigade was giving a magnificent account of itself. The Khalifa's

[From a Sketch by Lieut.-Col. C. Keith Falconer.]

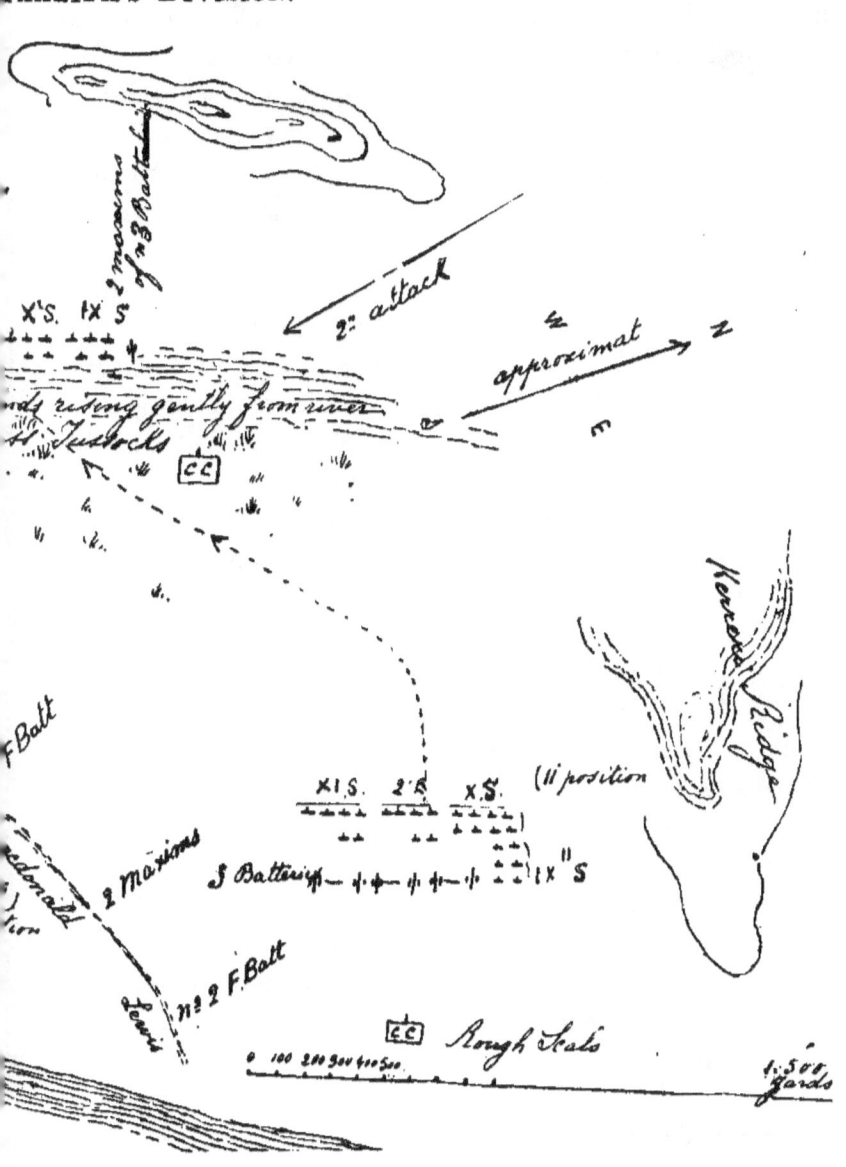

Dervishes were being hurled broadcast to the ground. Major Williams at last with his 15-pounders, our other batteries, and the Maxims were finding the range and ripping into shreds the solid lines of Dervishes. Still the enemy pressed on, their footmen reaching to within 200 yards of Macdonald's line. Scores of Emirs and lesser leaders, with spearmen and swordsmen, fell only a few feet from the guns and the unshaken Khedivial infantry. It is said one or two threw spears across the indomitable soldiery, and other Dervishes turned the flanks, but were instantly despatched. A few salvoes and volleys shook the looser attacking columns of Dervishes. The Khalifa's division had at length received such a surfeit of withering fire that the rear lines began to hold back, and the desperate rushes of the chiefs and their personal retainers grew fewer and feebler. But Sheikh Ed Din was at length within 1000 yards running with his confident legions to encompass and destroy the 1st Khedivial brigade. Macdonald, as soon as he saw that he could hold his own against the whole array of the Khalifa's personally commanded divisions, threw back his right, the 9th, and one and then another battery. He was now fairly beset on all sides, but fighting splendidly, doggedly. The Dervishes, taking fresh courage, made redoubled efforts to destroy him. It was by far the finest, the most heroic struggle of the day. A second battalion, the famous fighting 11th Sudanese, under Jackson, which lost so heavily at Atbara, swung round and interposed itself to Khalil's and Sheikh Ed Din's fierce followers. Furious as was the blast of lead and iron, the Dervishes had all but forged in between the 9th and 11th battalions, when the 2nd Egyptian, wheeling at the double, filled the gap. Without hesitation the *fellaheen*, let it be said, stood their ground, and, full of confidence, called to encourage each other, and gave shot and bayonet point to the few more truculent Dervishes who, escaping shot and shell, dashed against their line.

It was a tough, protracted struggle, but Colonel Macdonald was slowly, determinedly, freeing himself and winning all along the line. The Camel Corps came out to his assistance, and formed up some distance off on the right of the 11th Sudanese. Shells and showers of bullets from the Maxims on the gunboats drove back the rear lines of Sheikh Ed Din's men. Three battalions of Wauchope's got up to assist in completing the rout of the Khalifa. The Lincolns, doubling to the right, got in line on the left of the Camel Corps, and assisted in finishing off the retreating bands of the Khalifa's son. I then saw the Dervishes for the first time in all those years of campaigns turn tail, stoop, and fairly run for their lives to the shelter of the hills. It was a devil-take-the-hindmost race, and the only one I ever saw them engage in through half a score of battles. Beyond all else the double honours of the day had been won by Colonel Macdonald and his Khedivial brigade, and that without any help that need be weighed against the glory of his single-handed triumph. He achieved the victory entirely off his own bat, so to speak, proving himself a tactician and a soldier as well as what he has long been known to be, the bravest of the brave. I but repeat the expressions in everybody's mouth who saw the wonderful way in which he snatched success from what looked like certain disaster. The army has a hero and a thorough soldier in Macdonald, and if the public want either they need seek no farther. I know that the Sirdar and his staff fully recognised the nature of the service he rendered. A non-combatant general officer who witnessed the scene declared one might see 500 battles and never such another able handling of men in presence of an enemy. When the final rout of the Dervishes had been achieved it was about 10 a.m. The Sirdar wheeled his brigades to the left, into their original position, and marched them straightway towards Omdurman. Passing slowly over the battle-field the awful extent of the carnage was made evident. In my first wires I insisted that our total casualties were about 500, and the enemy's over 10,000 slain. Macdonald lost about 128 men. I subsequently ascertained that the total of our killed and wounded was about 524. The Dervish killed certainly numbered over 15,000, and their wounded probably as many more. Mahdism had been more than "smashed," it had been all but extirpated. So may all plagues end.

On the march the British troops having to swing aside from

MACDONAL

SECOND ATTACK.

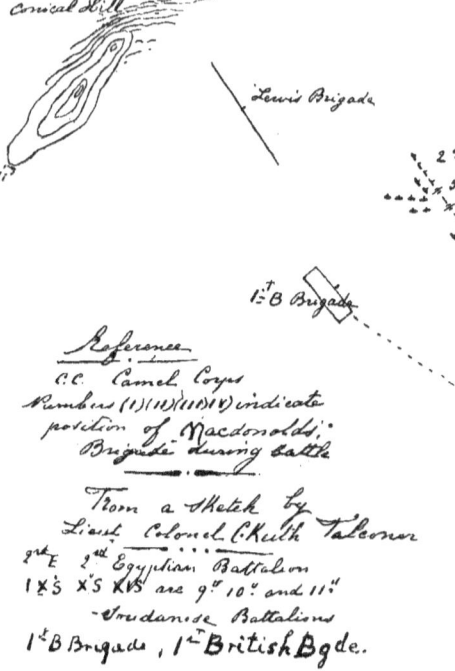

Reference
C.C. Camel Corps
Numbers (1)(11)(111)(1V) indicate
position of Macdonold's
Brigade during battle

From a Sketch by
Lieut Colonel C.Keith Falconer
9th E 2nd Egyptian Battalion
IX 5 X 5 XI5 are 9th 10th and 11th
Soudanese Battalions
1st B Brigade, 1st British Bgde.

LD'S BRIGADE.

SHEIKH ED DIN'S MEN.

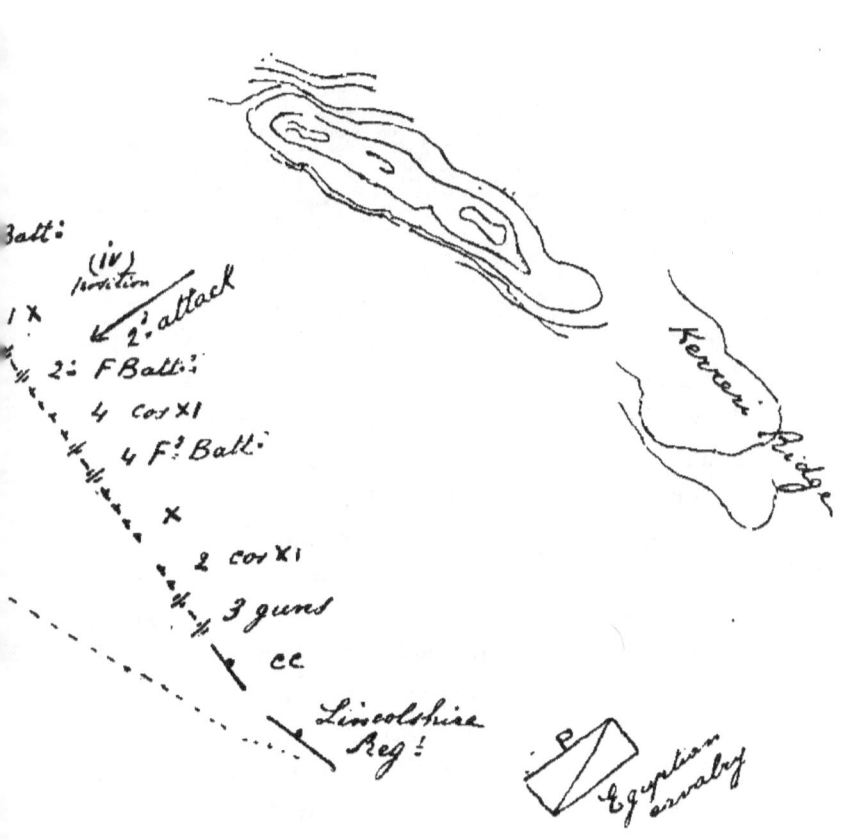

KHALIFA'S CAPTURED STANDARD (SIRDAR EXTREME LEFT)

where the Khalifa's black flag still stood, it fell into the hands of an Egyptian brigade, and was conveyed to the Sirdar by Captain Sir Henry Rawlinson and Major Lord Edward Cecil. It was given to an Egyptian orderly to carry behind the headquarters staff. Unfortunately, it attracted the attention of some of our own people on the gunboats who were unaware it had been captured. Several rounds were fired at the supposed Dervishes following it, and then it was discreetly furled for a time. By midday the army had arrived at the northern outskirts of Omdurman, where the troops were halted near the Nile to obtain food and water. I rode forward and saw that there were thousands of Dervishes in the town, many of them Baggara. The cavalry were sent as speedily as possible, after watering and feeding the horses, towards the south side of the town, and the gunboats were ordered up the river. Several deputations of citizens, Greeks and natives, came out and saw Slatin Pasha and the Sirdar. It was stated that the people would surrender, and that there would be no difficulty in occupying the place. The Khalifa, it was said, was in his house and must yield. Slatin Pasha, by the way, had gone over the battle-field and identified many of the slain Emirs. At 4.20 p.m., with two batteries, several Maxims and Colonel Maxwell's brigade leading, the Sirdar rode down the great north thoroughfare towards the central part of the squalid town. The houses, or more accurately huts, were full of Dervishes, hundreds of whom were severely wounded. Women and children flocked into the streets, raising cries of welcome to us. Of all the vile, dirty places on earth, Omdurman must rank first. There was no effort at sanitary observances, and dead animals, camels, horses, donkeys, dogs, goats, sheep, cattle, in all stages of putrefaction, lay about the streets and lanes. There were dead men, women, and children, too, lying in the open.

CHIEF THOROUGHFARE, OMDURMAN—
MULAZIM WALL, LEFT, OSMAN DIGNA'S HOUSE, RIGHT

We passed the big rectangular stone wall enclosing the Khalifa's special quarters. Within its area were his Mulazimin or body-guards' quarters, his granaries, treasuries, arsenal, the Mahdi's tomb, and the great praying square, misnamed the Mosque.

EFFECT OF SHELL FIRE UPON WALL (MULAZIM ENCLOSURE)

Except the tomb, the Khalifa's and his sons' houses, the town was void of buildings of any style or finish. I admit the great stone wall was of good masonry, and so was the well-finished praying-square wall. The Sirdar and party were frequently shot at, particularly on nearing the Khalifa's quarters. Abdullah slipped out with his treasures as the Sirdar arrived at his gate. It was long after sunset and dark when, with difficulty, the prison was reached, and Charles Neufeld brought out of his loathsome den, where he had spent eleven years in chains. He looked well, notwithstanding his long and irksome captivity, feeling, as he said, like a man drunk with new wine, on account of his release. That night I helped to relieve him from his fetters, freeing the limbs from the heavy bar and chains. Tired, worn out, without water or food, the Sirdar and his staff, as well as many more of us, were glad to escape out of Omdurman back to where the British camp was pitched in the northern outskirts. There I and others lay down and fell asleep on the bare desert, hoping to wake and find that our servants and baggage had turned up. Two of my colleagues had fared worse than I that day. Colonel F. Rhodes, of the *Times*, had been shot in the shoulder within the *zereba* early in the fight, and the Hon. Hubert Howard, of the *New York Herald*, was killed almost under my eyes, in the paved courtyard of the Khalifa, opposite the Mahdi's tomb. Such is the hasty record of as exciting and interesting a battle and a day's campaigning as it ever fell to mortal man to witness. Neither in my experience nor in my reading can I recall so strange and picturesque a series of incidents happening within the brief period of twelve hours.

CHAPTER 12

Stories of the Battle—Omdurman

There are numberless incidents and details remaining untold of the great battle and the fall of Omdurman. So singular and interesting an action is almost without parallel. "That villainous gunpowder" of former days was so sparingly used in the fight by the Sirdar's army that every part of the battle-field could be plainly seen. In the first stage the heaviest firing was by the British; the Lee-Metfords with cordite made little or no smoke. Maxwell's men of the Khedivial army, with their Martini-Henrys, never fired so fast as to cause any thick white cloud to shut out the view and hang between them and the enemy. Lewis's and Macdonald's brigades were never very heavily engaged whilst the troops remained *zerebaed*. Perhaps it was the light south wind which blew the men's rifle smoke behind us at once, but that was not what I thought. There seemed to be none to blow away. I recall that in the thick of the battle of Tamai with Davis's square, and at Abu Klea, the smoke cloud that hung like a curtain before our eyes was a source of danger. Save for the erratic, occasional whizzing of the enemy's bullets, the thud of a hit and the dropping, weltering in his blood, of a man here and there, watched from our firing lines the combat enlisted and fascinated the attention with barely a suggestion of danger to the onlooker. Few will ever see again so great and brave a show. A vast army, with a front of three miles, covering an undulating plain—warriors mounted and afoot, clad in quaint and picturesque drapery, with gorgeous barbaric display of banners, burnished metal, and sheen of steel—came sweeping upon us with the speed of cavalry. Half-a-dozen batteries smote them, a score of Maxims and 10,000 rifles unceasingly buffeted them, making great gaps and rending their ranks in all directions. With magnificent courage, without pause, the survivors invariably drew together, furiously, frenziedly running to cross steel with us. Their ardour and mad devotion won admiration on all sides in our own ranks. Poor, misguided *Jehadieh* and hocused Arabs of the spacious and cruel Sudan! With such troops disciplined and trained by English officers the policing of Africa would be an easy affair. Try and try as they did, they could not moving openly pass through our blasts of fire. Some few there were who got by subtler means to within 600 yards of the British front and 200 yards from Maxwell's blacks, there to yield their lives.

Among the earliest, if not the first man, wounded in the *zereba* on 2nd September was Corporal Mackenzie, of "C" Company Seaforth Highlanders. About 6.10 a.m. he was hit in the leg by a ricochet. The wound was dressed, and Mackenzie stuck to his post. At 6.30 a.m., when the action was almost in full swing, as Private Davis and Corporal Taylor, R.A.M.C., were carrying a wounded soldier upon a stretcher to the dressing hospital, Davis was shot through the head and killed, and Taylor was severely wounded in the shoulder.

Whilst our batteries were hurling death and destruction from the *zereba* at the Khalifa's army, Major Elmslie's battery of 50-pounder howitzers was battering the Mahdi's tomb to pieces and breaching the great stone wall in Omdurman. The practice with the terrible Lyddite shells was better than before, and the Dervishes, even more clearly than we, must have seen from the volcanic upheavals when the missiles struck, that their capital was being wrecked. It must have been something of a disillusion to many of them to note that the sacred tomb of their Mahdi was suffering most of all from the infidels' fire. Several of the gunboats assisted in the bombardment, but their chief duty was to drive all bodies of the enemy away from the river. Major Elmslie threw altogether some 410 Lyddite shells into Omdurman. Most of them detonated, but there were a few that merely flared. It was the fumes from these that imparted a chrome colour to the surrounding earth and stonework. Why the Khalifa did not make greater use of his artillery and musketry became more of a puzzle than ever when we saw how well provided he was in both respects. He had a battery of excellent big Krupps that were never fired, besides eight or ten machine guns. As for rifles, his men must have carried at least 25,000 into action against us. Had they employed these in "sniping" as at Abu Kru, the Sirdar would have had to march out and attack them.

The victory of Omdurman owed much to the masterly serving of the artillery. Even in Macdonald's severely contested action, the three batteries of Maxim-Nordenfeldt 12½-pounders did much to save the situation. These were Peake's, Lawrie's, and de Rougemont's, with, in the latter part of the fight, three Krupp guns of the horse artillery. The Camel Corps also brought up two Maxims to help at the close of the battle to repulse Sheikh Ed Din. Macdonald handled his guns as superbly as he did his infantry. At the Atbara against Mahmoud, the light powerful Maxim-Nordenfeldts had proved that they could be successfully fought side by side with infantry. Between the battalion intervals, therefore, the dauntless gunners stood firing point-blank at the Dervish columns. Throughout the battle Major Williams' 32nd Field Battery, R.A., fired 420 rounds. Three of the Maxim-Nordenfeldt batteries (all Egyptian) fired 100 rounds per gun, whilst Major Lawrie's battery, No. 4 Egyptian, also Maxim-Nordenfeldt guns, fired over that number, or 900 rounds in all. All these batteries were of six guns each. Captain Smeaton fired from his six Maxims, stationed in the *zereba* south-east corner, 54,000 rounds. One of the wants much felt by the gunners was the need of more shrapnel during the action. Twice at least the allowance supply was temporarily exhausted. Yet it is not to be assumed on that account that the reserve ammunition was difficult to be got at or that the firing lines were insufficiently fed. The arrangements in these respects were admirable. During the *zereba* action, the Grenadier Guards fired the largest number of rounds. The Camerons fired 34 rounds per man. Five companies of the Lincolns in the firing line, 32 rounds each man. The Northumberland Fusiliers fired in all 1200 rounds, and the Lancashire Fusiliers 400 rounds.

Many of our wounded were hit with bullets from elephant guns, brass cased Mausers, Remingtons, and repeating rifles. The great majority of the Dervishes carried Remingtons, and these, as a rule, were in passably good condition. Probably they were officers or crack shots among the *Jehadieh* and Arabs that fired into the *zereba* with the small bore Mausers. Most of their shooting was too high, though the direction was right enough. When the first phase of the action ceased at 8.30 a.m., hundreds, if not thousands of wounded Dervishes upon the field rose and moved away. Some of these were seen going back towards Omdurman, others walked towards the west to rejoin their friends. No attempt was made on our side to molest them, the order to "cease fire" having been given. It was either then or a little earlier that the large body of natives, possibly camp followers, behind the Khalifa's force, melted away, flowing back to the town. At that time some of our army camp followers, or servants, went forward from the *zereba* to pick up trophies from the field. A party of four went towards a small group of dead Dervishes lying about 300 yards on the left front of Maxwell's brigade. I noticed them picking up spears and swords. A correspondent rode out to join them, Mr Bennett Stanford, who was formerly in the "Royals." In company with another colleague I rode out from the British lines to join him, curious to see the effect of our fire. At the moment a Dervish arose, apparently unwounded, and spear in hand charged the servants, who incontinently bolted back to the *zereba*. My companion also turned back, but I was yet over 200 yards away, and so rode forward. One of the men attacked by the Dervish was a native non-commissioned officer. He had followed the others out. Dropping upon his knee he aimed at the Dervish, but his Martini-Henry missed fire. He fired again and missed, then, the Dervish being very near him, ran for the *zereba*. Mr Bennett Stanford, who was splendidly mounted, with a cocked four-barrelled Lancaster pistol aimed deliberately at the Dervish, who turned towards him. Waiting till the *jibbeh*-clad warrior was but a score of paces or so off, Mr Stanford fired, and appeared to miss also, for the Dervish without halt rushed at him, whereupon he easily avoided him, riding off. Then the Dervish turned to the soldier who, encumbered with his rifle, did not run swiftly. By that time I had drawn up so as to interpose between them, passing beyond the Dervish. I pulled up my rather sorry nag—my best was for carrying despatches—and took deliberate aim. The Dervish turned upon me as I wished. I fired and believe hit him, and as my horse was jibbing about fired a second shot from my revolver with less success, then easily got out of the Dervish's reach. He had a heavy spear and showed no sign of throwing it as I rode away, keeping well out of his reach. The camp followers by then were all safe, and so was the native soldier, Mr Dervish having the field very much to himself. Thereupon an A.D.C., Lieutenant Smyth, came galloping out and riding hard past, fired at the fellow but missed. Checking his horse Lieutenant Smyth wheeled it about, and he and the Dervish collided. The man, who by this time appeared somewhat weak, grabbed the Lieutenant and strove to drive his lance into him. With great hardihood Lieutenant Smyth fired his revolver in the Dervish's face, killing him instantly. It was a wondrous narrow escape for the Lieutenant. The instant afterwards I asked him if he had been badly wounded, but he declared that he was untouched, a statement I could scarcely credit, and so repeated my question in another form, to receive a similar answer. In the excitement of the moment he no doubt did not feel the slight spear wound he actually received upon the arm, which saved him from the thrust aimed at his body. An examination of the dead Dervish showed he had received four bullet wounds.

The following is a brief and well-balanced account of the charge of the Lancers furnished me by an officer who was present:—"We moved along to the left—*i.e.*, east of Surgham—following up the enemy on that flank. Our object was to prevent them retiring into Omdurman or, at any rate, delay their retreat. A body of Dervishes were seen crouching not far off to the right. Colonel Martin determined to push the enemy back and interpose between them and the town. The regiment, of four squadrons, was wheeled into line. When 300 yards off we started to charge, and were met by a heavy musketry fire from the enemy. At first it was ill-directed, but very soon casualties occurred in our ranks from it. Instead of a few Dervishes, we tumbled upon over 500 hidden in a fold of the ground. They were in a *khor*, or *nullah*, into which we had to drop, and they lined it twenty deep in places. Our weight, however, carried us through. The Dervishes, when we struck them, did not break, but "bunched" together, showing no fear of cavalry. There was half a minute's hacking, cutting, spearing, and shooting in all directions; then we cleared them, and rallied on the far side. Halting about 300 yards off, men were dismounted, and we opened a sharp fire from our carbines on the enemy, driving them to the westward in ten minutes. The charge was really successful in its object, as the retirement from that part of the field into Omdurman was stopped. We left perhaps sixty Dervishes on the field in the charge, and killed about 100 more with our subsequent fire." The Dervish leader who was sitting on a fine black Dongolawi horse was killed in the melee. A trooper met him in the *khor* and ran him through with his spear.

By far the finest feature of that morning of battles was the action fought by Colonel Macdonald with his brigade. The Dervish forces that sought to crush him numbered fully 20,000 men. To oppose them he had but four battalions, or in all less than 3000 Sudanese and Egyptian soldiers. With a tact, coolness, and hardihood I have never seen equalled, Colonel Macdonald manoeuvred and fought his men. They responded to his call with confidence and alacrity begotten of long acquaintance and implicit faith in their leader. He had led several of the battalions through a score of fierce fights and skirmishes, always emerging and covering himself and his men with glory, honour and victory. All of them knew him, they were proud of him, and reposed implicit confidence in their general. Unmistakably the Khalifa and his son, the Sheikh Ed Din, thought that their fortunate hour had come—that, in detail, they would destroy first Macdonald, then one by one the other Khedivial brigades. What might have been, had father and son arrived at the same time and distance on both sides of Macdonald, as they evidently intended, I will not venture to discuss. Happily the onslaughts of the wild, angry Dervishes did not quite synchronise, and Colonel Macdonald was able to devote virtually his whole firing strength to the overthrow of the Khalifa's division ere rapidly turning about first one then another of his battalions to deal with the Sheikh Ed Din's unbroken columns. The enemy on both sides got very close in, hundreds of them being killed almost at the feet of the men of the 1st Khedivial brigade. Dervish spears were thrown into and over the staunch and unyielding Sudanese and Fellaheen soldiery. Peake's, Lawrie's, and de Rougemont's batteries stood their ground, side by side with the infantry, never wavering, firing point-blank upon the Dervish masses. Majors Jackson, Nason, and Walter were, as usual, proud of the steadiness of their blacks—the 11th, 10th, and 9th battalions—whilst Major Pink, of the 2nd Egyptian, was elated with the stout way his soldiers doubled, wheeled, and at a critical moment rushed to fill up a gap near one of the batteries. The "Gippies" looked without flinching straight into the eyes of the Dervishes, and fired volleys that would have done credit to a British regiment. The hulking, physically strong "Fellah" had at last taken the measure of his enemy, and meant to prove himself the better man of the two. And he did—delighted with himself and his comrades, calling to them, chiding the Dervishes, and stepping out of the ranks to meet the onrush of those of the enemy who came near, to stop it with bullet or bayonet. But chief of all was Macdonald, going hither and thither and issuing his orders as if on parade, with a sharp snap to each command. Two armies saw it all, and one at least admired his intrepid valour. One hundred black-flag Taaisha, the Khalifa's own Baggara tribesmen and part of his body-guard, charged impetuously. Spurring their horses to their utmost speed leading the footmen, down they came straight for the brigade. Cannon, Maxims, and rifles roared, and, bold as the Taaisha rode, neither horse nor man lived to get within one hundred yards of our Sudanese and Gippies. Steady as a gladiator, with what to some of us looked like inevitable disaster staring him in the face, Colonel Macdonald fought his brigade for all it was worth. He quickly moved upon the best available ground, formed up, wheeled about, and stood to die or win. He won practically unaided, for the pinch was all but over when the Camel Corps, hurrying up, formed upon his right, after he had faced about to receive the Sheikh Ed Din's onslaught. The Lincolns, who arrived later on, helped to hasten the flight of the enemy, whose repulse was assured ere they or any of Wauchope's brigade were within 1200 yards of Macdonald. Lewis's brigade were not even able to assist so much, and such outside help as came in time to be of use was in the first instance from the guns of Major Williams' and another battery, and the Maxims upon the left near Surgham hurried forward by the Sirdar himself, as I saw. General Hunter came over to the headquarters-staff galloping to get assistance, and rode back with Wauchope's brigade, which doubled for a considerable distance, so serious was the situation and nervous the tension of that thrilling ten minutes. Had the brilliant, the splendid deed of arms wrought by Macdonald been done under the eyes of a sovereign, or in some other armies, he had surely been created a General on the spot. If the public are in search of the real hero of the battle of Omdurman there he is, ready-made—one who committed no blunder to be redeemed by courageous conduct afterwards. He boldly exercised his right of personal judgment in a moment of extreme peril, and the result amply justified the soundness of his decision.

It was about 11.50 a.m. when the Sirdar wheeled his army about to resume the march upon Omdurman. The Dervishes who had escaped slaughter had bent their bodies and run from the fatal field, going far off behind the western range of hills. Moving slowly and in echelon, as when we first set out, we passed over part of the battle-field. Groups of unwounded Dervishes, who insisted on fighting and sniping the troops, had to be dealt with as well as all others who persisted in being truculent. Like everybody else at the head of the column, I was shot at repeatedly. All of the enemy, however, who showed the least disposition to surrender were left unmolested. Hundreds of Dervishes who had been wounded hobbled on in front of our army. We could see the Khalifa's forces behind the hills watching us and streaming upon a parallel line towards Omdurman. But the Dervishes were no longer in compact military array or ranged in division under chiefs. They were mostly scattered in small groups and bands spread over a very wide area. It was a rabble, and had lost semblance of being an army with power of concerted action. When Macdonald's fight was over, the Egyptian cavalry under Colonel Broadwood returned and formed up near the camelry. They, with the Camel Corps, moved forward on the right as before during the final advance upon the Khalifa's capital. Men and horses had done a week of the hardest kind of work, but both were yet willing and full of spirit. As for the 21st Lancers, the few mounts remaining fit for work scarcely counted as a cavalry force. The gunboats and the infantry saw to our left, which was not difficult, for upon that hand the country was quite bare. About 2 p.m. the army reached the northern outskirts of Omdurman, the British division upon the left. Gatacre's men were nearest the Nile, Maxwell and Lewis being almost opposite one of the main thoroughfares of the town. A halt for water—the great necessity—food, and rest was ordered. Parties were instantly detailed to fill water-bottles and *fantasses*, iron tanks. The cooks, too, got to work, and fires were kindled with wood torn from neighbouring huts, and a meal was prepared. Under the burning sunshine, down upon the loose dirt and gravel, officers and men sprawled to rest themselves. There was a very muddy creek or inset near, and thither went thousands, parched with thirst, to drink, not hesitatingly but gulping down copious draughts of water, tough and thick as from a clay puddle. I wandered with my horse a little way into the town, and ultimately down towards the main stream of the Nile, where the water was cleaner and cooler than by the halting-place. There were plenty of Dervishes to be seen about, looking from lanes and walls, but they were far from being particularly aggressive at that part of the town. Indeed, several large groups of men, Arabs and negroes, came up bearing white rags on sticks in front of them. I went forward and met parties of them, and advised them to go into the British lines, where the soldiers would receive them as friends. Watering my horse, I let him feed on grass by the river's brink, filled my water-bottle, and then returned by a circuitous route. The natives were not all inclined to be friendly, for a few preferred shooting at the stranger. But their practice was very bad.

Returning to where the troops still lay, I found that a fresh movement was afoot. Report had been brought that hundreds of lesser sheikhs and leaders were in the town ready to surrender with their followers if their lives would be spared. The assurance sought was quickly conveyed to them. Slatin Pasha, who had been indefatigable on the battle-field, watching the course of events and locating the commands of the various important Dervish chiefs, had received news that the Khalifa was still in the town. The Pasha, on passing over the field, had searched around the black flag and other noted leaders' banners to see who lay there. In the heaped dead about the Khalifa's flag he had seen Yacoub, Abdullah's brother, and many more leaders, but the arch head of Mahdism, the Sheikh Ed Din and Osman Digna were nowhere to be found. Amongst the dead Emirs identified were Osman Azrak, leader of the cavalry, Wad el Melik, Ali Wad Helu, Yunis, Ibrahim Khalil, Mahmoud's brother, el Fadl, Osman Dekem, Zaki Ferar, Abu Senab, Mousa Zacharia, and Abd el Baki. The Khalifa had come into action riding a horse. As that did not suit him he changed for a camel and, finding the latter position too dangerously conspicuous, rode off the field on donkey-back. Perhaps the most concise summing up of the battle fell from a Tommy's lips: "Them Dervishes are good uns, and no mistake. They came on in thousands on thousands to lay us out, but we shifted them fast enough."

It was not quite four o'clock, afternoon. Slatin Pasha had got news from former friends that the fugitives and townspeople would gladly surrender, so the sooner the Sirdar marched in and took possession the better. True, the Khalifa with several hundreds of followers, or mayhap a thousand or more, was yet within the central part of Omdurman. Most of his *Jehadieh*, it was urged, would give in at once if an opportunity were afforded them, and Abdullah could be caught. With Maxwell's brigade, Major Williams' battery and several Maxims, the Sirdar and headquarters staff pushed along the wide thoroughfare that leads from the north past the west end of the great rectangular wall, towards the Mosque enclosure and Mahdi's tomb. The infantry, guns, and Maxims preceded but a few paces in front. Vile beyond description was Omdurman, its dwellings, streets, lanes, and spaces. Beasts pay more regard to sanitation than Dervishes. Pools of slush and stagnant water abounded. Dead animals in all stages of decomposition lay there in hundreds and thousands. There were besides littering the place camels, horses, donkeys, dead and wounded fresh from the battle-field. And there were many other ghastly sights. Dead and wounded Dervishes lay in pools of blood in the roadway. Several of the dying enemy grimly saluted the staff as we passed. An Emir who, horribly mauled by a shell, lay pinned under his dead horse waved his hand and fell back a corpse. Our guns and Maxims had opened once or twice to turn the armed fugitives from the town. The compounds and huts were full of wounded and unwounded Dervishes, most of the latter having Remingtons and waist-belts full of cartridges, besides carrying spears and swords. In the open thoroughfares there were many bodies of women and children lying stark and stiff. The majority of these victims were young girls. Many of the poor creatures had evidently been running towards the river to try and escape when caught and killed by jealous and cruel masters or husbands. The scenes were shocking, the smells abominable and quite overpowering to many who sought to ride in with the General.

There was something like a reception for the Sirdar on his entering the town. The women and children, mostly slaves, filled the thoroughfares, and in their peculiar guinea-fowl cackling fashion cheered the troops. Notables in *jibbehs*, which they had not yet had time to turn inside out, as nearly every native did afterwards, came and salaamed, smote their breasts, and kissed the hands and even the garments' hem of the Sirdar and his staff. In truly Oriental fashion they completed the ceremonial of obeisance and fealty by throwing dust upon their already frowsy enough heads. It was curious to watch the various recognitions extended to Slatin, and how the latter did not forget his old friends, who had been kind to him, or his Eastern manners in exchanging courtesies. When they realised that we were not cannibals, which they did very quickly, and that the Khalifa and others must have deceived them, they ran about amongst the troops. It was with difficulty at times the ranks were kept clear of them. Our Western leniency surprised them. The Sirdar shook hands with certain of the notables, including several of the Greeks and Jaalin. One of the most extraordinary incidents was the appearance of the Khalifa's own band with drums and horns to play in the 13th Sudanese. Evidently it was a case of black relations, for they played the battalion, Major Smith-Dorian's, out as well as into town on the following day.

The people were ordered to carry the good news about that none who gave up their arms would be killed or hurt, and that there was no intention on our part to sack the town or injure anybody. What? A captured city in the Sudan not to be given over to the victorious troops to do with as they liked! I am sure the natives of both sexes were amazed. And I cannot say all looked quite satisfied at the announcement. The crowd in the streets quickly increased; they evidently believed that we meant them no harm, and that they could do as they liked. In the bombardment the Lyddite shells had knocked down a gateway leading into the buildings and square mile of town enclosed by the great rectangular stone wall built by the Khalifa. For a space of fifty yards, several big holes had been blown in the structure, which was fourteen feet high and over four feet in thickness. Some of these breaches led into the beit-el-mal, or public granary. A few wretched, hungry slaves ventured to help themselves to the grain, chiefly dhura, that had partly poured out into the street. No one interfered with them. Within half an hour all the women and children in the town apparently, to the number of several thousands, were running pell-mell to loot the granary. Men also joined in plundering the Khalifa's storehouse. They ran against our horses, tripped over each other and fell in their crazy haste to fill sacks, skins, and nondescript vessels of all sorts—metal, wood and clay—with grain. Women staggered under burdens that would assure their households of food for months. It became a saturnalia and jubilee for the long, half-starved slaves, men and women. By-and-by looting became more general. The houses of Emirs who had run away or been killed were entered and plundered by the populace. Donkeys were caught and loaded with spoils

EFFECT OF SHELL FIRE UPON WALL (MULAZIM ENCLOSURE)

of war, and driven off to huts on the outskirts near where the troops bivouacked after their long and fatiguing day. During the earlier part of that night there was much noise and hubbub in Omdurman with constant firing of rifles. Maxwell's men, however, assisted by numbers of friendly Jaalin, finally succeeded in enforcing something like order and peace.

After the reception near the centre of the town the Sirdar proceeded with part of Colonel Maxwell's brigade along the west side of the big wall. Osman Digna's house was passed on the way. We got as far as the south-west corner into full view of the Mahdi's tomb, which was about 400 yards to the east. In the same direction and equidistant was the Khalifa's house. Beside us was the Praying Square or Mosque, a space of bare ground of about ten acres or so in extent. As soon as the troops got beyond the big wall and in sight of the tomb and Khalifa's house, a brisk fusillade from Remingtons by the Jehadieh body-guard protecting Abdullah was opened against us. Fortunately, the big stone wall was not loopholed on either side. Indeed there appeared to be no provision for its defenders to fire from it unless they mounted to the top. The Sirdar and staff fell back, and the guns and Maxims went forward a little. Maxwell's men then dealt with the enemy, and the Sirdar, still led by Slatin Pasha, whom the Dervishes called "Saladin," turned back to try and make his way through the breaches in the north wall. Troops were sent in to clear the compound of Dervishes, most of whom surrendered at once. But exit upon the south side was barred by interior walls and gates. Then the Sirdar essayed going along by the river's margin between the wall, the Nile, and the forts, to turn the south-east angle. A sharp and accurate fire from the Jehadieh stopped that advance for a time. Gunboats were ordered forward to drive the Dervishes from their cover. The soldiers pushed farther through the compound, and the gunboats swept the Jehadieh with Maxims and quick-firing cannon. About 5 p.m., with the shadows rapidly lengthening, the rough way between the river and the great wall was partly cleared of the enemy. Thereupon the Sirdar and staff forded a dirty, wide creek, the crossing being girth high, and trotted a few hundred yards up stream. With double teams, four guns of the 32nd Battery, Major Williams', were got across the pool, accompanying the headquarters.

Entering a gateway through the outer rectangular wall, the force moved towards the Mahdi's tomb and the Khalifa's chief residence or palace. The Sirdar and staff reined up before Abdullah's doorway, for the Dervish leader's house was surrounded by an inner wall and various small buildings. We were in a higgledy-piggledy looking corner, surrounded by rough shelters or stables for animals, horses and camels, and the unfinished but covered approaches to the Mahdi's tomb. The staff sat on horseback facing the doorway and dwelling; I pulled in opposite beside an angle of the wall. Upon the Sirdar's right were some corrugated iron roofed sheds, and a little in front the Praying Square. Behind was the Mahdi's tomb, and at no great distance various important Dervish buildings. Abdullah had so planted himself that he had easy and private access to all places of public resort as well as the official quarters.

Mahdi's tomb—effect of Lyddite shells

Slatin Pasha, Colonel Maxwell, and several soldiers, with one or two others, went in and searched for the Khalifa. A few minutes previously he had slipped out by a back door with the more important part of his personal treasures. His harem had been sent away earlier in the day. Mr Hubert Howard, correspondent of the New York Herald and the London Times, was near the headquarters staff. He came over to where I was and chatted. To a companion who had joined me he offered some cigarettes. He said it had been a splendid day, and he had seen much. Nothing could have been better than the way things turned out, and he was glad he had been through it from first to last, cavalry charge included. Then he said he would like to get a photograph or two of the surroundings and the Khalifa's house. I told him the light was spent and he could get no good results. He said he would try, and rode inside the courtyard. A minute or less later, there was the roar and crash of a shrapnel shell, which burst over our heads in very dangerous proximity. The iron and bullets struck the walls and rattled upon the corrugated iron roofs alongside. "That," I said to my companion and an artillery officer hard by, "was one of our own guns." The officer, Major Williams, I think, replied he feared indeed that it was so. A similar opinion was apparently entertained by the Sirdar and staff, for gallopers were sent to the officer in charge of the two guns of the 32nd Battery left on the west side of the wall in the main thoroughfare, to cease firing at once. Before riding up to the Khalifa's door the Sirdar had hailed the gunboats, and one of them, the "Sultan," came near enough inshore for us to converse with those on board and for the commander to receive orders to stop all firing at Abdullah's quarters. A few seconds after the first shrapnel burst, another pitched over our heads, aimed apparently like the previous one at the Khalifa's compound. Indeed, it appeared so later, for those of our men at the south-west corner of the wall saw a number of armed Jehadieh who were gathering behind Abdullah's compound. The Maxims also opened fire on what was probably a body of the enemy covering Ab-

INTERIOR MAHDI'S TOMB (GRILLE AROUND SARCOPHAGUS)

dullah's retirement, and who, at any rate, were firing at the troops. Immediately after the second shell exploded the Sirdar and headquarters rode off, returning by the road we entered, to the main thoroughfare upon the west side of the enclosing wall. I remained a few minutes longer, two shells bursting overhead in the interval, and with my companion retraced our steps, rejoining the headquarters' following. Mr Hubert Howard was struck upon the side of the head by a bullet or fragment of a shell and killed instantly. His body was removed and covered up by Colonel Maxwell and his men.

Arrangements were made for the instant pursuit of the Khalifa, who, I was told, only left his palace about five o'clock or sometime after we had penetrated into Omdurman. Notables and Dervishes who came in to us were freely used by the staff to run hither and thither conveying intimation to all their friends, that the war being over they should lay down their arms. In that way the news of the collapse of Mahdism was widely spread, and bands of thirty and forty of the Jehadieh and even of the Baggara surrendered. The presence of our Sudanese soldiers facilitated matters, for they saw in them, at any rate, countrymen. I had no difficulty in persuading several large groups of Dervishes, whom I could see from my horse inside their compounds, to come out into the lanes or roadway and lay down their rifles. By such means the headquarters' advance through the town was made possible and relatively easy. The sun had set and darkness was upon us before the Sirdar and staff, going at times in single file, reached the common prison where the Assouan merchant, Charles Neufeld, was confined. Whilst accompanying a convoy of rifles presented by the Egyptian Government in 1886 to Sheikh Saleh of the friendly Kabbabish tribe, Neufeld had been captured by a party of Dervishes. Like the other European prisoners who fell into their hands, he had undergone great hardships and experienced all the trials of misfortune. Neufeld and several hundred natives who had incurred the Khalifa's ire or distrust were found in a pestilential enclosure less than an acre in extent, surrounded by mud-walls. All of them wore heavy leg chains, and a few were handcuffed besides. The principal jail deliveries were by disease and the gallows; the latter were almost daily in use. Three rough sets of them stood together near the great wall. Limbs of trees

KHALIFA'S GALLOWS (CUTTING DOWN HIS LAST VICTIM)

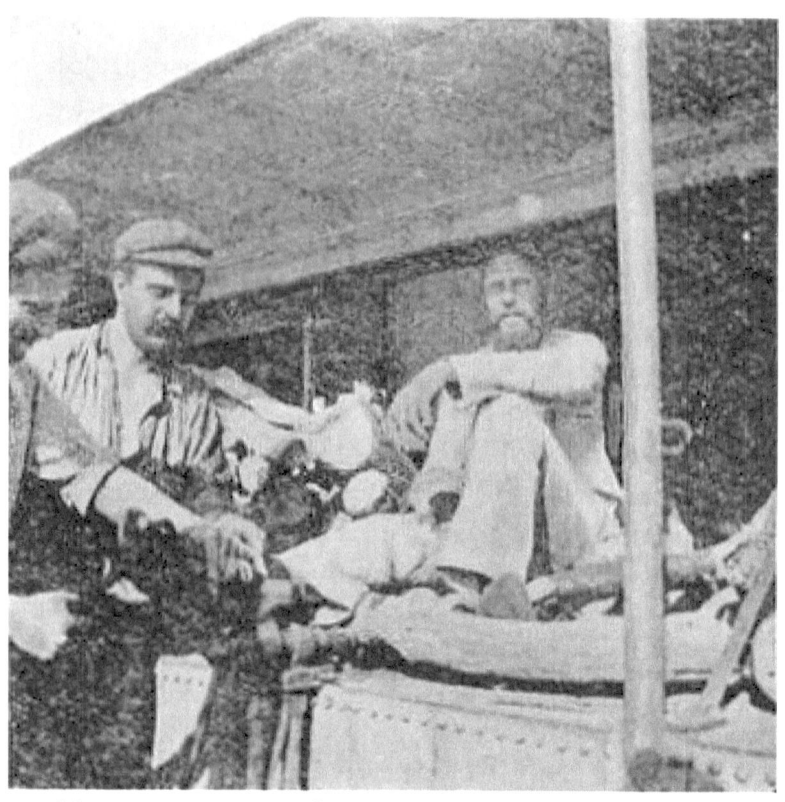

NEUFELD ON GUNBOAT SHEIK—CUTTING OFF HIS ANKLE-IRONS

stuck into the ground, with a cross-piece overhead, that was how the gallows were fashioned. A last victim of the Khalifa was cut down shortly after the troops entered Omdurman.

Neufeld was found under a mat-covered lean-to built against the mud-wall. There was no other protection for the prisoners from sunshine or rain than coarse worn matting spread upon sticks and laid against the walls. The enclosure was without any sanitary arrangements whatever. A well had been dug near the middle of the yard and from there the prisoners drew all the water they used. The Sirdar conversed with the prisoner, and a fruitless effort was made to find the jailer and have Neufeld's irons removed. Ultimately, when night had quite fallen and it was pitch dark, Neufeld was set upon an officer's horse, and the Sirdar and headquarters bringing him with them rode outside to where the main body of the army was bivouacking upon the desert, north of Omdurman. Later on I found means to have Neufeld's irons removed. He had three sets of leg irons fastened round his ankles; a heavy bar weighing fourteen pounds, and two thick chains above that. The heavy rings upon the legs we could not get off without other appliances than a hammer and iron wedge, so they were left to be removed next day on the gunboat "Sheik." It was found necessary on that occasion to grip the rings in a vice and cut them with a cold chisel. We, however, so freed his limbs that he could walk. Having written a second batch of despatches by the light of a guttering candle and handed them to the press censor, we lay down in our clothes to try and sleep—no easy thing to do when you had to hold the bridle of your hungry horse the while, and other equally restless Arab steeds were, after their manner, seeking to eat him or kick him to pieces. We were without food or water, for in the thrice altered camping grounds our servants had got lost. In a flurry between dozing and waking we spent the night, hoping for the morrow. When it came there was daylight but no breakfast. Indeed, it was not until the afternoon of the 3rd September that our servants and baggage re-appeared.

CHAPTER 13

Close of Campaign

Although the beginning of a campaign often drags, the ending is usually abrupt. With the defeat and flight of Abdullah, Mahdism became a thing of the past. True, there were several minor engagements fought later against isolated recalcitrant bodies of Dervishes who were too loyal to their old leaders. But these affairs in no way affected the result achieved upon the

Khalifa's chief eunuch (surrenders in British camp)

battle-field of Omdurman. During the night or early morning of the 2nd and 3rd of September, Colonel Macdonald's brigade advanced into the city to help to keep the peace, and to secure the surrender of all the armed bands of the enemy. Large bodies of Dervishes were still moving about both within and without Omdurman. I had myself seen many hundreds of natives set out about dusk to revisit the battle-field in search of plunder, to rescue wounded friends, and to bury their dead kinsmen. Those who showed a peaceable disposition were not molested, but all with arms were arrested and penned under guards in the Praying Square. Many prisoners were secured on the battle-field, but relatively only a few thousands. On 3rd September and following days enormous numbers surrendered, coming into town or being sent in by the cavalry and friendlies. In fact, they became so numerous that it was found almost impossible to deal with them. When Dervishes of the Jaalin and other tribes that had abandoned Mahdism came in they were at once told to behave themselves, and were allowed to go where they liked. The townsfolk and others who wished to be let alone, turned their *jibbehs* inside out, at once a renunciation of the Khalifa and his works as well as a sanitary gain. Some there were who, averse to over-cleanliness, simply tore the Dervish patches off their dress, thus also resuming their fealty to the Khedive. The roll of prisoners, however, in spite of convenient blindness in letting all the lesser men who wished to escape do so, swelled to about 11,000. In a house to house visitation the more important rebel sheikhs and Baggara in hiding were caught and kept under arrest with their followers. All the Greeks and the local chiefs whom Slatin Pasha knew to be secretly inimical to the Dervish rule, were from the first secured safe permits and absolute liberty. Among them were many of the Mahdi's relatives, former rulers of tribes, and Emirs once high in power. Of wounded Dervishes over 9000 were treated by the British and Egyptian Army Medical Staffs, although the doctors' hands were busy enough for two days with our own sick and wounded.

FRESH BATCH WOUNDED AND UNWOUNDED DERVISH PRISONERS
OMDURMAN, 4TH *SEPT.* 1898

Within twenty-four hours after the Sirdar's entry Omdurman began to assume the signs of orderly government. Thousands of the prisoners as well as the natives were set to work to clean up the place. The wounded were all carried into temporary hospitals and the dead were decently interred in Moslem burial-places out upon the desert. Then the thoroughfares were scrupulously scavengered by gangs of yesterday's furious foemen, blacks and Baggara. The dead things were put under ground, and the stagnant pools were drained or filled in. Within a week it became actually possible to walk without an attack of violent nausea in Omdurman. Visits were constantly paid to the battlefield for the double purpose of rescuing any wounded Dervishes there might be and counting the dead. The large number of the enemy who for days survived shocking wounds, to which a European would have instantly or speedily succumbed, was appalling. These wretched creatures had been seen crawling or dragging themselves for miles to get to the Nile for water or into villages for succour. Food and water were sent out to them by the Sirdar's orders on the day after the battle, when it was seen that the natives gave neither heed nor help to other than their own immediate kinsmen upon the field. Even in the town rations were distributed to the needy. The gunboats going up and down the river saw many sorry sights. Wounded Dervishes were lying by hundreds along the river's bank. Some, whose thirst had maddened them, had drunk copiously, and then swooned and died, their heads and shoulders covered with water and the rest of their bodies stretched upon the strand. General Gatacre and Lieut. Wood on riding to revisit the *zereba* near Kerreri, met a Dervish, part of one of whose legs had been blown off by a shell. The man was hobbling along, leaning upon a broken spear handle, making for Omdurman, with his limb burned and roughly tied up. They gave him food and water and passed on meeting others. A mile away, the mounted orderly drew the General's attention to an object upon the ground with the exclamation: "Blest if it isn't that bloke's foot!" which sure enough was the case. A number of officers were told off to count the enemy's dead upon the battle-field. Sections of the ground were assigned to each. The actual count was 10,800 dead bodies, which did not include all the slain, for there were those who died in Omdurman, and afar upon the desert. One of the officers wrote, "I won't enter into details of our day's work. It suffices to say, that a piece of cotton-wool soaked in eucalyptus placed in the nostrils and an ample supply of neat brandy were only just sufficient to keep us on our legs for the six hours that we were at the job." He and two others had undertaken to make a sketch in addition to helping to count the slain. Unfortunately, the sketch was lost.

And all might have been otherwise, for the Sirdar offered before the battle to treat with the Khalifa. Here is the copy of the letter, as translated and published, bearing upon the subject.

30th August 1898
Viz., 11 Rabi Akhar
1316 (M.E.)
From the Sirdar of the Troops
Sudan

To Abdulla, son of Mohamed El-Taaishi
Head of the Sudan

Bear in your mind that your evil deeds throughout the Sudan, particularly your murdering a great number of the Mohammedans without cause or excuse, besides oppression and tyranny, necessitated the advance of my troops for the destruction of your throne, in order to save the country from your devilish doings and iniquity. Inasmuch as there are many in your keeping for whose blood you are held responsible—innocent, old, and infirm, women and children and others—abhorring you and your government, who are guilty of nothing; and because we have no desire that they should suffer the least harm, we ask you to have them removed from the Dem (literally, enclosure) to a place where the shells of guns and bullets of rifles shall not reach them. If you do not do so, the shells and bullets cannot recognise them and will consequently kill them, and afterwards you will be responsible before God for their blood.

Stand firm you and your helpers only in the field of battle to meet the punishment prepared for you by the praised God. But if you and your Emirs incline to surrender to prevent blood being shed, we shall receive your envoy with due welcome, and be sure that we shall treat you with justice and peace.

(Sealed) Kitchener
Sirdar of the Troops in the Sudan

Colonel Maxwell was appointed Commandant of Omdurman, and his brigade was quartered in the town, detachments occupying the principal buildings. Among the places so held were the Arsenal, the Khalifa's and his son the Sheikh Ed Din's houses, the Treasury, Tomb and Mosque enclosure. The rest of the troops were moved two miles to the north of the town, where a camp was formed along the river bank. Omdurman was too abominably dirty to risk keeping a single soldier in the place other than was absolutely necessary. Not an hour was wasted. The Sirdar's practice was—abundant work for each day and all plans prepared ahead for the next. The submission of sheikhs and their followers had to be received, the pursuit of the Khalifa pressed, wounded Dervishes and prisoners provided for, as well as the thousands of poor in Omdurman helped in various ways. Then there had to be arranged-for the disposal of the spoils of war, repatriation for many of Abdullah's enforced subjects, the formal re-occupation of Khartoum, and the immediate despatch back to Lower Egypt of the British troops whose services were no longer required. All this and much more was done, nor am I aware that anything was neglected, not even the correspondents, who were evidently too seldom far removed from the General's thoughts. Hurrying into the town early on Saturday morning, 3rd September, to attend Howard's funeral, I found that within half an hour after sunrise all the dead Dervishes, with the murdered women and children, had been removed to the native burial-grounds outside Omdurman. In my rambles in the capital that day I visited the only two passable dwellings in the place, Abdullah's and his son Osman's. Both houses had a pretence of tidiness and comfort, particularly the Sheikh Ed Din's. There were paved courtyards, doors, windows with shutters, plastered walls, cupboards, benches, and ottomans. In each there were several rooms furnished in a rude style with articles of European manufacture. Of glass-ware, crockery, and large mirrors there was an abundance. The Khalifa's favourite reception-room and a chamber in the harem were almost covered with big looking-glasses. Angry Jaalin and others who had forced an entrance on the previous day, or else mayhap the Lyddite bombs, had smashed the mirrors and most of the domestic ware into atoms. Spears and swords had been freely used to hack the furniture and fittings about. A wealth of printed and manuscript books and papers in Arabic characters were scattered, torn, and thrown into a shed.

    The kitchens, stables and outhouses were odorously barbaric in squalor. They were in strange contrast to any of the rooms in the rabbit warren of attached dwelling-places within the Khalifa's private compound. Around the Mahdi's tomb were great splashes of human blood. On the previous evening I had seen many dead Dervishes lying in that vicinity. In their credulous faith in Mohamed Achmed they had flocked there for safety, only to be killed by our fire. Of 120 who were praying around the tomb when a 50-lb. Lyddite shell burst, but eighteen escaped alive, and these were sorely wounded. The tomb, carefully stuccoed over inside and out, was built of stone and well-burned bricks. The base of the square wall from which the cone-shaped dome sprang was over six feet thick, the vaulted roof tapering to about eighteen inches at the apex. Great holes had been knocked in the north-east side, and the rubbish had tumbled in, breaking the brass and iron grille round the catafalque. Beneath, covered by two huge blocks of stone, lay Mohamed Achmed's remains. Early that day violent hands were laid on the brass rails in the outer windows and grille. The catafalque was stripped of its black and red cloth covering, and the wood-work was totally destroyed. All the yellow lettered panels, with texts from the Koran and the Mahdi's prayer-book, as well as the blue and yellow scroll work, were smashed or carried off by relic-hunters. The false prophet was so speedily discredited that not a Dervish amongst the tens of thousands but regarded these and the subsequent proceedings with complete indifference. To destroy utterly the legend of Mohamed Achmed's mission, when the British troops had returned to Cairo the Mahdi's body was disinterred. It had been roughly embalmed and the features were said to be recognisable. The common people who saw the remains almost doubted their senses, for it had been given out that the Mahdi had merely gone off on a visit to heaven and would shortly return. That his body was found surprised them, as they thought he had gone aloft in the flesh, the object of the tomb being to mark the spot where he took leave of the earth and would return to it. Perhaps it may be deplored that Mohamed Achmed's remains were broken up, part being cast into the Nile, whilst the head and other portions of the body were retained for presentation, it is said, to medical colleges. There were those who thought that the wisest course would have been to expose the remains for all to see them who cared to, and then to hand them over to the natives to bury in one of their cemeteries as if he had been an ordinary man. But the Sudan is not Europe, nor are its inhabitants amenable to measures eminently satisfactory to civilised northern races. The tomb was subsequently levelled to the ground by an explosion of gun-cotton and the debris was cleared away.

I had a good look over the Khalifa's war arsenal. There were plenty of cannon, old and new, as well as machine guns, rifles, pistols, and fowling pieces of all kinds. Musical instruments, war-drums, elephants' tusks used as horns, coats of chain-mail old and new, and steel helmets. Most of the latter are quite modern, being part of 600 supplied by a London firm of sword makers—Wilkinson & Co., Pall Mall, to a former Khedive's body-guard. Somehow these plate and chain crusader-like head-pieces seem all to have drifted south. There were hundreds of Dervish battle flags, including several duplicate black silk banners such as the Khalifa carried during the action, and thousands of native spears, swords, and shields. In short, it would be easier to tell what was not in that extraordinary storehouse than what was. Among other articles I saw were: Ivory, powder, percussion caps, old lead, copper, tin, bronze, cloth, looms, pianos, sewing machines, agricultural implements, boilers, steam-engines, ostrich feathers, gum, hippopotamus hides, iron and wooden bedsteads, drums, bugles, field glasses—Lieutenant Charles Grenfell's, lost at El Teb in the Eastern Sudan in 1883, were found there—bolts, zinc, rivets, paints, India-rubber, leather, boots, knapsacks, water-bottles, flags, and clothes. There were three state coaches—one of them might at a pinch have served for the Lord Mayor—and an American buggy. They needed a little retrimming, but there was harness and material enough to have rigged out the four vehicles in style. In short, the arsenal held the jettisoned cargo of the whole aforetime Egyptian Sudan, with much besides drawn from Abyssinia and Central Africa. Truly, the Khalifa must have been a strange man, with a fine acquisitive instinct abnormally cultivated.

NEUFELD, WITH ABYSSINIAN WIFE AND CHILDREN;
ALSO FELLOW PRISONER

Neufeld, quite contrary to Slatin Pasha's way of speaking, declared to me that the Khalifa was not at all a bad sort of man, nor an exceptionally cruel Arab task-master, and certainly not a monster. The Khalifa, he said, had often come and chatted with him. Abdullah had vowed to him, that if he were able to have his own way he would make a close friend of him, and have him always near his person. The Khalifa asserted he liked white men, admired their knowledge and ability, and would, were he permitted, have many of them in Khartoum. As everybody knew, he befriended the Greeks, because he could do that with safety, for the natives were not so jealous of them as of other white men. The Taaisha were, he declared, absurdly suspicious of his intercourse with Neufeld, and were always bringing him tales, to try and get him to kill all the white men without exception. His countrymen's jealous, narrow fanaticism annoyed him, but what, he asked, could he do, for he was very much in their power, and unable to afford to fly in their faces? Abdullah often spoke thus, according to Neufeld, and, as the latter also said, frequently that leader of the fanatical Dervishes exhibited keen interest in acquiring information about Europe and its people. He hoped to make peace some day with the outside world, and be allowed thereafter to rule the Sudan. All this, I submit, is rather puzzling, in view of the filthy den the Khalifa kept Neufeld shut up in, and the manner in which he loaded him with heavy leg-irons. During his captivity, Neufeld had with him an Abyssinian girl, or rather woman. She was taken prisoner with him. Thereafter she devotedly ministered to his wants, fetched water and food, and made, under his tuition, really eatable bread. Neufeld, who said he met me in 1884-85, up the Nile, when he was attached to the army, gave me a piece of this bread, and I found it quite palatable. Yeast is easily made in the Sudan with sour dough and sugar.

As arsenals mayhap date back to the eras of Tubal Cain and Vulcan, it was to be expected the Khalifa would also have his modern smithy. He made his own gunpowder, shells, and bullets, and the metallic cases for his troops' Remington rifles. The country was laid under contribution to supply copper for that purpose, and he essayed the filling of percussion caps with fulminate, not over successfully I hope. He had his cartridge manufactory, and a very well equipped engineer shop as well. Yea, the potentate was setting up a Zoo, wherein I saw three young lions chained to posts by neck collars, as though those savage beasts were watch-dogs. As for the engineer shop, with foundry and smithy attached, the Beit el Mauna, it was part of a cleverly planned square of buildings with a river frontage and a spacious yard. The designer was one El Osta Abdullah, a former employee of General Gordon's in Khartoum Arsenal. There were several steam engines; the principal one driving the main shafting was of 28 horse-power. The fly-wheel was 4 feet in diameter. There were five lathes, one cat-head lathe—36 inch, three drills, and other tools including a slotting machine, all in perfect going order. The machinery had formed part of the dismantled Khartoum Arsenal, and had been removed into Omdurman to be nearer the watchful eyes of Yacoub, who superintended the workshops, though destitute of mechanical knowledge. El Osta was the foreman and had numbers of natives, free and prisoners, under him. There were plenty of crucibles for iron as well as brass smelting. The blasts of furnaces and smithy fires were served from fanners driven by machinery. There were paint shops and stores, the floors of which were laid in bricks. In truth, the arsenal was in process of extension. Two more engines for the shop were in course of completion. The steamers disabled or wrecked in the 1885 campaign had all been recovered and overhauled by the Dervishes. They were sagacious enough to make use of all the skilled labour to be found amongst the Turkish and Egyptian prisoners who fell into their hands. Although the Khalifa's river steamers, recaptured by the Sirdar, could steam fully as well as ever, their hulls and decks were dreadfully rotten and dilapidated, not a pound of paint nor any fresh timber having been used upon them in all the intervening years.

"Is that mean, dirty compound, with those squalid mud-huts, facing the Khalifa's big wall, Osman Digna's house?" I asked.

"Yes," said my native informant, "that is the house of the robber-chief, Osman Digna."

I entered and found within only a few wretched slaves and poor Hadendowas. Osman, like the Khalifa, had given us the slip, leaving behind such of his people as he thought of no value, and hurrying away with all his women and treasure towards the south. They had horses and camels, and upon the best of them they decamped. Several of the notorious Osman Digna's tribal retainers were caught. These wretched Hadendowas were, I was told, glad to be permitted subsequently to return to their own country. Over 300 Abyssinians were amongst our prisoners. They had volunteered or been coerced into joining the Dervish ranks. All of them were surprised to find themselves kindly treated. In due course, those who cared to go—men, women and children—were provided with free passages back to Abyssinia. The Sirdar held several receptions, whereat the principal native leaders and sheikhs attended. Amongst others delighted at the overthrow of the Khalifa were all the survivors of the old

Khedivial army, who had been abandoned to their fate for years. Of these were the former Governor of Senaar, a native artillery officer who had been with Hicks Pasha, and Gordon Pasha's native medical attendant.

During the week after the battle the British and Khedivial troops, by brigades, made triumphal marches into and through Omdurman. Proceeding from our camp with flags flying and bands playing, they went along the main thoroughfares to the Tomb and Mosque, returning by a circuitous route to quarters. The ex-Dervishes and other natives flocked in thousands to see the finely-equipped and well-disciplined battalions led by the Sirdar. It was an exhibition of power they quite understood, and one which won from them open praise at the gallant bearing of our soldiery. The immediate effect was to produce a feeling of deep respect for the authority of the new order of things.

When it was found that the Khalifa had escaped by the south end of Omdurman, Colonel Broadwood, with his two regiments of Egyptian cavalry and the Camel Corps, started in pursuit. Gunboats also proceeded up the White Nile to head off the fugitives. Unfortunately as there had been a very general rainfall, the desert routes towards Kordofan were not absolutely waterless. The cavalry soon found that they were upon a hot trail; and men, women, and children, who had been unable to keep pace with the flying Khalifa and Osman Digna, were picked up. Some of these, no doubt, had purposely given their master the slip. It was in that way that Abdullah's chief wife, the Sheikh Ed Din's mother, was caught and brought in by the "friendlies." One poor woman, just confined, had the babe, a male, taken away by her lord, whilst she was left to shift for herself. Happily, her life was saved.

As I have said relatively little about the Egyptian cavalry, I will let one of their officers tell what they did. Colonel Broadwood had under him a magnificent body of officers, British and Egyptian. Captain Legge of the 20th Hussars was the brigade-major. The narrative in question was given to me a few days after the victory.

The Sirdar's orders on the morning of the battle to Colonel Broadwood were, to take up successive positions on his (the Sirdar's) right flank, and to prevent the enemy's left from overlapping too far. The fear was that the Dervishes might attack upon the north or weakest side of the *zereba*. After rejoining the infantry towards the end of the assault made on Macdonald's brigade we were formed into two lines. Turning our backs to the Nile, that is, facing west, we galloped in pursuit of the retreating Dervishes. For four miles we rode forward without check. Then we wheeled to the left, towards Omdurman, and swept the country on the right front of the Sirdar over a width of four miles. We were shot at repeatedly, and sometimes heavily, by bands of fugitives, but we never drew rein, using lance and sword upon all who showed fight. In that draw we made 1000 prisoners, breaking the Remingtons of those who had rifles and sending our captives under escort of a squadron to the Sirdar. When close to Omdurman we came across a large body of Dervishes full of 'buck.' Four of our squadrons went for them. They charged clean through them, wheeled, and charged back again. That took the sting out of them, though there were still individual Dervishes who would keep trying to charge us. Colonel Broadwood came up at that juncture with the supports, whereupon the enemy all bolted for the hills. At 2 p.m. we reported to headquarters, and, following the infantry, went to water our horses at the Nile. The same afternoon we passed through part of Omdurman and went out upon the open desert to the south-west. At 6.30 p.m. Slatin Pasha brought us orders to start immediately in pursuit of the Khalifa. We went on as best we could until 8.30 p.m., without food or water. Trying to run in towards the river to procure both, for a gunboat was to carry our supplies, we found it was impossible to get within two miles of the Nile owing to the overflow having turned the margin into boggy land. Besides, the bushy inaccessible ground was teeming with hostile Dervishes. We had missed our way. Without offsaddling, we bivouacked where we were, forming square. At 4 a.m. we mounted and rode on, going until 8.30 a.m., when we got down to the river. There Slatin Pasha quitted us, returning to Omdurman. We halted for an hour, watered and fed our poor horses, and had a bite for ourselves. Then we remounted and rode fifteen miles farther south. We had reached a point just thirty-five miles south of Omdurman. Our horses had been going almost continuously for four days previously, the forage was finished, and the animals exhausted, so we again halted. Supplies had been ordered forward to that spot, but the overflow prevented us from being able to get near enough the native boats to draw upon them for stores. We decided to bivouac there and take our chance of being able somehow to get at the boats. Next morning we were ordered back into Omdurman. Slatin Pasha had learned from fugitives and natives that the Khalifa was still twenty-five miles ahead of us. Abdullah had with him 100 Taaisha Baggara, and had procured fresh camels and horses, so was 'going strong,' too good for us to catch up. The riverside country people could not credit that we had defeated the Khalifa and taken Omdurman. On our way back we picked up six of Osman Digna's Hadendowas. They said Osman was riding with the Khalifa, showing him the tracks and bypaths, with all of which he was familiar. We heard that neither Osman nor the Khalifa was wounded, and that Sheikh Ed Din was likewise untouched.

It has been too readily accepted that the Black, although an incomparably fine infantry-man, would not make a good trooper. There are Blacks and Blacks as there are "Browns and Browns." Many of the negroid races of the Central Sudan are excellent horsemen. The dash of the Khalifa's mounted men was superb. So it came about that after Omdurman the Sirdar decided to reinforce the Egyptian cavalry with a newly raised squadron or two composed entirely of Blacks. Ex-Dervishes of suitable smartness and physique were permitted to join the new body, the ranks of which were filled in a very short time, for hundreds eagerly volunteered. The accounts I have since heard of the 1st Black Cavalry are eminently favourable. There can be no doubt about one thing—whatever may be said of *fellaheen* troopers, the Blacks will charge home.

Another matter that merits a little more detail is the action fought by Major Stuart Wortley's "friendlies," and the work accomplished by the flotilla under Commander Keppel, R.N. It was the gunboats that transported the British infantry from their camps at Dakhala and Darmali so smartly to Wad Habeshi. Their assistance in that respect reduced the campaign from one of months to days, and lessened the risks to the troops. Eight steamers arrived at Dakhala on one occasion, and the transport department did its duty so well that they were loaded and despatched back up stream within twenty-four hours. Royan Island had not only been made a depot of stores, but a sanatorium where sick officers and men were sent as a "pick 'em up." An order from the Sirdar on the 30th of August was wired to Royan, to find 235 men and 8 officers who were well enough to man the gunboats, to be in short amateur marines. At that date there were 327 sick upon the island. Most of them were eager to get to the front, but the doctors would not certify that any of them were able to bear the fatigue of marching. There was therefore great rejoicing among the more convalescent, for they had begun to despair of seeing the fight. The hospital state showed that there were then at Royan 46 men of the Warwicks, 69 of the Lincolns, 62 of the Seaforths, 36 of the Camerons, 19 of the Grenadier Guards, 42 of the Northumberland Fusiliers, 42 of the Lancashire Fusiliers, and 21 of the Rifles. From 25 to 40 men were marched on board each of the gunboats the same day. Captain Ferguson of the Northumberland Fusiliers became marine officer on board the *Sultan*, Lieutenant Allardice went to the *Sheik*, Lieutenant Seymour of the Grenadier Guards to the *Melik*, Captain Ritchie to the *Nazir*, Lieutenant Arbuthnot to the *El Hafir*, and Lieutenant Jackson and other officers respectively to the *Tamai, Fatah, Metemmeh*, etc.

On the 31st of August the *Melik* kept abreast of the cavalry acting as a screen. At noon of the same day the *Sultan* and the *Melik* and *Nazir* were sent to shell the Dervish tents and *tukals* seen to the east of Kerreri village. The enemy were found in some force, about 3500 strong. Eight or ten shrapnel were fired into their *zerebaed* camp. Right in the middle of the tents the first shell burst. The Dervishes struck their camp instantly, and mounted men and footmen ran to the hills, their flight quickened by the gunboats' Maxims. Their *zereba* was burned. South Kerreri village was found unoccupied. The steamers proceeded a little further up stream, had a look at Tuti Island, and on the west bank caught sight of a body of Dervishes, Emir Zaccharia's men, who also had a taste of shrapnel and Maxims.

On the 1st of September at 5.30 a.m. the steamers *Sultan, Melik, Sheik, Nazir, Fatah, Tamai*, and *Abu Klea* went again up the river to destroy the forts and land the 50-pounder Lyddite howitzer battery on Tuti Island, whence it was to shell Omdurman. Major Stuart Wortley and part of his force were also to be transferred to that island to support Major Elmslie's battery and clear off any Dervishes. It was found, as I have already stated, that Tuti was unsuitable as a position, and the Lyddite guns were landed instead upon the east or right bank of the river. The *Sultan* opened the attack, firing at the forts and pitching shells into Omdurman. In a short time the other gunboats came to her assistance, and the mud forts, of which there were a dozen or more, were promptly silenced. Several of the Dervish gunners' shells, however, only missed the steamers that were their target by a very few yards. Happily the embrasures of the forts were so badly made, that the enemy had but a small angle of fire. It was in more than one instance impossible for the Dervish guns to train except straight to their front. The flotilla passed down behind Tuti Island, going by the east bank, and were brought-to below the island. There the 37th R.A. Battery was landed, and the Lyddite shell fire was directed against the great wall and the Mahdi's tomb, the range of the latter being 3200 yards. Many Dervishes were seen in and around Omdurman, and a number were noticed upon the right bank. Two of the gunboats remained all night to protect the Lyddite battery, using their electric search-lights to detect any lurking Dervishes. The steamers fired that day several hundred shells and 8000 rounds from their Maxims. Captain Prince Christian Victor was attached on board the *Sultan*, and Prince Teck, who had a sharp attack of fever and had temporarily to abandon his squadron in the Egyptian cavalry, saw that and the next day's battle from one of the other gunboats.

On the 2nd of September the *Melik* ran a little way up stream before sunrise and then returned. In the first stage of the battle the *Nazir*, *Fatah*, *Sheik*, *El Hafir* and another protected the south front of the Sirdar's camp, whilst the *Sultan*, *Melik* and *Tamai* guarded the north end of it. There were over 100 shells were fired from the *Sultan* at 3000 to 2800 yards ranges. The *Melik* found the enemy's columns with their quick-firing 15 pounders at under 1500 yards range on one occasion. During the second phase of the battle, the *Melik* dropped again downstream, and struck Sheikh Ed Din's column as the enemy advanced to attack Macdonald's brigade, treating the Dervishes to all her artillery. When Omdurman was occupied by the troops the flotilla again rendered valuable help. After the action the gunboats were sent, part up the White, part up the Blue Nile, to carry the good news and break up any Dervish camps. The *Sultan*, *Melik*, *Sheik*, *Nazir*, and *Fatah* proceeded up the White Nile. Commander Keppel went 115 miles south of Omdurman. He saw but few of the enemy. The country was much overflowed, the river was nearly 6 miles wide in several places, the wooded banks and bush being under water.

On the 2nd of September Major Stuart Wortley and his friendlies had a brisk engagement with Emir Isa Zaccharia. Major Elmslie had begun the day's battle at 5.30 a.m. with a salvo of his six guns, throwing the 50 lb. Lyddite shells into Omdurman. Wortley's friendlies, later on, advanced in fine style, in open order, and drove about 800 *Jehadieh* out of a village. About 350 were killed, including their leader. The remainder bolted off towards the Blue Nile, pursued by the Jaalin and others. At the close of the action Major Wortley, Captain Buckle, Lieut. C. Wood, and two non-commissioned English officers walked down towards the point from which Major Elmslie's battery was firing. They were seen and charged by about twenty-five Dervish horsemen. Luckily, heavy, boggy land intervened, and Lieut. Wood and Major Wortley dropped the leading horsemen, when some of the Jaalin rallied and came to their assistance. The rout of the Baggara was completed, the Dervish horsemen leaving eleven dead upon the field.

On Sunday morning, 4th September, the Press were invited by Headquarters to go over by steamer to Khartoum. We were told that an official ceremony which we ought not to miss was about to take place. There were an unusual number of correspondents. The previous restrictions and military objections to their presence had been made ridiculous by the widest throwing open of the door to all. The Sirdar and Headquarters embarked upon the *Melik*. We found that representative detachments from all the commands in the army were being ferried over in boats and *giassas* towed by the steamers. From every British battalion there were present eighty-one officers and men. The 21st Lancers were represented by ten officers and twenty-four non-commissioned officers and men. Two officers and seven men were sent by each battery of artillery, and two officers and five men from the Maxim batteries. There were also representative sections from the Khedivial forces. As the steamers drew up alongside the stone-wall quay before the ruined Government House where General Gordon made his last stand, the soldiers were seen to be already in position. There was but little space between the quay wall and the buildings, for the debris of bricks and stone from the overturned structure nearly blocked up the former open promenade facing the muddy Blue Nile. The ruined walls and forts looked picturesque in their deep setting of dark-green palms, mimosa, and tall orange-trees. Compared with treeless, brown, arid Omdurman, Khartoum wore an air of romance and loveliness that well became such historic ground. An odour of blossom and fruit was wafted from the wild and spacious Mission and Government House gardens, which even the Dervishes had not been able to wreck totally.

DISTANT VIEW, KHARTOUM (FROM BLUE NILE)

Two flagstaffs had been erected upon the top of the one-storied wall fronting the Blue Nile. The Sirdar ranged facing the building and the flagstaffs. Behind him were the Headquarters Staff, the Generals of division, and others. To his left, formed up at right angles, were the representative detachments of the Egyptian army, the 11th Sudanese, with their red heckles in their fezzes, in the front line. Upon the Sirdar's right were the detachments of Gatacre's division, each in its regimental order of seniority. Standing a few paces in front of the Sirdar, but facing him, upon a mound of earth and bricks, were the four chaplains attached to the British infantry—Presbyterian, Church of England, Roman Catholic, and Wesleyan. *En passant*, though it is an army secret, in nothing was the Sirdar's power and strong will more manifest than in securing the presence that day in amity of the four representatives of religion. One of the reverend gentlemen, presumably on the strength of the superior claims of his orthodoxy, refused to join in any service in which clergymen of any other denomination bore a part. The Sirdar sent a peremptory order, without a word of explanation, for that cleric to embark forthwith and return to Cairo. Instead, he hastened to Headquarters and made his peace, and had the order withdrawn. Upon their right was a small body of Royal Engineer officers, Gordon's own corps. A hundred natives or more had gathered on the outside, wondering what was going to happen. The Sirdar himself had been the first to land upon the quay and walk towards the building, the windows of which Gordon had caused to be filled in to stop entrance of the Dervish bullets from Tuti. There were plenty of marks of the enemy's musketry fire, as well as the dents of shell and round shot. The former official entrance was within a littered courtyard upon the opposite side of the building. It was whilst descending the interior stairway to meet the Dervishes that Gordon was hacked and slain by the fierce fanatics and his body cast into the courtyard.

Ten o'clock was the official hour notified for the ceremonial, which commenced upon a signal from the Sirdar. A British band played a few bars of "God Save the Queen." Whilst all were saluting, Lieutenant Stavely, R.N., and Captain J. Watson, A.D.C., standing on the west side of the wall ran up a brilliant silk Union Jack to the top of their flagstaff, hauling the halyard taut as the flag flapped smartly in the breeze. It had barely begun to ascend when Lieutenant Milford and Effendi Bakr, at the adjacent pole, ran up the Egyptian flag. Thereupon an Egyptian band played at some length the Khedivial hymn. At its close the Sirdar called for three cheers for "The Queen," which were given voluminously, even the natives shouting, though, perhaps, they didn't quite know why. Three cheers for the Khedive were also heartily given. Meantime the *Melik*'s quick-firing guns were rolling out a royal salute, and, as usual with them, making things jump aboard the lightly built craft and smashing glass and crockery in all directions.

Ere the echo of cannon had died away another ceremony had begun. The British band played softly the "Dead March in Saul," and every head was bared in memory of Gordon. His funeral obsequies were at last taking place upon the spot where he fell. Then the Egyptian band played their quaint funeral march, and the native men and women, understanding that, and whom it was played for, raised their prolonged, shrill, wailing cry. Count Calderai, the Italian Military Attaché, who stood near the Sirdar, was deeply affected, whilst Count von Tiedmann, the German Attaché, who appeared in his magnificent white Cuirassier uniform on the occasion, was even more keenly impressed, a soldier's tears coursing down his cheeks. But there! Other eyes were wet, and cheeks too, as well as his, and bronzed veterans were not ashamed of it either. Sadness and bitter memories! So the Gordon legend, if you will, shall live as long as the English name endures. A brief pause, and in gentle voice and manner the Rev. John M. Sims, Presbyterian Chaplain—Gordon's faith—broke the silence. In his brief prayer he said:

HOISTING FLAGS, KHARTOUM

"Our help is in the name of the Lord who made heaven and earth." Then he observed, "Let us hear God's word as written for our instruction," reading from Psalm XV. the following verses: "Lord, who shall abide in Thy tabernacle? Who shall dwell in Thy holy hill? He that walketh uprightly, and worketh righteousness, and speaketh the truth in his heart. He that backbiteth not with his tongue, nor doeth evil to his neighbour, nor taketh up a reproach against his neighbour. In whose eyes a vile person is contemned; but he honoureth them that fear the Lord. He that sweareth to his own hurt, and changeth not. He that putteth not out his money to usury, nor taketh reward against the innocent. He that doeth these things shall never be moved.

"And to God's great name shall be all the praise and glory, world without end. Amen."

When Mr Sims had concluded, the Rev. A. W. B. Watson, Church of England Chaplain, recited the Lord's Prayer. Following him the Rev. R. Brindle, Roman Catholic Chaplain, prayed, saying:

"O Almighty God, by whose providence are all things which come into the lives of men, whether of suffering which Thou permittest, or of joy and gladness which Thou givest, look down, we beseech Thee, with eyes of pity and compassion on this land so loved by that heroic soul whose memory we honour before Thee this day. Give back to it days of peace. Send to it rulers animated by his spirit of justice and righteousness. Strengthen them in the might of Thy power, that they may labour in making perfect the work to which he devoted and for which he gave his life. And grant to us, Thy servants, that we may copy his virtues of self-sacrifice and fortitude, so that when Thou callest we may each be able to answer, 'I have fought the good fight,'—a blessing which we humbly ask in the name of the Father, Son, and Holy Ghost. Amen."

When Father Brindle had concluded, the pipers, accompanied by muffled drums, played the Coronach as a lament. The weird Highland minstrelsy seemed quite in keeping with the place and solemn scene. Then the Khedivial band played a hymn tune, *Thy Will be Done*, and the sad ceremony was closed to the boom of minute guns. Generals Rundle, Gatacre, and Hunter then stepped forward and congratulated the Sirdar upon the successful completion of his task, and the commanding officers and others, following their example, did the same. Sir Herbert acknowledged their greeting, and announced that the men would be allowed to break off for half an hour or so to go over the ruins and gardens if they wished. Everybody availed himself of the opportunity. In a few minutes a throng of officers and men who had scrambled over the debris filled the roofless rooms and packed the stairway where Gordon was struck down. I was surprised to find that even the youngest, most callow soldiers knew their Khartoum and the story of Gordon's fight and death. So deep and far had the tale travelled. There were speculations and suggestions as to how the end exactly came about that were a revelation to me, so full of information and pregnant of observation were many of the men's remarks. Throng succeeded throng in the rooms and stairways, whilst others went to explore the outhouses and the gardens. The passion flowers and the pomegranates were in bloom, but the oranges and limes were in fruit. Leaves and buds were plucked by all of us as souvenirs. Brigade-Major Snow, who was with the Camel Corps in 1884-85 across the Bayuda desert, produced a tiny bottle of champagne that was to have been drunk in Khartoum when we got there. He opened it, and shared the driblet with a few of the old campaigners. By one p.m. we were all back again in Omdurman, leaving behind two companies of the 11th Battalion to hold Khartoum for the two flags, the hoisting of which, side by side, the Egyptians regarded as natural and most proper.

Chapter 14

The Official Despatches

It was decided by the Sirdar, from whom no successful appeal was possible, that, after the occupation of Khartoum, the war correspondents had no longer any pretext for remaining in the country. There were no questions raised by the military to excuse their ruling. No more was heard about the difficulties of transport, the scarcity of provisions, and everything being required for the soldiers. Had not the keen Greek sutlers, as usual, followed the army in shoals, managing somehow to convey themselves and their goods to the front? We had not been two days encamped at Omdurman before some of these traders arrived, and, dumping their sacks and boxes by the wayside, started selling forthwith. The natives, too, speedily reassured, brought out and squatted before baskets of dates, onions, and other comestibles they were anxious to dispose of for English or Egyptian money. Rightly contemning the Khalifa's coinage as practically valueless, they refused to accept it in payment, and proffered to sell all they possessed at the price of old copper. The British troops made their triumphal entry into Omdurman on the 5th of September, and several of the correspondents left for England the same day. We who remained had a sort of Hobson's choice, either to return to Cairo on the 8th September or to remain in Omdurman out of which we should not be allowed to stir until all the British troops had gone, when we should have to leave with the last batch. Which course we should adopt was with fine humour left to be decided by a majority of ourselves. For once the Press was practically unanimous and elected to shake the dust of the Sudan from their feet, and so it came about that the war correspondents had to fold their tents and go, disposing of their quadrupeds as best they could. There was no alternative in the case of the horses between accepting any price for them or shooting them, for, in the Sudan, there being no grazing, a horse must have a master or starve. I disposed of a £40 animal for £1 and got but little more for three others. The camels and stores fetched somewhat better prices. Our servants we took back to their homes.

Yet for sundry reasons I was anxious to be allowed to remain longer in the Sudan. There was news of fighting and movement up the Blue Nile. Emir Ahmed Fadl bringing a force of 3000 Dervishes from Gedarif to assist the Khalifa had been driven back by the gunboat *Sultan*. More important still, rumours had reached us that the French, under Marchand, were at Fashoda. I knew that the Sirdar intended sending a force upon the gunboats up the White Nile to Fashoda and Sobat, so I made both verbal and written requests to the General for permission to accompany the expedition. That, I was told, could not be granted. We had full confirmation of the fact that Major Marchand was at Fashoda brought down to Omdurman on the 7th September by the Dervish steamer *Tewfikieh*. I boarded her and had a long chat with the captain (*reis*) and members of the crew, all of whom wore *jibbehs*. The little craft was an ex-Thames, above-the-bridges, penny steamer with Penn's oscillating engines. She was one of the boats Gordon sent from Khartoum in 1884 to meet the Desert Column at Metemmeh. She was, if possible, more dilapidated-looking than ever. By guarded questioning I ascertained that the *Tewfikieh* was three days out from Fashoda. She and the *Safieh*, another Dervish steamer, had been hotly fired upon by the French who were occupying the old Egyptian fort with 100 Senegalese or natives of Timbuktu. A number of local natives, Shilluks, who had long been hostile to the Dervishes, were co-operating with the strangers. The *reis* accurately described the French flag which was flying over the works and the appearance of the Europeans. I was also able to procure several of the Lebel rifle bullets that had entered the upper structure of the steamer. The censor struck out from my telegrams all allusion to the presence of the French at Fashoda, and I had to wait until I returned to Lower Egypt to transmit the news to London. I openly held that the Fashoda affair should be promptly and fully disclosed to the British public, and I acted upon that conviction.

The *Safieh* remained up the Nile, making fast to the bank about 100 miles north of Fashoda, to await the return of the *Tewfikieh* with orders from the Khalifa and reinforcements to destroy the French. No doubt there was an attempt made to carry out an Anglophobe idea of effecting a friendly alliance with the Mahdists so as to secure to France the right of access to the Nile and the Bahr el Ghazal. It was an effort to achieve the impossible, to negotiate a treaty with wild beasts. Had the Dervishes, or even the *Safieh's* people who were drumming up recruits, been granted a fortnight to do it in the Marchand expedition would have been totally destroyed. The *Tewfikieh* arrived in a dust-storm and passed the Sirdar's gunboats unseen, and it was not until she got to Omdurman that the Dervish *reis* and crew realised what had happened. With quick wit the skipper acted, for those who go upon waters are of a catholicity of creed and good-fellowship very different from ordinary landsmen. He ran his craft to the bank, landed with one of his crew and paid a visit to headquarters, where he surrendered himself and his craft. Both were at once accepted, and during the course of the same day the *Tewfikieh* again hoisted the Khedivial flag and was employed in towing and ferry work. The captain and crew stood by their ship working her, and though dressed as Dervishes were on the flotilla muster-roll for wages and rations. The like befell the other Dervish steamers that came into the Sirdar's hands. For two days there was a sale of the loot captured by the army. Arms, drums, flags, and nearly all the smaller articles found in the arsenal were auctioned. Some £4000 or more of ivory and other merchandise were put aside. On the first day big prices were paid by officers and men for trophies, but the following day spears and swords were sold for trifling sums. The money derived from the sale was set aside for distribution as prize money. All the battalions, batteries, and corps had, however, free gifts of guns, flags, or other trophies for souvenirs. On the afternoon of the 8th September the correspondents and their belongings proceeded on the horribly frowsy, rat-overrun, Dervish steamer *Bordein* to Dakhala, the railhead. The steamer was packed upon and below deck with British soldiers, about 50 of whom were sick, whilst several were wounded. Stowed almost like cattle, sitting, squatting, lying anywhere, anyhow, without shade or shelter, we underwent two days of it on board. It was found necessary to tie up occasionally for wood (fuel), and at night the steamer was always moored to the bank. These occasions provided the needed opportunity to prepare and partake of meals, and find space to sleep upon the shore. But it was war-time, and extra roughing-it is always an accompaniment of the game in uncivilised countries. Within a week, thanks to the desert railway and the post-boats, we were back enjoying the delicious flesh-pots of Egypt, first on board Messrs Cook's magnificent Nile steamers, and thereafter in Shepheard's hotel, Cairo.

On the way down I saw something and heard more of the excellent base-hospital established at Abadia, of which Lieut.-Col. Clery, R.A.M.C., was in charge. Landing stages had been erected for receiving the sick and wounded, and wells were dug from which, owing to infiltration, clear water was drawn for use in the hospital. All water, however, used for food or drink was in addition filtered and boiled. The percentage of recovery by patients was eminently satisfactory. Major Battersby, R.A.M.C, had a Röntgen Ray apparatus which was employed in twenty-two cases to locate bullets and fractures. In connection with the treatment of the sick and wounded, it is to be regretted that earlier and greater use was not made of the National Aid Society's offer to provide steamers properly fitted for carrying invalids. A railway journey in Egypt or the Sudan is, at the best, a painful experience for even those who are well. From Assouan to Cairo every invalided soldier could and should have been transported by water, on just such a craft as the hospital, *Mayflower*, which the Society promptly and admirably equipped the moment the authorities gave their consent. As early as June 1898 Lieut.-Col. Young, on behalf of the Red Cross Society, wrote intimating a desire to assist, entirely at their own expense, in the expedition. This application met with a refusal, and it was not until the 1st of August 1898 that the Foreign Office replied to a subsequent appeal that the Sirdar would gladly accept their proffer. Had the matter been settled in June, instead of August, there could have been three hospital ships plying, enough to transport every sick soldier by water. By the 6th of September the *Mayflower* was ready with a crew and a complement of nurses. The army provided their own medical staff, the Society running the steamer and supplying the cuisine, which was under the direction of a French "chef." The *Mayflower* was able to convey, in most comfortable quarters, with every possible attention to their needs, seventy-two sick and wounded soldiers. Pyjamas, socks, shirts and other necessaries were given free to every patient. The steamer did good service, making at least three round trips to bring down patients.

The wounds received in battle had scarce been dressed before the Sirdar was seeking to give effect to his schemes for the well-being of the Sudanese. Means were taken for the speedy connecting by telegraph of Suakin and Berber, Suakin, Kassala, Gedarif, Khartoum. The wire from Dakhala to Nasri was brought on to Omdurman a few days after the victory. Arrangements were further made to bridge the Atbara and carry forward the Wady Halfa-Abu Hamed-Dakhala line along the east bank to a point upon the Blue Nile opposite Khartoum. That railway will be completed in 1899, and there will be through train service from Wady Halfa to the junction of the two Niles. With the suitable steamers already in hand, there should be, all the year round, water communication up the Blue Nile for hundreds of miles, and upon the White Nile, with a few porterages, to the Great Equatorial Lakes, and west through the Bahr el Ghazal country. So much was for commerce, for material benefaction, but there was besides recognition of what was due to higher needs. I knew the Sirdar had long entertained the idea of fitly commemorating General Gordon's glorious self-abnegation in striving to help the natives, single-handed, fighting unto death ignorance and fanaticism. A scheme that would provide for the education of the youth of the Sudan, conveying to them the stores of knowledge taught in the colleges of civilised countries, was what he aimed at. The desired institution should be founded in Khartoum, which was to become a centre of light and guidance for the new nation being born to rule Central Africa. As the Mussulman is nothing if not fanatical whenever religious questions are introduced, it was to be a foundation solely devoted to teaching exact knowledge without any *ism*.

I had the opportunity afforded me of several conversations with the Sirdar upon the subject so dear to him, "a Gordon Memorial College in Khartoum." The substance of these interviews I cabled fully to the *Daily Telegraph*, which, with most other journals, warmly advocated the carrying out of the scheme. It was certain that Gordon and Khartoum would remain objects of interest to our race, and that public sentiment demanded the erection of some proper memorial of the sad past. Nothing better than the founding of a People's College could be thought of. Lamentable ignorance of the world and all therein was and yet is the direct curse of the land. The natives have had no opportunity of learning anything beyond the parrot-smattering of the Koran, the one book of Moslem schools. The rudimentary knowledge common to British schoolboys transcends all the learning of the wise in the Sudan. The people, Arabs and blacks, are docile and capable of readily learning everything taught in the ordinary scholastic curriculum at home. With a minimum annual income of £1500 a year, teachers and apparatus could, it was said, be provided, although in addition five or six thousand pounds sterling would be required for preliminary outlay. The land and part of the necessary buildings, the Sirdar intimated, would probably be presented as a gift by the Egyptian Government. It would be futile, as all knew, trying to succeed with a staff of native teachers. Tribal relations and other causes stood in the way, and unless the college was to be doomed to failure it would have to be launched and conducted by virile European professors. Much if not all of the food required for the staff and scholars could be purchased cheaply or might be raised in the college grounds by the pupils themselves. Technical training would be taught hand in hand with the ordinary courses. These were the outlines of the Sirdar's communications, who, by the way, at that date was already being known as Lord Kitchener of Khartoum. It having been noticed that certain dignitaries and others were, through the press, ruining the scheme by attempts to foist upon it theological and medical schools, a complete answer was found for their statements by a near relative of Gordon Pasha. In the course of conversation he referred to what I knew to be the facts, that the British and Egyptian army doctors wherever stationed in the Sudan, or from Assouan south, were wont to give medicines and professional services to the civil population free of charge. General Gordon, I was authorised to state, was no narrow-spirited Christian, for he always put the need of giving education before attempts at proselytising. It is not generally known amongst strait-laced sectarians or churchmen that Gordon Pasha, at his own expense, built a mosque for the devout Mohammedans whom he ruled, and that his name, as worthy to be remembered in Moslem annals, is inscribed upon the walls of the Mosque at Mecca. That General Gordon was a staunch Christian goes without saying, but he was no churl who could not esteem and respect the faith of his fellow-men. But the case is well summed up in Lord Kitchener's subsequent letter to the press. The Sirdar wrote:

> *Sir*,—I trust that it will not be thought that I am trespassing too much upon the goodwill of the British public, or that I am exceeding the duties of a soldier, if I call your attention to an issue of very grave importance arising immediately out of the recent campaign in the Sudan.

That region now lies in the pathway of our Empire, and a numerous population has become practically dependent upon men of our race.

A responsible task is henceforth laid upon us, and those who have conquered are called upon to civilise. In fact, the work interrupted since the death of Gordon must now be resumed.

It is with this conviction that I venture to lay before you a proposal which, if it met with the approval and support of the British public and of the English-speaking race, would prove of inestimable benefit to the Sudan and to Africa. The area of the Sudan comprises a population of upwards of three million persons, of whom it may be said that they are wholly uneducated. The dangers arising from that fact are too obvious and have been too painfully felt during many years past for me to dwell upon them. In the course of time, no doubt, an education of some sort, and administered by some hands, will be set on foot. But if Khartoum could be made forthwith the centre of an education supported by British funds and organised from Britain, there would be secured to this country indisputably the first place in Africa as a civilising power, and an effect would be created which would be felt for good throughout the central regions of that continent. I accordingly propose that at Khartoum there should be founded and maintained with British money a college bearing the name of the Gordon Memorial College, to be a pledge that the memory of Gordon is still alive among us, and that his aspirations are at length to be realised.

Certain questions will naturally arise as to whom exactly we should educate, and as to the nature of the education to be given. Our system would need to be gradually built up. We should begin by teaching the sons of the leading men, the heads of villages, and the heads of districts. They belong to a race very capable of learning and ready to learn. The teaching, in its early stages, would be devoted to purely elementary subjects, such as reading, writing, geography, and the English language. Later, and after these preliminary stages had been passed, a more advanced course would be instituted, including a training in technical subjects specially adapted to the requirements of those who inhabit the Valley of the Upper Nile. The principal teachers in the college would be British and the supervision of the arrangements would be vested in the Governor-General of the Sudan. I need not add that there would be no interference with the religion of the people.

The fund required for the establishment of such a college is £100,000. Of this, £10,000 would be appropriated to the initial outlay, while the remaining £90,000 would be invested, and the revenue thence derived would go to the maintenance of the college and the support of the staff of teachers. It would be clearly impossible at first to require payment from the pupils, but as the college developed and the standard of its teaching rose, it would be fair to demand fees in respect of this higher education, which would thus support itself, and render the college independent of any further call upon the public. It is for the provision of this sum of £100,000 that I now desire to appeal, on behalf of a race dependent upon our mercy, in the name of Gordon, and in the cause of that civilisation which is the life of the Empire of Britain.

I am authorised to state that Her Majesty the Queen has been graciously pleased to become the patron of the movement. His Royal Highness the Prince of Wales has graciously consented to become vice-patron.

I may state that a general council of the leading men of the country is in course of formation. Lord Hillingdon has kindly consented to accept the post of hon. treasurer. The Hon. George Peel has accepted to act as hon. secretary, and all communications should be addressed to him at 67, Lombard Street, London, E.C. Subscriptions should be paid to the Sirdar's Fund for the 'Gordon Memorial

College' at Khartoum, Messrs Glyn, Mills, Currie, & Co., 67, Lombard Street, London, E.C.

Enclosed herewith is a letter from the Marquis of Salisbury, in which he states that this scheme represents the only policy by which the civilising mission of this country can effectively be accomplished. His lordship adds that it is only to the rich men of this country that it is possible for me to look, yet I should be glad for this appeal to find its way to all classes of our people.

I further enclose a letter from the Baroness Burdett-Coutts, whose devotion to the cause of Africa has been not the least of her magnificent services. I forward, besides, an important telegram from the Lord Mayor of Liverpool, and letters of great weight from the Lord Provost of Edinburgh, and the Lord Provost of Glasgow. I would venture to address myself to the other great municipalities of the Kingdom.

Above all, it is in the hands of the Press of this country that I place this cause. I look with confidence to your support in the discharge of this high obligation.—I have the honour to remain, yours faithfully,

(Signed) *Kitchener of Khartoum*

Lords Salisbury and Rosebery, and many more distinguished personages, followed the example of the Sovereign and the Prince of Wales and became supporters of the proposed institution. In the Metropolis as well as in all the chief towns of the Kingdom the matter was taken up enthusiastically. An influential committee was formed. The subscriptions were showered in from home and abroad, wherever the English tongue was spoken and Gordon had been known. In less than a month the £100,000, and considerably more, were subscribed, and the establishment of the Memorial College assured.

Lieut.-Colonel C. S. B. Parsons, R.A., Governor of Kassala and the Red Sea littoral, to whom I have previously referred when we were advancing against Omdurman, was menacing the Dervish outpost of Gedarif. Later on, when Ahmed Fadl was marching to reinforce his master the Khalifa, Colonel Parsons was leading his Egyptians, Abyssinian irregulars, and friendlies from Kassala up the head waters or *khor* of the Atbara, far to the southward, and thence to a tributary of the Blue Nile where the enemy had long had a garrison. The fifteen years' campaign against Mahdism was nigh over, but not quite concluded, with the victory of Omdurman. On receiving the check from the gunboats, Fadl and his Dervishes retreated up the Blue Nile to where they had come from, their own country upon the borders of Abyssinia. News seems to have reached them of Colonel Parsons' advance, and it became a race for Gedarif. The Egyptians had a good start, and managed to reach and capture the place and occupy the two forts, one on either side of the river, or, what it is more frequently, the *khor*, before the Dervishes got back. Fadl was a man of mettle and resolutely assaulted the town and forts of which he had so long been governor. A desperate action ensued, but Fadl was beaten off with a loss of 700, it is said, in killed and wounded. The casualties in Colonel Parsons' force were about 100. But the Dervishes, though severely beaten, soon returned to attack the forts. With increased numbers they sat down before the place and began to harass sorely the Egyptian troops, cutting their communications with Kassala, whence by wire to Massowah over the Italian lines and up the Red Sea to Egypt the Sirdar was able to keep in touch with Colonel Parsons. They endeavoured again, on several occasions, to storm one or other of the forts, which were about half a mile apart, but happily they were invariably repulsed. Still they persisted in their tactics of worrying, evidently determined to recapture the place. At last matters grew so serious that Major-General Rundle was sent with a brigade of infantry and several batteries to deal with Ahmed Fadl's Dervishes. Advancing up the Blue Nile in gunboats, the Egyptian force cleared the banks of all the many wandering armed bands of the enemy. Through the aid of the wily Abyssinian scouts, information was sent to and received from Colonel Parsons and a plan arranged for catching Fadl and his men between two attacking columns. Seventeen hundred men of the Omdurman force attacked the Dervishes on one side, whilst Colonel Parsons' garrison assailed them from the other. The enemy were completely routed and scattered in all directions. Hundreds of Dervishes were slain, and ultimately many who escaped were so closely pressed by friendlies and Abyssinians that they surrendered. A thousand fugitive Baggara or so vainly tried to make their way up the Blue Nile, in order to retire to their former country in Kordofan. They were caught crossing far up stream, near Rosaires, by Colonel Lewis, vigorously attacked, defeated, and finally scattered. Thus the last Dervish army in the field was destroyed, and the country reclaimed to the side of peace, order, and civilised government.

The following are the official despatches of Lieutenant-General Sir Francis Grenfell, who commanded the British troops in Egypt, and of the Sirdar, relating to the battle of Omdurman:

The Official Despatches

Headquarters
Cairo
September 16, 1898

Sir,—1. I have the honour to forward a despatch from Major-General Sir H. Kitchener, K.C.B., Sirdar, describing the later phases of the Sudan Campaign, and the final action on 2nd September.

2. The Sirdar, in this despatch, recounts in brief, simple terms the events of the closing phase of one of the most successful campaigns ever conducted by a British General against a savage foe, resulting in the capture of Omdurman, the destruction of the Dervish power in the Sudan, and the reopening of the waterway to the Equatorial Provinces.

3. The concentration of the army on the Atbara was carried out to the hour, and the arrangements for the transport of the force to the vicinity of the battle-field were made by the Sirdar and his staff with consummate ability.

All difficulties were foreseen and provided for, and, from the start of the campaign to its close at Omdurman, operations have been conducted with a precision and completeness which have been beyond all praise; while the skill shown in the advance was equalled by the ability with which the army was commanded in the field.

The Sirdar's admirable disposition of the force, the accurate fire of the artillery and Maxims, and the steady fire discipline of the infantry, assisted by the gunboats, enabled him to destroy his enemy at long range before the bulk of the British and Egyptian force came under any severe rifle fire, and to this cause may be attributed the comparatively small list of casualties. Never were greater results achieved at such a trifling cost.

4. The heavy loss in killed and wounded in the 21st Lancers is to be deeply regretted. But the charge itself, against an overwhelming force of sword and spear men over difficult ground, and under unfavourable conditions, was worthy of the best traditions of British cavalry.

5. As regards the force employed, I can say with truth that never, in the course of my service, have I seen a finer body of troops than the British contingent of cavalry, artillery, engineers, and infantry placed at the disposal of the Sirdar, as regards physique, smartness, and soldierlike bearing. The appearance of the men speaks well for the present recruiting department, and was a source of pride to every Englishman who saw them.

6. While thoroughly endorsing the Sirdar's recommendations, I desire to call attention to the good work done by Major-General Henderson, C.B., and staff at Alexandria, who conducted the disembarkation of the force, and by my own staff at Cairo.

On Colonel H. Cooper, Assistant Adjutant-General, and Lieut.-Colonel L. A. Hope, Deputy-Assistant Adjutant-General, fell the brunt of the work in the despatch of the British Division to the front.

I also desire to acknowledge the services of Brevet-Colonel A. O. Green, Commanding Royal Engineer; Surgeon-General H. S. Muir, M.D., Principal Medical Officer; Lieut.-Colonel F. O. Leggett, Army Ordnance Department; Colonel F. Treffry, Army Pay Department; Veterinary-Captain Blenkinsop, and the junior officers of the various departments.

Major Williams, my C.R.A., was indefatigable in organising the mule transport for the 32nd and 37th Field Batteries.

7. I have received the greatest assistance from the Egyptian Railway Administration in the movements of the troops both going south and returning.

Thanks to the admirable system organised by Iskander Bey Fahmy, the traffic manager, all the services were rapidly and punctually carried out.

8. I am sending this despatch home by my *Aide-de-camp*, Lieutenant H. Grenfell, 1st Life Guards, who acted as Orderly Officer to Brigadier-General Honourable N. G. Lyttelton, C.B., commanding Second British Brigade in the Sudan.—I have, &c.,

Francis Grenfell
Lieutenant-General
Commanding in Egypt

The despatch from Major-General Sir Herbert Kitchener, Sirdar, to Lieutenant-General Sir Francis Grenfell, commanding in Egypt, was as follows:—

Omdurman
September 5, 1898

Sir,—It having been decided that an expeditionary force of British and Egyptian troops should be sent against the Khalifa's army in Omdurman, I have the honour to inform you that the following troops were concentrated at the North End of the Sixth Cataract, in close proximity to which an advanced supply depot had been previously formed at Nasri Island.

British Troops.—21st Lancers; 32nd Field Battery, Royal Artillery; 37th Howitzer Battery, Royal Artillery; 2 40-prs., Royal Artillery. Infantry Division:—1st Brigade: 1st Battalion Warwickshire Regiment, 1st Battalion Lincolnshire Regiment, 1st Battalion Seaforth Highlanders, 1st Battalion Cameron Highlanders, 6 Maxims, Detachment Royal Engineers. 2nd Brigade: 1st Battalion Grenadier Guards, 1st Battalion Northumberland Fusiliers, 2nd Battalion Lancashire Fusiliers, 2nd Battalion Rifle Brigade, 4 Maxims, Detachment Royal Engineers.

Egyptian Troops.—9 Squadrons, Cavalry; 1 Battery, Horse Artillery; 4 Field Batteries; 10 Maxims; 8 Companies, Camel Corps. 1st Brigade: 2nd Egyptian Battalion; 9th, 10th, and 11th Sudanese Battalions. 2nd Brigade: 8th Egyptian Battalion; 12th, 13th, and 14th Sudanese Battalions. 3rd Brigade: 3rd, 4th, 7th, and 15th Egyptian Battalions. 4th Brigade: 1st, 5th, 17th, and 18th Egyptian Battalions. Camel Transport.

On 24th August the troops began moving by successive divisions to Jebel Royan, where a depot of supplies and a British communication hospital of two hundred beds were established.

On 28th August, the army marched to Wadi el Abid, and on the following day proceeded to Sayal, from whence I despatched a letter to the Khalifa, warning him to remove his women and children, as I intended to bombard Omdurman unless he surrendered.

Next day the army marched to Sururab, and on September 1 reached the village of Egeiga, two miles south of the Kerreri hills, and within six miles of Omdurman. Patrols of the enemy's horsemen were frequently seen during the march falling back before our cavalry, and their outposts being driven in beyond Egeiga, our advanced scouts came in full view of Omdurman, from which large bodies of the enemy were seen streaming out and marching north. At noon, from the slopes of Jebel Surgham, I saw the entire Dervish army some three miles off advancing towards us, the Khalifa's black flag surrounded by his Mulazimin (body-guard) being plainly discernible. I estimated their numbers at 35,000 men, though, from subsequent investigation, this figure was probably under-estimated, their actual strength being between forty and fifty thousand. From information received, I gather that it was the Khalifa's intention to have met us with this force at Kerreri, but our rapid advance surprised him.

The troops were at once disposed around the village of Egeiga, which formed an excellent position with a clear field of fire in every direction, and shelter-trenches and *zerebas* were prepared.

At 2 p.m. our vedettes reported that the enemy had halted, and later on it was observed that they were preparing bivouacs and lighting fires. Information was received that the Khalifa contemplated a night attack on our position, and preparations to repel this were made, at the same time the Egeiga villagers were sent out to obtain information in the direction of the enemy's camp with the idea that we intended a night attack, and, this coming to the Khalifa's knowledge, he decided to remain in his position; consequently, we passed an undisturbed night in the *zereba*.

Meanwhile the gunboats, under Commander Keppel, which had shelled the Dervish advanced camp near Kerreri on 31st August, proceeded at daylight on 1st September, towing the Howitzer Battery to the right bank, whence, in conjunction with the Irregulars under Major Stuart Wortley, their advance south was continued. After two forts had been destroyed and the villages gallantly cleared by the Irregulars, the Howitzers were landed in a good position on the right bank, from whence an effective fire was opened on Omdurman, and, after a few rounds, the conspicuous dome over the Mahdi's tomb was partially demolished, whilst the gunboats, steaming past the town, also effectually bombarded the forts, which replied with a heavy, but ill-directed fire.

At dawn on the following morning (2nd September), our mounted patrols reported the enemy advancing to attack, and by 6.30 a.m. the Egyptian Cavalry, which had been driven in, took up a position with the Horse Artillery, Camel Corps, and four Maxims on the Kerreri ridge on our right flank.

At 6.40 a.m. the shouts of the advancing Dervish army became audible, and a few minutes later their flags appeared over the rising ground, forming a semi-circle round our left and front faces. The guns of the 32nd Field Battery opened fire at 6.45 a.m. at a range of two thousand eight hundred yards, and the Dervishes, continuing to advance rapidly, delivered their attack with all their accustomed dash and intrepidity. In a short time the troops and Maxims on the left and front were hotly engaged, whilst the enemy's riflemen, taking up positions on the slopes of Jebel Surgham, brought a long-range fire to bear on the *zereba*, causing some casualties, and their spearmen, continually reinforced from the rear, made attempt after attempt to reach our lines.

Shortly after 8.0 a.m. the enemy's main attack was repulsed. At this period a large and compact body of Dervishes was observed attempting to march round our right, and advancing with great rapidity they soon became engaged with our mounted troops on the Kerreri ridge. One of the gunboats which had been disposed to protect the river flanks at once proceeded downstream to afford assistance to the somewhat hardly-pressed mounted troops, and coming within close range of the Dervishes inflicted heavy loss on them, upwards of 450 men being killed in a comparatively circumscribed area. The Artillery and Maxims on the left face of the *zereba* also co-operated, and the enemy was forced to retire again under cover of the hills. All attacks on our position having failed, and the enemy having retired out of range, I sent out the 21st Lancers to clear the ground on our left front and head off any retreating Dervishes from the direction of Omdurman. After crossing the slopes of Jebel Surgham they came upon a body of Dervishes concealed in a depression of the ground; these they gallantly charged, but finding, too late to withdraw, that a much larger body of the enemy lay hidden, the charge was pressed home through them, and, after rallying on the other side, they rode back, driving off the Dervishes, and remaining in possession of the ground. Considerable loss was inflicted on the enemy; but I regret to say that here fell Lieutenant R. Grenfell (12th Lancers) and twenty men.

Meanwhile I had ordered the army to follow in echelon of brigades from the left. At 9.30 a.m. the front brigades having reached the sand ridge running from the west end of Jebel Surgham towards the river, a halt was ordered to enable the rear brigades to get into position, and I then received information that the Khalifa was still present in force on the left slopes of Surgham; a change of front half-right of the three leading brigades was, therefore, ordered, and it was during this movement that Macdonald's brigade became hotly engaged, whilst taking up position on the right of the echelon.

Learning from General Hunter, who was with Macdonald's brigade, that he might require support, I despatched Wauchope's brigade to reinforce him, and ordered the remaining brigades to make a further change half-right.

No sooner had Macdonald repelled the Dervish onslaught than the force, which had retired behind the Kerreri hills, emerged again into the plain and rapidly advanced to attack him, necessitating a further complete change of front of his brigade to the right. This movement was admirably executed, and now, supported by a portion of Wauchope's brigade on the right and by Lewis's brigade enfilading the attack on the left, he completely crushed this second most determined Dervish charge.

Meantime Maxwell's and Lyttelton's brigades had been

pushed on over the slopes of Jebel Surgham, and driving before them the Dervish forces under the Khalifa's son, Osman Sheikh ed Din, they established themselves in a position which cut off the retreat on Omdurman of the bulk of the Dervish army, who were soon seen streaming in a disorganised mass towards the high hills many miles to the west, closely pursued by the mounted troops, who cleared the right front and flanks of all hesitating and detached parties of the enemy.

The battle was now practically over, and Lyttelton's and Maxwell's brigades marched down to Khor Shambat, in the direction of Omdurman, which was reached at 12.30 p.m., and here the troops rested and watered. The remainder of Hunter's division and Wauchope's brigade reached the same place at 3 p.m.

At 2 p.m. I advanced with Maxwell's brigade and the 32nd Field Battery through the suburbs of Omdurman to the great wall of the Khalifa's enclosure, and, leaving two guns and three battalions to guard the approaches, the 13th Sudanese Battalion and four guns (32nd Field Battery) were pushed down by the north side of the wall to the river, and, accompanied by three gunboats which had been previously ordered to be ready for this movement, these troops penetrated the breaches in the wall made by the howitzers, marched south along the line of forts, and turning in at the main gateway found a straight road leading to the Khalifa's house and Mahdi's tomb; these were speedily occupied, the Khalifa having quitted the town only a short time before our entry, after a vain effort to collect his men for further resistance.

The gunboats continued up the river clearing the streets of Dervishes, and, having returned to the remainder of the brigade left at the corner of the wall, these were pushed forward, and occupied all the main portions of the town. Guards were at once mounted over the principal buildings and Khalifa's stores, and after visiting the prison and releasing the European prisoners, the troops bivouacked at 7 p.m. around the town, after a long and trying day, throughout which all ranks displayed qualities of high courage, discipline, and endurance.

The gunboats and Egyptian Cavalry and Camel Corps at once started in pursuit south; but owing to the exhausted condition of the animals and the flooded state of the country, which prevented them from communicating with the gunboat carrying their forage and rations, they were reluctantly obliged to abandon the pursuit after following up the flying Khalifa for 30 miles through marshy ground. The gunboats continued south for 90 miles, but were unable to come in touch with the Khalifa, who left the river and fled westward towards Kordofan, followed by the armed friendly tribes who took up the pursuit on the return of the mounted troops.

Large stores of ammunition, powder, some sixty guns of various sorts, besides vast quantities of rifles, swords, spears, banners, drums, and other war materials, were captured on the battle-field and in Omdurman.

The result of this battle is the practical annihilation of the Khalifa's army, the consequent extinction of Mahdism in the Sudan, and the submission of the whole country formerly ruled under Egyptian authority. This has re-opened vast territories to the benefits of peace, civilisation, and good government.

On 4th September the British and Egyptian flags were hoisted with due ceremony on the walls of the ruined Palace of Khartoum, close to the spot where General Gordon fell, and this event is looked upon by the rejoicing populations as marking the commencement of a new era of peace and prosperity for their unfortunate country.

It would be impossible for any Commander to have been more ably seconded than I was by the General Officers serving under me. Major-Generals Hunter, Rundle, and Gatacre have displayed the highest qualities as daring and skilful leaders, as well as being endowed with administrative capabilities of a high order. It is in the hands of such officers that the Service may rest assured their best interests will, under all circumstances, be honourably upheld, and while expressing to them my sincere thanks for their cordial co-operation with me, I have every confidence in most highly recommending the names of these General Officers for the favourable consideration of Her Majesty's Government.

The manner in which the Brigadiers handled their respective brigades, their thorough knowledge of their profession, and their proved skill in the field, mark them out, one and all, as fitted for higher rank, and I have great pleasure in submitting their names for favourable consideration:—Brigadier-Generals N. G. Lyttelton and A. G. Wauchope; Lieutenant-Colonels J. G. Maxwell, H. A. Macdonald, D. F. Lewis and J. Collinson.

Macdonald's brigade was highly tested, bearing the brunt of two severe attacks delivered at very short intervals from different directions, and I am sure it must be a source of the greatest satisfaction to Colonel Macdonald, as it is to myself and the whole army, that the very great care he has for long devoted to the training of his brigade has proved so effectual, enabling his men to behave with the greatest steadiness under most trying circumstances, and repelling most successfully two determined Dervish onslaughts.

I should also mention under this category the excellent services performed by Colonel R. H. Martin, commanding 21st Lancers; by Lieut.-Colonel Long, commanding the combined British and Egyptian Artillery; and by Lieut.-Colonel R. G. Broadwood, commanding the Egyptian Cavalry; as well as by Major R. J. Tudway, commanding the Camel Corps. I consider that these various arms could not have been more efficiently commanded than they were throughout the recent operations. The best result was, I believe, attained, and it is due to the skilful handling of their respective commands that the Dervish defeat was so complete.

The Medical Department was administered with ability and skill by Surgeon-General Taylor, Principal Medical Officer, who was well assisted by Colonel M'Namara, whilst the medical organisation of the Egyptian Army fully maintained its previous excellent reputation under the direction of Lieut.-Colonel Gallwey and his staff. The general medical arrangements were all that could have been desired, and I believe the minimum of pain and maximum of comfort procurable on active service in this country was attained by the unremitting energy, untiring zeal, and devotion to their duty of the entire medical staff.

Owing to the long line of communications by rail, river, and desert, the work of maintaining a thoroughly efficient supply and transport system, both by land and water, was arduous in the extreme, and that a large British and Egyptian force was brought up to within striking distance of Khartoum, amply supplied with all its requirements, reflects the greatest credit on the supply and transport system. I wish to cordially thank the officers of the Supply, Transport and Railway Departments for the satisfactory results which have attended their labours.

I consider that the excellent ration which was always provided kept the men strong and healthy and fit to endure all the hardships of an arduous campaign, enabling them, at a critical moment, to support the exceptional fatigue of continuous marching and fighting for some fourteen hours during the height of a Sudan summer.

The Intelligence Department were, as usual, thoroughly efficient, and their forecasts of the intentions and actions of the enemy were accurate. Colonel Wingate and Slatin Pacha worked indefatigably, and, with their staff, deserve a prominent place amongst those to whom the success of the operations is due.

The excellent service performed by the gunboats under Commander Keppel and his subordinate officers of the Royal Navy is deserving of special mention. These gunboats have been for a long time past almost constantly under fire; they have made bold reconnaissances past the enemy's forts and rifle pits, and on the 1st and 2nd September, in conjunction with the Irregular levies under Major Stuart Wortley, and the Howitzer Battery, they materially aided in the capture of all the forts on both banks of the Nile, and in making the fortifications of Omdurman untenable. In bringing to notice the readiness of resource, daring, and ability of Commander Keppel and his officers, I wish also to add my appreciation of the services rendered by Engineer E. Bond, Royal Navy, and the engineering staff, as well as of the detachments of the Royal Marine Artillery and the gun crews, who have gained the hearty praise of their commanders.

The Rev. R. Brindle, the Rev. J. M. Simms, the Rev. A. W. B. Watson, and the Rev. O. S. Watkins won the esteem of all by their untiring devotion to their sacred duties and by their unfailing and cheerful kindness to the sick and wounded at all times.

To all my personal staff my thanks are specially due for the great assistance they at all times rendered me.

In conclusion, I have great pleasure in expressing my appreciation of the services rendered by the detachments of the Royal Engineers, Army Ordnance Corps, and Telegraph and Postal Departments.

The names of a large number of officers, non-commissioned officers, and men who had been brought to the Sirdar's notice for good service were appended to the despatch.

Two other documents call for notice, the Queen's message and the Sirdar's general order to his army after the victory.

From the Queen to the Sirdar, Khartoum: I congratulate you and all your brave troops under fire on the brilliant success which you have achieved. I am grieved for the losses which have been sustained, but trust the wounded are doing well. *Victoria*

The Sirdar congratulates all the troops upon their excellent behaviour during the general action to-day, resulting in the total defeat of the Khalifa's forces and worthily avenging Gordon. The Sirdar regrets the loss that has occurred, and, while warmly thanking the troops, wishes to place on record his admiration for their courage, discipline, and endurance.
(Signed) *H. M. L. Rundle*

Long lists of honours and promotions were subsequently published in the *Gazette*. Of these, the more prominent officers who received such recognition of their distinguished services were as follows: The Sirdar was raised to the peerage as Lord Kitchener of Khartoum. In addition thereto the dignity G.C.B. was conferred upon the Sirdar, and Sir Francis Grenfell. Major-Generals W. F. Gatacre, A. Hunter, and H. M. L. Rundle were created K.C.B.'s, and the dignity of Companion of the Bath was granted to Surgeon-General William Taylor, Colonel V. Hatton, Colonel L. C. Money, Colonel T. E. Verner, Colonel W. H. M'Namara, R.A.M.C., Lieut.-Col. R. A. Hope, Lieut.-Col. Collingwood, Lieut.-Col. D. F. Lewis, Lieut.-Col. J. Collinson, Lieut.-Col. W. E. G. Forbes, Lieut.-Col. M. Q. Jones, Lieut.-Col. F. R. South, Lieut.-Col. R. H. Martin, Lieut.-Col. W. G. C. Wyndham, and Commander C. R. Keppel, R. N. Colonel F. R. Wingate was made a Knight Commander of the Order of St Michael and St George, and a like dignity was conferred upon Colonel R. Slatin Pasha. Distinguished Service Orders were granted to the Rev. R. Brindle, Lieut.-Col. C.V. F. Townshend, Lieut.-Col. G. A. Hughes, Lieut.-Col. C. J. Blomfield, Lieut.-Col. F. Lloyd, Major E. J. M. Stuart Wortley, Major E. M. Wilson, R.A.M.C., Major G. Cockburn, Major Hon. C. Lambton, Major N. E. Young, Major C. E. Laurie, and Major F. J. Maxse, Captain C. C. Fleming, R.A.M.C., Lieutenant G. C. M. Hall, Lieutenant F. Hubbard. The Khedive conferred the Medjidieh and Osmanlieh orders on a large number of officers. Others, whose names did not appear in the order list, figured in that of army promotions. Victoria Crosses were given to Captain P. A. Kenna, 21st Lancers, Lieutenant R. H. L. J. de Montmorency, 21st Lancers, Private Thomas Byrne, 21st Lancers (for turning back in the charge and rescuing Lieutenant Molyneux), Captain N. M. Smyth, 2nd Dragoon Guards.

Lieut.-Col. H. A. Macdonald, C.B., D.S.O., was made an extra A.D.C. to the Queen.

The Sirdar on his return to Lower Egypt met with an enthusiastic reception. Lord Cromer, Sir Francis Grenfell and all the notables in Cairo met him and the troops turned out to escort him to his residence. He was entertained in Cairo at a grand banquet. When he visited England even a heartier and grander welcome was extended to the victor of Omdurman and the destroyer of Mahdism. The public acclaimed him, and honours and dignities were showered upon him ere he returned to resume his self-imposed task of reconstructing the Sudan.

Colonel Hector A. Macdonald alone seems as yet to have had extended to him scant military recognition of his invaluable services. The post of A.D.C. to Her Majesty is a coveted dignity, but a mere honorary office, carrying neither pay nor emolument. Indeed it is the other way, for the accessories required to bedeck the person will cost at least £25. But the fact cannot be forgotten, or cried down, that Colonel Macdonald saved the situation. He fought a single-handed battle against tremendous odds and won. First he faced the Khalifa and fought him to a finish, and then faced about and served Sheikh Ed Din's unbeaten Dervishes in much the same fashion. For reasons that could be given, and which reflect no discredit upon the other brigadier, Colonel Lewis' force was not moved promptly up to Macdonald's support. Honour lists and promotion lists still keep cropping up, and possibly the military authorities are yet deliberating what is the right thing to do in Macdonald's case. In the Scotch press, and particularly in that of the Far North, there has been much adverse comment on the ungenerous treatment accorded their countryman. The Highlanders, as is their nature, write and speak passionately of the matter, and pertinently ask if the authorities wish no more Highland recruits. From the paper of his own district, the Dingwall *North Star*, I quote the following lines:

> *In glen and clachan, England's tardy debt*
> *The clansmen's pride will adequately pay:*
> *Round Nor'land hearths when lamplit nights are long,*
> *Thy fame shall ever live in many a tale and song.*

The battle of Omdurman was not the only occasion in which Colonel Macdonald has exhibited magnificent tactical skill combined with soldierly dash and undaunted courage. It is not so long since the Atbara was fought, and in half a score of engagements before that he quitted himself equally well. He was deservedly promoted from the ranks, and to Field-Marshal Lord Roberts is due the credit of having discovered and properly appreciated the gallant Highlandman. His record is one for any man to be proud of, for to his own hand he owes his present distinguished position. I again quote from the *North Star*:

> Colonel Macdonald was born at Rootfield, in the parish of Urquhart, in the county of Ross and Cromarty, and on the property of Mr Mackenzie of Allangrange. He began life as a stable-boy with Bailie Robertson, of the National Hotel, Dingwall, when tenant of the farm of Kinkell, Conon Bridge. At the age of seventeen he went to Inverness and became an apprentice draper with Mr William Mackay, late of the Clan Tartan Warehouse. In this capacity he served two years, but finding mercantile life distasteful to him, he enlisted in the 92nd Regiment. Here his qualities procured for him rapid promotion. He successively and successfully discharged the duties of drill-instructor, pay-sergeant, and other non-commissioned offices, and held the rank of colour-sergeant at the commencement of the Afghan campaign, wherein he repeatedly so greatly distinguished himself.
>
> Macdonald's first engagement with an enemy was at Jagi Thanni. On that occasion General Roberts, escorted by

the 9th Lancers and 5th Punjab Cavalry, advanced from Ali Kheyl to Kushi, and, while passing by Jagi Thanni, he was attacked by about 2000 Mangals and Machalgah Ghilzais, who there lay in ambush. Fortunately, early intimation of the Mangals' hostile intentions reached Fort Karatiga, a mile or two off, and a party of 45 men of the

Col. H. Macdonald at Omdurman, with officer and non-commissioned officer of 1st Brigade

3rd Sikhs, under Jemander Shere Mahomed Khan, was at once sent out to reconnoitre, and, as firing was soon afterwards heard in the direction the party had gone, Colour-Sergeant Macdonald promptly turned out with 18 men of his own regiment, and overtaking the Sikhs, he took over command of the whole, and, gallantly leading his little force across a difficult river and up a steep hill, he boldly attacked and dislodged the enemy from a strong position on the crest, but not before four of the Sikhs were killed, and Deputy-Surgeon-General Townsend, who rode near General Roberts, severely wounded. The enemy's loss here was about 30 killed. Macdonald's brilliant services on this occasion averted something like a disaster. In a Divisional Order, Roberts wrote:

> The above non-commissioned officer and a native officer, with a handful of soldiers, drove before them a large body of Mangals, who had assembled to stop the road, ... the great coolness, judgment, and gallantry with which they behaved.

In his despatch, dated Kabul, 15th October, and published in the *Gazette*, General Roberts further said:

> Meanwhile, a warm engagement had for some time been carried on in the direction of Karatiga, and presently large numbers of the enemy were seen retreating before a small detachment of the 92nd Highlanders and 3rd Sikhs, which had been sent out from Karatiga, and which was, with excellent judgment and boldness, led up a steep spur commanding the defile. The energy and skill with which this party was handled reflected the highest credit on Colour-Sergeant Hector Macdonald, 92nd Highlanders, and Jemander Shere Mahomed, 3rd Sikhs. But for their excellent services on this occasion, it might probably have been impossible to carry out the programme of our march.

In the same *Gazette* was published another despatch from Sir F. Roberts, dated Kabul, 20th October, in which he says:

> Colour-Sergeant H. Macdonald, a non-commissioned officer, whose excellent and skilful management of a small detachment when opposed to immensely superior numbers in the Hazardarakht defile was mentioned in my despatch of the 16th instant, here again distinguished himself.

This refers to his conduct at Charasiab, at the close of which action our brave countryman was sent for by Roberts, who publicly complimented and thanked him personally for 'the ability and intelligence with which he handled the party under his command' at the battle. Macdonald's commission was conferred on the recommendation of General Roberts, that distinguished officer having witnessed repeated proofs of his valour and capacity.

In 1885 Colonel Macdonald joined the then reorganised Egyptian Constabulary and received rapid promotion. From these, on other changes being made, he passed into the Khedivial army, drilling and training new Sudanese levies. So thorough a soldier is too valuable to be longer left in the Sudan now that peace is assured.

CHAPTER 15

The Fashoda Affair

France is following in the footsteps of Spain. A fatality dogs her schemes of empire and colonisation. In truth she has no colonies—they are but military possessions. She has set her face, alone and in conjunction with others, in America, Asia, and Africa to hoop our enterprises in with bands of iron. Failure attended her policy across the Atlantic, in India, in Burma, and but the other day at Fashoda. Her object in that last instance was to connect her possessions in West and East Africa, so that the red British lines which are steadily extending from North and South Africa should never be joined. France is the largest holder of territory upon the Dark Continent, and she probably regarded that fact as the best justification for her subtle move, through the Marchand and Abyssinian Missions, to add still more to her dominions. She had been permitted to hoop us about at Bathurst and Sierra Leone upon the West Coast and has all but completed the same process round Ashanti and the Niger countries, not to speak of elsewhere. Madagascar she had grabbed without a shadow of excuse, but time and South African civilisation will make it a bigger Cuba. Already her failures at government in that vast African island are grievous. Less than five years ago, to use a phrase I have employed elsewhere, property and life were ridiculously safe in that country. But then the Hovas and Prime Minister Rainilaiarivony ruled the land. Other changes predicted have come about there. The one native who showed honesty and courage in successfully opposing them at Tamatave the French subsequently executed. The Queen and Prime Minister were banished. Speaking English, the chief foreign language spoken, has been tabooed. Natives who are heard using it, or suspected of employing our mother tongue, are thrust into prison and kept there, *pour encourager les autres*, until they promise to discontinue speaking it. Association of natives with English or Americans renders them marked persons. The Protestant missions are regarded as centres of treason and enmity to French authority. Quickly, as foretold, has come about their reward(?) for non-interference politically in the early days of French intrigue. Had they insisted, with the British Government of a bygone day, in saving the island for the Malagasy, they would have succeeded. Our commerce has also had to suffer, for the French *instruct* the natives that they must only buy articles of French manufacture. The native who purchases British or American goods soon discovers, from the severe handling he receives through the local officials, that he has made a serious mistake. Robbery and lawlessness are rife, and in many places neither life nor property is safe beyond rifle-shot of the French garrisons. The facts are notorious and are in possession of the Foreign Office in Downing Street.

It had leaked out a day or two after the battle that the Sirdar intended accompanying the expedition to Fashoda. The troops ordered to proceed up the Nile with him were paraded outside Omdurman on the morning of the 8th of September. These were 600 men of the 11th Sudanese under Major Jackson, 600 men of the 13th Sudanese under Major Smith Dorrian, 100 men of the Cameron Highlanders under Captain the Hon. A. D. Murray, and Captain Peake's battery of 12½-pounder Maxim-Nordenfeldt guns. At the same time the force that was to be sent across to reoccupy and assist in rebuilding the ruined Government buildings in Khartoum also turned out for inspection. Nothing was left to chance. Care was taken that only those fit and well should proceed on the gunboats and barges to Fashoda. Provision was made that the work of reconstruction should go on in his absence, and that Khartoum and Omdurman should be left in a proper state of defence. A great air of official mystification and secrecy prevailed respecting everything that happened at that time. Particulars were difficult to glean of the actual condition of affairs up the Blue and White Niles. Even the plans for the removal of the military headquarters and the re-establishment of the central authority in Khartoum were sealed against us. As the telegraph service was in the Sirdar's hands, much of the pains bestowed to keep news from us was surely unnecessary. But the Sirdar has a way of bestowing confidences on no one—simply issuing orders when the occasion arrives.

Since my return to England a reference to the correspondence disclosed in the official despatches or Fashoda Blue-book proves the correctness of the information that reached me even at that early stage. From the summary of the documents which appeared in the *Daily Telegraph* of 10th October, we learn that "before the battle of Omdurman Lord Salisbury had given instructions to the Sirdar through Lord Cromer," as follows:

> It is desirable that you should be placed in possession of the views of Her Majesty's Government in respect to the line of action to be followed in the event of Khartoum being occupied at an early date by the forces now operating in the Sudan under the command of Sir Herbert Kitchener.
> Her Majesty's Government do not contemplate that after the occupation of Khartoum any further military operations on a large scale, or involving any considerable expense, will be undertaken for the occupation of the provinces to the south. But the Sirdar is authorised to send two flotillas, one up the White and the other up the Blue Nile. You are authorised to settle the composition of these two forces in consultation with the Sirdar.
> Sir Herbert Kitchener should in person command the White Nile flotilla as far as Fashoda, and may take with him a small body of British troops, should you concur with him in thinking such a course desirable.
> The officer in command of the Blue Nile flotilla is au-

thorised to go as far as the foot of the cataract, which is believed to commence about Rosaires. He is not to land troops with a view to marching beyond the point on the river navigable for steamers. Should he, before reaching Rosaires, encounter any Abyssinian outposts, he is to halt, report the circumstance, and wait for further instructions. In dealing with any French or Abyssinian authorities who may be encountered, nothing should be said or done which would in any way imply a recognition on behalf of Her Majesty's Government of a title to possession on behalf of France or Abyssinia to any portion of the Nile Valley.

Although everybody engaged in the Fashoda expedition was repeatedly warned not to disclose anything about it, and to forget all they had seen or heard, I was enabled very shortly after the event to wire, day by day, the whole story of the enterprise. It was General Grant, who, during the Civil War in the United States of America, terribly vexed at the newspaper correspondents, on one occasion vowed he would send them all away and not have a press-man in his army.

"Then, General," said the American journalist addressed, "may I ask what are you going to do without soldiers, every man of them can speak and write?"

General Grant saw the absurdity of the position and smiled, and there was an end of the matter. It was, perhaps, a choice of one of two evils, either accepting and making the best of the situation to allow the trained journalists to remain, or to prepare to meet a tremendous inundation of wild letter-writing from all ranks that would find its way into the public press and do incalculable harm. "Other times, other manners," and those modern generals discredit themselves who fail to recognise at the close of the nineteenth century that the schoolmaster and the press must be reckoned with.

The information given me by the *reis* of the *Tewfikieh* proved accurate in almost every detail. I confess that, at the time, knowing the Arab indifference to exactness in dates, I did not credit his assertion that Marchand had reached Fashoda six weeks before the Dervishes attacked him. Floating down stream in a small steam launch, aluminium row-boats, and other craft, the Frenchmen arrived off Fashoda on the 10th of July. In 1892-93 the French Government had begun sending military or quasi-scientific missions from the west and east African coasts to obtain treaties and pre-emption claims to territory in the interior. That the French flag should wave from sea to sea was their confessed desire. Their incentive was to forestall and annoy Great Britain and render worthless the blood and treasure our country might spend in smashing the Dervishes. Major Marchand set out from the west coast or French Congo in 1896, with a small body of Europeans and about 500 Senegalese troops. With indomitable zeal and courage he pushed east, reaching the vast basin lands of the Bahr el Ghazal after sore hardships and the loss of many of his men, chiefly from sickness. The spirit that animated the leader and his followers may be gathered from the following lines which were written some time ago by a non-commissioned officer of Senegalese Rifles to his relatives.

> We have no rest, not even for a single day, as a moment's delay might render all our exertions useless. All that we shall have done will be wasted if the English or others occupy our route when we want to pass. When you read this letter we shall either be on the Nile or our bones will be slowly whitening in the Egyptian brushwood under a torrid sun. I verily believe that if we are destroyed I shall retain regret for our failure in another world.

Fashoda is 444 miles by river south of Omdurman. It is situated upon the west bank, on a low headland which at high Nile becomes an island. Before the Mahdist rising, Fashoda was a fortified Egyptian station with a garrison of 1000 men, and a native population of nearly 4000. The place was enclosed within a ditch and a sun-dried brick wall. From its position it commanded the passage of the Nile, which was less than half a mile in width. The Dervishes allowed the place to fall into ruins, only maintaining a very small garrison—less than 100 men—to raid for grain to supply Omdurman with, and to collect revenue from the native boats. Like the rest of the Sudan, the Shilluk country, in which Fashoda is situated, had suffered terribly and been sadly depopulated. The country of the Shilluk negroes used to extend for several hundred miles northward down the left bank of the Nile from the Bahr el Ghazal. It was but a strip, ten miles or so in width, their nearest neighbours, with whom they were usually at war, being the Baggara Arabs. Like so many other *riverain* tracts susceptible of cultivation, it once teemed with people, the villages along the banks appearing to be one continuous row of dwellings. Helped by the Shilluks, Major Marchand had no difficulty in capturing Fashoda. The old fortification was built upon the only accessible strip of dry land, at high Nile, available for miles along the bank in that vicinity. Seen from the river, the works consisted of a rectangular mud-wall about 200 yards in length, protected by horse-shoe bastions at the corners. The Khalifa being as usual in need of supplies sent out a small foraging expedition many weeks before our arrival on the scene. Starting in the steamers *Safieh* and *Tewfikieh*, they collected grain and cattle, shipping them down to Omdurman. Learning that Europeans had been seen at Fashoda, part of the force proceeded there, and engaged the French, attacking them by land and water. The date was the 25th of August. Behaving with great steadiness, and helped by Shilluks, after a stiff fight the Dervishes were driven off, after losing a number of men, by Marchand's little garrison.

"If they had had cannon," said the Dervish skipper to me, "they fired so well that they would have sunk our steamers."

The Dervish captains then ran their boats downstream to collect their followers and return to assault the position. About 100 miles north the *Safieh* stopped to collect the raiders, who numbered about a thousand with four brass guns.

At six o'clock on the morning of the 10th September, the Sirdar set out from Omdurman with his expeditionary force. The troops were embarked upon the gunboats *Sultan*, *Sheik*,

Fatah, and barges towed by these vessels. Colonel Wingate, Major Lord Edward Cecil, Captain J. K. Watson, A.D.C., and other officers, accompanied the General on the stern-wheel steamer *Dal*, which had for armament several Maxims. A Union Jack, as well as an Egyptian flag, was hoisted on the boat. Abundance of ammunition and two months' provisions for the force were carried on the steamers and tows. The steamers went along very leisurely, going only by daylight. In the afternoon, or towards sunset, the flotilla made fast to some suitable bank. The troops then formed a sort of camp, and parties went out with saws and axes to cut timber for fuel for the boilers. The hard gummy mimosa and *sunt*, when there is not too much sap in it, burns fiercely with a glow almost equal to ordinary coal. South of Omdurman, the river still being in full flood, the Nile had overspread the low banks for miles. There were places where it resembled a lake, two to six miles wide, dotted with islands. Landing was not always easily effected, for the banks were frequently marshy. There was plenty of good sizable wood to be had all along the river, the only difficulty being to reach and cut it. More than once, in order to "fill up" the vessels for next day's steaming, the Camerons and Sudanese soldiers laboured far into the night, hewing and carrying timber for fuel by candle-light and the electric beam. Nearing Fashoda the Nile in places ran through channels but 400 yards in width. The water was deep and relatively clear, with a current of but two miles or less an hour. Unfortunately, it rained heavily nearly every night, and the troops quartered upon the barges got drenched to the skin, the water pouring, in so many shower-baths, through the cracked boarded coverings. It is a peculiarity of most tropical climates, that Jupiter Pluvius does most of his work between the hours of sunset and sunrise. The natives met with as a rule were disposed to be friendly. Those with whom the men talked would not quite credit the statement that the Khalifa had been defeated, his army destroyed, and that he had run away. On Saturday the 17th September, the gunboat *Abu Klea* caught up with and joined the flotilla.

During the same night, Dervish deserters, blacks, and Arabs came in. They stated that a short way further up there was a camp of the enemy. On Sunday morning, 18th September, when near Kaka, some 65 miles north of Fashoda, the Dervish steamer *Safieh* was sighted, lying at the east bank close by the enemy's camp. The *Sultan* forged ahead and began shelling the enemy with all her guns, using the Maxims as well. With great alacrity the Dervishes on shore replied, if indeed they did not fire first. A few shots also came from the *Safieh*. With their rifled guns from behind screens of bushes the enemy bravely stood up, making excellent practice at the gunboats. The *Sultan* had several very narrow escapes, shells passing close over her bows and stern. When the other gunboats got up, what with cannon, quick-firing guns, and Maxims brought to bear upon the Dervish camp, it was speedily wrecked and torn. The enemy bolted into the bush, leaving over 200 dead and wounded behind, including several Baggara and the chief Emir. A few shells from the *Sultan* had hulled and shattered the *Safieh*, so the victory was complete. Detachments were landed from the gunboats and the Dervishes driven still further afield. Their camp was looted and burned, and the *Safieh* and several *nuggars* temporarily repaired and sent down to Omdurman. It was found that the patch put upon the *Safieh*'s boiler by chief-engineer Benbow in 1885 was intact. That steamer went to rescue Sir Charles Wilson's party who were wrecked on their return from Khartoum. Near Shabluka she was attacked by a Dervish fort and hulled. Lord Charles Beresford, who was in command, stuck to the vessel after the boiler blew up, and during the night it was repaired. On Sunday, 18th September, the Sirdar despatched a Shilluk runner to go by land with a letter to Major Marchand telling him of the approach of the Egyptian flotilla. Next morning a reply was brought out to the *Dal* when it was within sight of Fashoda by an officer in a row-boat flying the French flag, that the garrison would receive him as a friendly visitor. Major Marchand furthermore declared that by treaty the territory belonged to France and he had communicated the fact to his Government, sending his despatches through Abyssinia. Precise details of what had been done were included.

It was 10 a.m. of the 19th September when the expedition reached Fashoda and saw the French flag flying over the fort. A Senegalese sentry was walking beneath the *tricolor*, and a row of these black riflemen's heads peeped from the walls and trenches. All of them had evidently been turned out under arms. Apparently there were about 300 people—not more—in the fortification. Steaming close in without being hailed, the vessels hove to opposite the works. A row-boat manned by Senegalese pushed from the shore and made for the *Dal*. From the stern staff drooped the French flag, and by the tiller sat Major Marchand and an officer, M. Germain. The Major was dressed in a suit of white ducks. Below the medium height, of spare habit, with something like Dundreary side whiskers, he looked elderly and worn, almost twice his years, for he is still a young man. As he stepped aboard the steamer, he was received at the side. He and his companion shook hands with the Sirdar and the other members of the headquarters staff. A relatively brief conference ensued, at which the Sirdar stated the object of his mission and his official instructions to recover the lost provinces for Egypt. He intended, he said, to occupy and hold them. Major Marchand intimated that he had established a prior claim for his Government, and had entered into treaties with the local rulers securing rights for France to the country along the Nile south and through the Bahr el Ghazal. He had established posts at Meshra er Rek and elsewhere in that region. Without express orders to the contrary from his Government, he would not abandon the old Egyptian fort, nor concede an inch of the territory he had acquired. The Sirdar said he meant to land, and although he would avoid a collision if possible with the Major and his party, yet he would not be dissuaded from carrying out his orders because it might be unpleasant. Would, he asked, the Major oppose him with force; his means were inadequate to do so with any hope of success. Major Marchand replied, "No," he was not in a position to justify any attempt to contend with arms against the strong flotilla and land army that could be brought against him by the Sirdar. Still, he would neither yield nor withdraw without the order of his Government. The Sirdar stated he was not adverse to letting the two Governments settle the matter, meantime they as soldiers could remain on amicable terms. In the course of an hour or so he would land his troops and occupy a position as near the fort as possible. Major Marchand protested, but said that he, under the circumstances, would have to accept the situation.

Refreshments are always in order on board a ship where the Royal Navy is in command. Over a friendly glass of champagne Marchand and the Sirdar chatted on topics of general interest. The Major intimated that he was rather short of ammunition and stores. He had sent his steam launch south to try and bring up supplies and reinforcements from his other stations. The doctor was anxious to obtain the assistance and advice of some of the British medical staff as to the best treatment of beri-beri or sleeplessness sickness, which had appeared among them. Several of the mission had succumbed to that weird disease. It is not unknown in the United Kingdom, a case having recently occurred at Richmond Asylum, Dublin. After spending about half an hour on board, Major Marchand and M. Germain, accompanied by Colonel Wingate and Commander Keppel, went ashore together in the row-boat. Landing at the fort, the party were received by the garrison with military honours. The two British officers were shown every courtesy, and escorted over the works, which had been considerably strengthened. A morass or small lagoon cut the fortification off in rear from the mainland. It was a position which could not easily have been carried by assault, but was indefensible against cannon. The Senegalese Tirailleurs forming the garrison were paraded for their inspection. There appeared to be about 120 of them, all stalwart, soldierly fellows, beside whom the Frenchmen looked shrunken and diminutive. In addition to the Senegalese, or rather natives of Timbuktu, for such they were, about 150 Shilluks and nondescript natives made up the remainder of the garrison. Including Major Marchand there were nine Europeans, or five commissioned and four non-commissioned officers. Of four others who had succumbed on the way, two died of beri-beri, one was killed by a fall from a tree, and a third by a crocodile. The Nile in that vicinity was found to be teeming with animal life. Not only crocodiles but hippopotami were seen by those on board the flotilla.

Eventually the five steamers crept as close inshore towards the north end of the fort as the shallow overflown land admitted. Colonel Wingate and Commander Keppel having returned on board, all the troops were ordered to disembark. The steamers were made fast to the banks, and planks were placed ashore. They were of little use, for officers and men had to flounder and wade through the shallows before they reached firm ground 300 yards from the bank. Four of the guns of Peake's battery were also landed. The force having been formed up was marched a short distance to the south. It was halted behind and exactly covering the French position from the land side, the flanks overlapping and enclosing the old line of Egyptian works. A tall flag-pole which was brought ashore was set up on a ruined bastion in line with the French *tricolor* and about 300 yards behind it. Then the Sirdar and staff came and stood around the pole. An instant later, the order having been given, the Egyptian flag was hoisted to the top, and the Sudanese bands played a few bars of the Khedivial anthem. Ere the music ceased, the Sirdar, setting the example, called for three cheers for His Highness the Khedive. The British flag, the Union Jack, was meanwhile flying inshore from the *Dal*. None of the French officers attended the ceremony, but the Senegalese and the natives watched the proceedings with great interest. In fact, as many of the soldiers of the 11th and 13th Sudanese battalions were Shilluks, there had been numerous greetings and interchanges of courtesy between them. The worthy old Lieutenant Ali Gaffoon, a Shilluk, who had been in his youth a sheikh and soldier, and who had fought in Mexico for Maximilian, and since entered the Khedive's service, soon had crowds of his countrymen and countrywomen flocking to see him. Immediately after the flag was hoisted, Major Jackson was appointed commandant of the Fashoda district, and left with a garrison of the 11th Sudanese battalion and four guns of Captain Peake's battery. A large quantity of stores of various kinds was landed for their use. Meanwhile E Company of the Cameron Highlanders and the rest of the troops returned on board ship. The bands and pipers again played as the troops marched away, the Highlandmen stepping off to the tune of the *Cameron Men*. E Company of the Camerons numbered exactly 100 rank and file under five officers: Captain Hon. A. Murray, Lieutenants Hoare, Cameron, Alderson, and Surgeon-Captain Luther.

The fraternisation of the Sudanese soldiers and the Shilluks became thorough. An informal reception of the natives, sheikhs, and headmen, some of whom were attended by their wives, was held by the Sirdar ashore and afterwards on board the *Dal*. It was observed that, although hundreds of natives were seen, they were only brought forward in batches of less than a dozen to be presented. Besides, a considerable interval always elapsed before the arrival of the succeeding groups. Ali Gaffoon and his countrymen-comrades in the ranks, with pardonable tribal pride, were adverse to bringing their relatives and friends forward until the natives put on some clothes. For that purpose they had borrowed or got together about a dozen Arab dresses of kinds, wherewith to cover the bodies and limbs of the unsophisticated Shilluks. The national costume for men is a state of nudity, but they occasionally sprinkle their bodies with red or grey ashes. The women usually wear scant leather or thong aprons.

When the Sirdar ascertained the true cause of the delay, time pressing, he intimated he would waive for the nonce their putting on of ceremonial attire. "Let them all come as they are," and they did. They evinced the liveliest interest and pleasure in all they saw and heard in camp and aboard ship. The chiefs declared they had signed no treaty with the French nor conceded any of their country. All of them asserted that they were subjects of the Khedive, to whom they renewed their allegiance forthwith. The French mission had been short of food and they had helped them only by giving supplies. Incidentally it may be stated that the Shilluk country is exceedingly fertile. At one time it was the most densely populated region of the Sudan for its acreage, containing a population of over 2,000,000 souls, living under an ancient dynasty of kings. From 1884 the Shilluks repeatedly warred with the Dervishes. In 1894 they rose again and fought for a long time before their Queen was slain and they were put down. On that occasion the Mahdists behaved with more than usual ferocity, putting thousands to the sword. Strange to say, great numbers of Shilluks, like other Sudan blacks, fought against us under the Khalifa's banners. The moment, however, they were captured, with great readiness they enlisted in the Khedivial army. Latterly so many deserters and prisoners brought by their friends offered themselves as soldiers, that only the smartest and strongest were chosen.

That afternoon the *Dal* and two of the gunboats left Fashoda and steamed away up the Nile towards Sobat. Before leaving, the Sirdar sent a formal written document to Major Marchand, protesting against any usurpation by another Power of the rights of Great Britain and Egypt to the Nile Valley. He stated that he would refuse to recognise in any way French authority in the country. There was found to be large quantities of grass weed and *sudd* in the Nile at no great distance from Fashoda. In several places the clear channels were less than 150 yards wide. As the steamers made southing, the river became narrower and the obstacles to navigation more serious—floating islands of weeds and banked *sudd* blocking the fairway, leaving it but 50 yards or less in width. It is about 62 miles from Fashoda to the Sobat river, that Abyssinian tributary to the Nile. There was formerly an Egyptian station and fort on the neck of land at the junction of the two rivers. Other stations were also held by Khedivial troops further up the river in the old days before the Mahdi's rebellion. It was on the 20th September, the date as officially given, that the flotilla reached Sobat. The place was overgrown with bush, as compared with what had formerly been the case. Only a few natives were seen upon the mainland and islands, and they were friendly disposed. The Sobat, though but 150 yards or so wide, is 30 feet deep when in flood. Its yellow stream runs at two knots an hour, the current driving far into the wider and slacker waters of the Nile, which is about three-quarters of a mile wide at that point. The banks were accessible, and a landing of the troops was much more easily effected than had been the case at Fashoda. As soon as the soldiers and the two remaining guns of Captain Peake's battery were got ashore, the Egyptian flag was formally hoisted and greeted. It was the Sirdar who directed the whole proceedings. The ceremonial observance attending the re-occupation was precisely similar to that which had taken place at Fashoda. Major Smith Dorian was placed in command of the post and district. Three companies of the 13th Sudanese were left as a garrison together with the two Maxim-Nordenfeldt guns. A gunboat was also detailed to proceed a little way up the Sobat and the Bahr el Ghazal.

Next morning the vessels having been filled up with fuel, the Sirdar, with the Camerons and the remainder of the troops not detached for garrison duty, steamed away back towards Omdurman. No news had penetrated to that remote region about the overthrow of the Dervishes and very little was known about the passing mission under Major Marchand. The same day, 21st September, Fashoda was reached, and a short stay was made. All was quiet and the two flags were flying just as the Sirdar had left them. But the place had been transformed all the same. A military camp had arisen that looked like a village. *Tukals* and shelters covered the clearing behind the French lines. Trenches also had been dug and Marchand's party were completely hemmed in from the landward side as well as by water, the gunboats controlling the river. The Shilluks had all gone over and put themselves under Major Jackson and the Khedivial flag. A sort of bazaar had been started and the country was already making for peace. There was universal rejoicing at the downfall of the Khalifa. A determination was expressed of promptly dealing with him or Osman Digna, should either of them pass that way.

The new twin-screw gunboats *"Sultan"* and *"Sheik"* had nine days' rations for troops put aboard. They were then detached, being ordered to remain behind for patrol duty. Their instructions were to keep the river and banks clear of all armed bands of Dervishes, and, if necessary, afford assistance to the posts at Sobat and Fashoda. They were also bidden to prevent the transport of war material, or conveyance of reinforcements, except by accredited Khedivial officers. The Sirdar in a note informed Major Marchand that he had prohibited the transport of all war material upon the Nile. Thereafter the Sirdar resumed the journey downstream. The long and fertile island of Abba—it extends for 20 miles—was passed without seeing anything of the fugitive Khalifa and his followers. It was to Abba island the Mahdi went, and it was there the rebellion first broke out. Subsequently it was ascertained that Abdullah and Osman Digna with their retainers sought shelter in the heavy woods opposite Abba island, and they were stated to be in hiding there at the end of December 1898. The Sirdar and headquarters got back to Omdurman on the 25th of September.

Popular feeling ran very high at home when it was ascertained that, despite repeated notification, the French had tried to grasp the fruits of the British victory over the Dervishes. A Liberal statesman had, years before, declared, that any attempt on the part of France to occupy the Upper Nile valley lands would be regarded as an unfriendly act by this country. Conservative statesmen had endorsed that official pronouncement; yet, in face of these declarations, the thing had been done with every evidence of a fine contempt for British feeling and self-respect. The enemies of England in Egypt and elsewhere were sniggering. Our diplomatic and military chiefs were making unusual efforts to keep the Marchand affair a profound secret. At every stage down the Nile from Omdurman to Cairo, the Camerons and all who had been to Fashoda and Sobat were officially warned to keep the matter a profound secret. The case I thought was too serious to be left hidden in the breasts of a few where the issues involved were so tremendous. So I openly set myself to learning what had happened, and wiring every scrap of information for publication. Several officers were sent down from Omdurman with special despatches. Long before they arrived even in Cairo, cypher messages extending to many folios had been forwarded day after day direct from Khartoum to Downing Street.

The Sirdar reached Cairo on the 6th of October and left for England on the 21st of the same month. By that time much had happened. The official despatches had been published in a Parliamentary paper and there were ominous preparations for war in both France and Great Britain. Fleets were being got ready for sea and feverish activity prevailed in Gallic and British arsenals. The insistence of the Parisian Ministers in seeking to have other questions discussed side by side with the demand for the evacuation of Fashoda and their dilatory tactics but increased the feeling of irritation in the United Kingdom. Statesmen seemed to be undecided and diplomacy, as usual, revolving in a circle. Happily, this country was never better prepared for war, and that in the end, as has so often been the case, proved the best advocate for peace. It would be uncharitable to emphasise the fact of the French Government slipping away from one after another of the positions they had taken up in reference to the whole question. That being Frenchmen they felt acutely the false moves they had made goes without saying. Whilst war was impending and the French Government seemed bent upon driving our Government to that point, the anti-British Pashas and the Gallic set in Egypt were jubilant. The Turkish Pashas and Beys were openly chuckling and romancing about unheard-of things. It is in Egypt, as it is in Armenia and was in the Balkans: the Turk is the enemy of good government and freedom for the people. A check to British policy and rule meant to them a possible return of the old corrupt days when they did as they liked, treating *fellaheen* and negroes as slaves. Had Great Britain in this instance yielded a jot of her just rights to the intriguing and bellicose spirit of French officialism Egypt would have been made an impossible place for our countrymen to remain in. Being in Cairo and Alexandria at the time I was privately assured by scores of my countrymen, men in business and in public offices, that they would be obliged to quit Egypt if France succeeded in her pretensions to the Nile Valley. Petty annoyances, tyranny, all manner of injustice and even violence would be resorted to, to force them to leave and to drive British interests to the wall.

I avail myself again of the excellent synopsis of the official despatches dealing with the Fashoda incident, which appeared in the *Daily Telegraph*. The Parliamentary papers in question were issued on the 9th of October last. The official papers opened with a despatch from Sir Edmund Monson to the Foreign Secretary, bearing date December 10, 1897. Therein the British Ambassador says:

> The despatches which I have recently addressed to your lordship respecting the reports of the massacre of the Marchand Expedition, and the comments made in connection with this rumoured disaster by the French Press, will have already shown your lordship how necessary it has become to remind the French Government of the views held by that of Her Majesty as to their sphere of influence in the Upper Nile Valley; and it has been with great satisfaction that I have found myself so promptly authorised to make a communication upon the subject to M. Hanotaux. Made in the way in which it has been suggested by your lordship, I see no reason why this communication should prejudice the chances of our coming to a satisfactory arrangement upon the question with which we are dealing in connection with the situation in West Africa.

Sir Edmund Monson enclosed in the despatch a copy of a note he had addressed to M. Hanotaux, at that period French Minister of Foreign Affairs, as follows:

> The other point to which it is necessary to advert is the proposed recognition of the French claim to the northern and eastern shores of Lake Chad. If other questions are adjusted, Her Majesty's Government will make no difficulty about this condition. But in doing so they can-

not forget that the possession of this territory may in the future open up a road to the Nile; and they must not be understood to admit that any other European Power than Great Britain has any claim to occupy any part of the Valley of the Nile. The views of the British Government upon this matter were plainly stated in Parliament by Sir Edward Grey some years ago during the Administration of the Earl of Rosebery, and were formally communicated to the French Government at the time. Her Majesty's present Government entirely adhere to the language that was on this occasion employed by their predecessors.

To this M. Hanotaux replied:

In any case the French Government cannot, under present circumstances, refrain from repeating the reservations which it has never failed to express every time that questions relating to the Valley of the Nile have been brought forward. Thus, in particular, the declarations of Sir Edward Grey, to which the British Government has referred, gave rise to an immediate protest by our representative in London, the terms of which he repeated and developed in the further conversations which he had at the Foreign Office on the subject. I myself had occasion, in the sitting of the Senate on April 5, 1895, to make, in the name of the Government, declarations to which I consider that I am all the more justified in referring from the fact that they have called forth no reply from the British Government.

The speech to which M. Hanotaux refers is published at length in an appendix, and, so far from being a reply to Sir Edward Grey, it gives the French position completely away.

I now come, gentlemen, to the question of the Upper Nile. I will explain the situation to the Senate in a few words; for I think it will be useful to complete the explanations which M. de Lamarzelle has already given on this subject. Between the country of the lakes and the point of

Wady Halfa, on the Nile, extends a vast region, measuring twenty degrees of latitude, or 2000 kilometres, that is, more than the breadth of Western Europe from Gibraltar to Dunkirk. In this region there is at this moment, perhaps, not a single European; in any case, there does not exist any power derived, by any title, from a European authority. It is the country of the Mahdi! Now, gentlemen, it is the future of this country which fills with an uneasiness, which we may describe as at least premature, the minds of a certain number of persons interested in Africa. The Egyptians who occupied this vast domain for a considerable time have moved to the north. Emin Pasha himself was compelled to withdraw. The rights of the Sultan and the Khedive alone continue to exist over the regions of the Sudan and of Equatorial Africa.

That is to say, after the Mahdi, who was the *de facto* ruler, the authority over the whole basin of the Upper Nile reverted to the Khedive and the Sultan as his suzerain, which is exactly the position taken up by Lord Salisbury in his despatch of September 9, 1898.

Major Marchand has had various titles conferred upon him, and in the penultimate despatch contained in the papers he is described by Lord Salisbury as "a French explorer who is on the Upper Nile in a difficult position." To M. Delcassé, however, is reserved the honour of giving him an official designation. On September 7 the French Foreign Minister, in an interview with Sir E. Monson, after handsomely complimenting the British Government on the victory of Omdurman, expressed his anxiety about a possible meeting of the Sirdar and M. Marchand.

> Should he (M. Marchand) be met with, his Excellency said that he had received instructions to be most careful to abstain from all action which might cause local difficulties, and that he had been enjoined to consider himself as an 'emissary of civilisation' without any authority whatever to decide upon questions of right, which must proper-

ly form the subject of discussion between Her Majesty's Government and that of the French Republic.

M. Delcassé therefore begged me to inform your lordship of this fact, and expressed the hope that the commander of Her Majesty's naval forces on the river might be instructed to take no steps which might lead to a local conflict with regard to such questions of right.

It may be remarked, in passing, that this view of the position of the emissary of civilisation does not tally with that which M. Marchand subsequently gave to the Sirdar, to whom he stated—

> .... that he had received precise orders for the occupation of the country and the hoisting of the French flag over the Government buildings at Fashoda, and added that, without the orders of his Government, which, however, he expected, would not be delayed, it was impossible for him to retire from the place.

The instructions given by Lord Salisbury, through Lord Cromer, to the Sirdar, have been given elsewhere in this chapter.

On September 11 our Ambassador informed M. Delcassé of the advance of the Sirdar up the Nile, and on the 18th the French Foreign Minister stated further:

> As a matter of fact, there is no Marchand Mission. In 1892 and 1893 M. Liotard was sent to the Upper Ubanghi as Commissioner, with instructions to secure French interests in the north-east. M. Marchand had been appointed one of his subordinates, and received all his orders from M. Liotard. There could be no doubt that for a long time past the whole region of the Bahr-el-Ghazal had been out of the influence of Egypt.

Sir E. Monson left M. Delcassé in no doubt as to the view Her Majesty's Government took of the situation. Of the interview referred to, he reports to Lord Salisbury as follows, under date September 22:

Although his Excellency made two or three allusions to the reasons for which, in his opinion, the French might consider that the region in question was open to their advance, he himself volunteered the suggestion that discussion between us would be inopportune.

In this I, of course, concurred, reminding him of the terms of your lordship's telegram of the 9th inst.; but I told him, as emphatically as I could, that I looked upon the situation at Fashoda, if M. Marchand had occupied that town, as very serious, inasmuch as Her Majesty's Government would certainly not acquiesce in his remaining there, nor would they consent to relinquishing the claims of Egypt to the restoration of all the country latterly subject to the Khalifa, which had heretofore been a portion of her territory. I felt it to be my duty, I said, to speak with extreme frankness, and to assure him that on this point no compromise would be possible.

M. Delcassé listened to me with grave attention, but his reply was chiefly to the effect that if the two Governments discussed the matter with calmness and a sincere desire to avoid a conflict, there could be no doubt of our arriving at a peaceable and satisfactory solution. France does not desire a quarrel. In saying this he could speak with absolute certainty. All his colleagues in the Government are, like himself, anxious for good relations with England. If this anxiety is reciprocated on the other side of the Channel (and the tone of the English Press inspires him with doubts of this) there can be no danger.

I replied that Her Majesty's Government have no desire to pick a quarrel with France, but that nothing could be gained by my concealing from him the gravity of the situation as I regarded it, or the fixed determination of Her Majesty's Government to vindicate claims of the absolute justice of which they hold that there can be no question. I, of course, avoided the use of any expression which might sound like a menace, but short of this I did my best to make my declaration of the impossibility of the French being allowed to remain at Fashoda as clear and distinct as could be expressed in words.

On 25th September, the day the expedition returned from Fashoda to Omdurman, Mr Rennell Rodd, who during the absence of Lord Cromer in Europe was in charge of affairs in Egypt, telegraphed to Lord Salisbury the following despatch, which had been received from the Sirdar:

> I found at Fashoda, whence I have just returned, M. Marchand with 8 officers and 120 men. The French flag had been hoisted over the old Government buildings in which they were located. I sent a letter announcing my approach on the day before my arrival at Fashoda. On the following morning, September 19, a reply was brought to me from M. Marchand by a small rowing-boat carrying the French flag. It stated that he had arrived at Fashoda on July 10, having been instructed by his Government to occupy the Bahr-el-Ghazal up to the confluence of the Bahr-el-Jebel, and also the Shilluk country on the left bank of the White Nile as far as Fashoda. It went on to say that he had concluded a treaty with the Shilluk chiefs by which they placed the country under the protection of France, and that he had sent this treaty to his Government for ratification by way of Abyssinia, as well as by the Bahr-el-Ghazal. He described his fight with the Dervishes on August 25, and stated that, in anticipation of a second and more serious attack, he had sent his steamer south for reinforcements, but that our arrival had prevented a further attack.
>
> When we arrived at Fashoda, M. Marchand and M. Germain came on board our steamer, and I at once informed them that the presence of a French party at Fashoda and in the Nile valley must be considered as a direct infringement of the rights of Egypt and of the British Government, and I protested in the strongest terms against the

occupation of Fashoda by M. Marchand and his party, and the hoisting of the French flag in the dominions of his Highness the Khedive. M. Marchand stated, in reply, that he had received precise orders for the occupation of the country and the hoisting of the French flag over the Government buildings at Fashoda, and added that, without the orders of his Government, which, however, he expected would not be delayed, it was impossible for him to retire from the place. I then inquired of him whether, in view of the fact that I was accompanied by a superior force, he was prepared to resist the hoisting of the Egyptian flag at Fashoda. He hesitated, and replied that he could not resist. The Egyptian flag was then hoisted, about 500 yards south of the French flag, on a ruined bastion of the old Egyptian fortifications, commanding the only road which leads into the interior from the French position. The latter is entirely surrounded to the north by impassable marshes.

Before leaving for the south I handed to M. Marchand a formal written protest on the part of the Governments of Great Britain and Egypt against any occupation of any part of the Nile valley by France, as being an infringement of the rights of those Governments. I added that I could not recognise the occupation by France of any part of the Nile valley.

I left at Fashoda a garrison of one Sudanese battalion, four guns, and a gunboat under Major Jackson, whom I appointed Commandant of the Fashoda district, and I proceeded to Sobat, where the flag was hoisted and a post established on September 20. We did not see or hear anything of the Abyssinians on the Sobat, but were informed that their nearest post was about 350 miles up that river. The Bahr-el-Jebel being entirely blocked by floating weed, I gave orders for a gunboat to patrol up the Bahr-el-Ghazal in the direction of Meshra-er-Rek. As we passed Fashoda on the return journey north, I sent M. Marchand a letter stating that all transport of war material on the

Nile was absolutely prohibited, as the country was under military law. The chief of the Shilluk tribe, accompanied by a large number of followers, has come into Major Jackson's camp. He entirely denies having made any treaty with the French, and the entire tribe express the greatest delight at returning to allegiance to us.

M. Marchand is in want of ammunition and supplies, and any that may be sent to him must take months to arrive at their destination. He is cut off from the interior, and is quite inadequately provided with water transport. Moreover, he has no following in the country, and nothing could have saved his expedition from being annihilated by the Dervishes if we had been a fortnight later in crushing the Khalifa.

The gist of this despatch was communicated to the French Government, accompanied by a notification that the Sirdar's "language and proceedings" had the complete approval of Lord Salisbury. M. Delcassé was evidently at his wits' end to escape from an *impasse* which was chiefly of his own creation.

In an interview with Sir E. Monson on September 27 he wished to put off a final decision till he had received the despatches which M. Marchand had forwarded in duplicate by way of the French Congo and Abyssinia respectively. Our Ambassador writes:

To gain time, M. Delcassé wished that I should request your lordship to consent to a telegram being sent by the French agent at Cairo to Khartoum, to be forwarded from thence up the Nile to Fashoda. The telegram would contain instructions to M. Marchand to send at once one of the French officers serving on his mission to Cairo with a copy of his above-mentioned report, so that the French Government might learn its contents as soon as possible. They were, of course, ready to bear all the expense.

Stress was laid by M. Delcassé upon the great desire entertained at Paris to prevent any serious difficulty from arising; at the same time, he felt convinced, especially in view of the conduct of the Sirdar at Fashoda, acting as he undoubtedly was under instructions, that Her Majesty's Government were as anxious as the French Government to avoid a conflict.

I told M. Delcassé in reply that I must conclude from the language which he had held that the French Government had decided that they would not recall M. Marchand before receiving his report, and I asked if I was right in this conclusion. I pointed out to his Excellency that M. Marchand himself is stated to be desirous of retiring from his position, which appeared to be a disagreeable one. Such being the case, I must urgently press him to tell me whether he refused at once to recall M. Marchand.

After considering his reply for some few minutes, his Excellency said that he himself was ready to discuss the question in the most conciliatory spirit, but I must not ask him for the impossible.

I pointed out that your lordship's telegram of the 9th inst., which I had communicated to him at the time, had made him aware that Her Majesty's Government considered that there could be no discussion upon such questions as the right of Egypt to Fashoda.

To this Lord Salisbury replied next day:

Her Majesty's Government cannot decline to assist in forwarding a message from the French Agent in Egypt to a French explorer who is on the Upper Nile in a difficult position, and your Excellency is authorised to inform M. Delcassé that Her Majesty's Acting Agent at Cairo will be instructed to transmit to Omdurman immediately any such message, and at the same time to request Sir H. Kitchener to forward it thence to its destination by any opportunity which may be available.

Her Majesty's Government do not desire to be made acquainted with the purport of the message. But you must explain that they are unable to accept any responsibility for the results to the safety or health of the explorer which the delay in quitting his present situation may bring about.

The official papers closed with the following laconic despatch from Lord Salisbury to Sir E. Monson, bearing date 3rd October.

I request your Excellency to inform the French Minister for Foreign Affairs that, in accordance with his wish, his message for M. Marchand has been transmitted to Khartoum, and will be forwarded thence to its destination. In order to avoid any misunderstanding, you should state to M. Delcassé that the fact of Her Majesty's Government having complied with his Excellency's request in regard to the transmission of the message does not imply the slightest modification of the views previously expressed by them. You should add that, whether in times of Egyptian or Dervish dominion, the region in which M. Marchand was found has never been without an owner, and that, in the view of Her Majesty's Government, his expedition into it with an escort of 100 Senegalese troops has no political effect, nor can any political significance be attached to it.

In the appendix were given past speeches and despatches by M. Decrais, M. Hanotaux, Lord Kimberley, Sir E. Grey, etc.

The rest can be quickly told. Military and naval preparations for war in both countries were redoubled and the public tone was bellicose. Consols were affected and war appeared almost inevitable. It was an occasion for union among all who rightly set patriotism above party. Lord Rosebery, Late Premier, with splendid grace and disinterestedness, in a speech, 13th October, voiced the sentiment of the masses and classes. His lordship said:

Behind the policy of the British Government in this matter there is the untiring and united strength of the nation itself. (Cheers.) It is the policy of the last Government deliberately adopted and sustained by the present Government. (Cheers.) That is only a matter of form, but it is the policy of the nation itself, and no Government that attempted to recede from or palter with that policy would last a week. (Loud cheers.) I am perfectly certain that no idea or intention of any weakening on this point or this question has entered the head of Her Majesty's present advisers.

Messages were transmitted up the Nile to Major Marchand at Fashoda. In response thereto he sent Captain Baratier down with despatches. That officer arrived with Slatin Pasha in Cairo on the 20th October. His despatches were wired to Paris, for which Baratier himself started next day. It happened that the Sirdar, who also left for England on that date, was a fellow-traveller with him. Another hitch occurred, the French Government stating that Marchand's report made no allusion to the meeting with the Sirdar at Fashoda. That they would have to wait for before giving an answer. Marchand, it was alleged, had not had time to bring his report down to date, when Baratier left him. They had not long to wait, for suddenly the announcement was sprung that Major Marchand, acting on his own volition, had left Fashoda and was coming down by Khedivial transport, to Cairo. He arrived in that city on the evening of 3rd November, and got a deservedly hearty reception from the English as well as the French community. Prominent officials, civil and military, were there to greet the brave and hardy explorer. His companion, Captain Baratier, who had been to Paris and had hastened back intending to return to Fashoda, met the Major next day in Cairo. But on the very day that Major Marchand reached Cairo, the French Government had issued an official note stating it had been decided to evacuate Fashoda, as the position had been reported untenable. So saying "No, no, they would ne'er consent," they consented.

At the Mansion House banquet given to the Sirdar, on 4th November, Lord Salisbury said:

> I received from the French Ambassador this afternoon the information that the French Government had come to the conclusion that the (Fashoda) occupation was of no

sort of value to the French Republic, and they thought that under those circumstances, to persist in an occupation which only cost them money and did harm, merely because some of their advisers thought they would be an unwelcome neighbour, would not show the wisdom with which the French Republic has uniformly been guided. They have done what I believe every Government would have done in the same position—they have resolved that the occupation must cease. A formal intimation to that effect was made to me this afternoon, and it has been conveyed to the French authorities at Cairo. I do not wish to be misunderstood as saying that all causes of controversy are by this removed between the French Government and ourselves. It is probably not so, and it may be that we shall have many discussions in the future, but a cause of controversy of a singularly acute and somewhat dangerous character has been removed, and we cannot but congratulate ourselves upon it.

In the same connection it is of interest to learn what Major Marchand had to say. The full text of his speech made at a banquet given to him and Captain Baratier by the French Club at Cairo on the 7th October appeared in the Press. In the presence of the Acting French Diplomatic Agent and others, Major Marchand said:

Monsieur le Ministre de France, Monsieur le Président, Messieurs—There are two reasons why you will not expect a speech from me. In the first place I am only a soldier and no orator; and then one cannot be talkative on a day of reflection, a day which brings to me personally a great sorrow, the official abandonment of Fashoda. Fashoda! it was only a point—it is true that it synthesised everything. But if we lose the point we abandon nothing of our thesis. To reflect is not to despair—on the contrary. The experiences of this world teach us that the sum of our sorrows is not greater than that of our joys. The more the black period may be prolonged the more quickly will approach the dawn of proud aspirations at length realised. And the granite Sphinx which near at hand dreams on the desert sands, the Sphinx which saw the passage of Bonaparte, which saw Lesseps and his work, has not yet uttered its last word, has not murmured the supreme sentence. The more fiercely evil fortune may pursue us the more should we call to our aid the great hopes which swell the heart and fortify the will. The French colony in Cairo, moreover, has shown more than ten times over already that it knows no discouragement. I should like, my dear and valiant compatriots, to give you some small recompense. Listen! When, nearly three years ago, the Congo-Nile mission left France, it was not in order to make a more or less famous journey of exploration. No, its aim was far higher. You have already guessed it. Why, then, proclaim it here? We desired (here the speaker paused a moment) to carry across French Africa to the French in Egypt a hand-grip from the French of France. The road was long, sometimes hard; we have reached our destination, however, since I have the honour to greet you here to-day. Do you not see a symbol in this? Fortune, which detests broad and easy paths, is perhaps at this moment on her way, bringing you the succour so patiently looked for. We must never despair, and who can say that the Sphinx may not be about to smile? It is for this that I have come to tell you that if we are few to-day we shall be many to-morrow—who forget nothing, who abandon nothing. It is with this thought that I drink to your health, gentlemen, the health of the French colony in Egypt. To the Greater France!

It is easy to feel great sympathy with so gallant and hardy a soldier, who, having successfully accomplished the perilous mission entrusted to him by his Government, found support denied him and his work fruitless. Major Marchand and Captain Baratier again availed themselves of the Egyptian military transport to return to their comrades. At half-past 8 a.m., 11th December, the French hauled down their flag at Fashoda, and left for the Sobat river. They were intending to make their way up that stream to the nearest Abyssinian post, and thereafter, striking through Menelik's country, hoped to arrive on the East African coast at Djibutil. Their sick comrades they entrusted to the Egyptian military authorities to send home by the Nile through Lower Egypt. The invalided Frenchmen and Senegalese in question reached Cairo at the end of the year.

Perhaps it was only to be expected that the French press and politicians would display increased virulence against this country over the Fashoda settlement. But their persistence in that course, and the fact of their present extraordinary naval expenditure, can only mean getting ready for war against Great Britain. This may lead our people to consider whether it would not be cheapest and wisest to settle the quarrel off-hand. True, delay makes for peace, but a peace that is to be a struggle to overtop one another in armaments may be more costly in every sense than sharp and decisive warfare. The chief cause of the soreness in France against us is our presence in Egypt. Yet the French have no such vital interest there as this country has. To many of our colonies and dependencies the shortest way lies through Egypt. Again, the French form quite a minority in numbers and wealth among the foreign communities in Egypt. Since 1882, the year of occupation, Great Britain has been careful to avoid interference with the privileges and rights of all foreigners. In what community controlled by France through sixteen years would it have been allowed that an alien language should be maintained in use in public places. No official step has been taken to diminish the use of French in street nomenclature, or public conveyances, or public departments in Egypt until last year. Arabic is the language of the people, and English is the language of commerce in the country. A sensible change in the direction indicated is at last evident, even in Cairo and Alexandria. Shops and warehouses are displaying Anglo-Saxon signs, and the natives are discarding French and are speaking English as the one foreign language necessary to acquire.

There has been talk among our neighbours of emulating the Sirdar's enterprise and founding French colleges at Khartoum and Fashoda. But urged by less disinterested motives they may find it necessary instead to devote their funds to the cultivation of the Gallic tongue in Lower and Upper Egypt, rather than in the Sudan. In the year 1897, in Tantah, the third largest town in the Delta, there were 130 scholars learning French and but 40 studying English. In 1898 there were 98 at the English classes and but a moiety at the French. The scholastic year 1899, according to the officials of the Public Instruction Department, will see a farther and even more serious decline in the study of the French language. The French officials themselves are painfully aware that the Gallic speech, for colloquial intercourse between educated natives and Europeans, is doomed if matters continue as at present. In Assouan, where during 1897 much the same state of things prevailed as at Tantah; in 1898 there were 118 scholars learning English and but three at the French classes.

Until quite recently, it was wont to be the case in Lower Egypt that there were always two pupils learning French to one devoting attention to acquiring English. In Upper Egypt of late years the difference had not been so marked, the proportion of French and English students being about equal. These figures refer to primary classes in Upper Egypt, and to secondary, as well as primary, classes in Cairo and Alexandria. As a matter of fact, the results of the examinations did not follow in quite the same proportion in the Delta. About three pupils have passed in French to two in English. Shortly after the battle of Omdurman, applications had to be made for entrance into the school classes for English and French tuition. In a great number of schools, in both Upper and Lower Egypt, especially in the stronghold of the French tongue—the Delta—not a single application was made by candidates for entrance to the second primaries, in which French teaching begins. That means to say that there will a dearth and practically a cessation of French teaching in 1899 in the primary schools, and subsequently, or in 1900, the year of the Exposition Universelle at Paris, a total discontinuance of it in the secondary schools. Taking the secondary schools examinations throughout the whole of Lower Egypt by themselves, I learn that in 1898, although there were a larger proportion of candidates for French certificates of proficiency, yet the numbers that actually passed in each language were about the same. The Examining Commissioners are Egyptian, English, and French.

It is in Egypt as in certain other countries. The great ambition of every lad is to get into the Government service, and failing that to become a lawyer. Law schools are therefore well attended. Heretofore budding lawyers have been taught in French classes only. An English-speaking law section was started in 1898. The natives are quick to appreciate any change which is to their advantage. Pupils in the secondary schools have now opened to them careers which have heretofore been closed. There is in truth a silent, but certain to be effective, educational and social revolution begun in Egypt. No more will every whim and caprice of those who seek to obstruct the advance of the Egyptians be tolerated. In 1899 for the first time examining educational centres will be established at Assouan and Suakin. All those south of Assiut will be for English students only, for French will be quite dropped. Not only will there be a college at Khartoum but one at Kassala, where English as well as Arabic will be taught. In a new and thorough manner has the regeneration of Egypt and the Sudan been undertaken. The dream of a red English through-traffic line from Cairo to Cape Town will have a speedy realisation. Possibly within eighteen months the railway will be carried to the Sobat. Certainly before 1899 is ended there will be through communication with Khartoum. Mr Cecil Rhodes is busy with his South African lines, which by that time should be up to the Zambezi, and within three years after there will possibly be open rail and water communication from the Mediterranean to Cape Town. But before then the telegraph wire will bind North and South Africa together, and to the United Kingdom.

Postscript

This volume was written and in the printer's hands when an article by a Mr E. N. Bennett appeared in the columns of *The Contemporary Review*, entitled "After Omdurman." That gentleman made a series of grave charges reflecting upon the Anglo-Egyptian arms, not only during the Khartoum Expedition, but also on their conduct in Egypt and the Sudan since 1882. In the Daily Telegraph and elsewhere I have deservedly stigmatised Mr Bennett's allegations as untrue, stupid, and wantonly mischievous.

In the pages of The Khartoum Campaign, 1898, can be read the detailed version of events which happened in the field before as well as after Omdurman. I venture to think that abundant refutation will be found in the Work of most of Mr Bennett's scandalous assertions. Although it may seem to lend further temporary importance to what that gentleman has written, as his accusations were made public under the cover of a respectable magazine, perhaps a few words more may not be out of place.

Mr Bennett's article was seemingly framed on the specious pretext of, under a discussion of the principles of international law, questions of belligerency, Geneva Convention rules, and so forth, to base thereon a claim for the treatment of Dervishes as combatants entitled to all the amenities of civilised warfare. Several pages of his composition are given up to treating upon that matter. For instance, he says—

Moreover, it is worth remembering that the Dervishes were not 'savages' in the sense in which the word is applied to the followers of a Lobengula or a Samory. On the contrary, they satisfied all the requirements for recognition as an armed force.

Now, that is an aspersion upon Lobengula and Samory in particular. For unredeemed devilishness, the Dervishes have had no equals. The fact is, that the Mahdists made it a constant practice to ruthlessly slaughter all prisoners in battle, wounded or unwounded; to enslave, torture, or murder their enemies, active or passive; to loot and to burn; to slay children and debauch women. To set up a pretext that such monsters are entitled to the grace and consideration of the most humane laws, is to beggar commonsense and yap intolerable humbug. Yet British self-respect was such, Mr Bennett to the contrary notwithstanding, that the Dervishes were treated as men, and not as wild beasts.

Started upon his false pursuit, Mr Bennett proceeds from error to error, abounding in reckless misstatements, atrocious imputations, and scattering charges void of truth. As briefly as possible, I will deal with his accusations. One of his first deliverances is as follows:

> It is, of course, an open secret that in all our Sudan battles the enemy's wounded have been killed. The practice has, ever since the days of Tel-el-Kebir, become traditional in Sudanese warfare. After the battle of Atbara, it was announced that 3000 Dervishes had been killed. There was practically no mention of the wounded.... How, then, was it that no wounded were accounted for at the Atbara?

Again he writes:

> But I cannot help thinking that if the killing of the wounded had been sternly repressed at Tel-el-Kebir and during the earlier Sudan campaigns, our Dervish enemies would have learned to expect civilised treatment, etc.

Gaining courage, probably from his own audacity, Mr Bennett

had the hardihood to virtually declare that the cruelties permitted by British officers made the Dervishes what they were.

Now, I went through the 1882 war in Egypt as well as most of the campaigns in the Sudan. I am therefore in a better position than he to declare, that his allegations are a perversion of the truth. It was neither the practice at Tel-el-Kebir nor subsequent thereto for British led troops to kill wounded men. The insinuation that they did so, or connived at such slaughter, is a stupid or a malicious falsehood. In every battle within the period referred to, large numbers of wounded and unwounded prisoners were taken, and invariably great lenience was shown. Surgical treatment also was, whenever possible, always promptly rendered. Indeed, they were in countless cases treated as tenderly as our own wounded. This further: in action there are no soldiers less prone to needless blood-spilling, or men readier to forgive and forget, than "Tommy Atkins." Official returns exist setting at rest the fiction about Tel-el-Kebir and the Sudan battles. At Tel-el-Kebir many thousand prisoners were made, and in other engagements our hands were always full of Dervish wounded. At El Teb, Tamai, Abu Klea, Abu Kru, Gemaizeh, Atbara, and elsewhere, wounded Dervishes fell into our hands, and received every attention from the medical staff. And in some of these actions our troops were themselves in sore straits. Several hundred Dervishes were picked up within and without the Atbara den, including the leader Mahmoud and his two cousins. Be it remembered, our troops only remained there a few hours, marching back to the Nile.

Still further abominable charges Mr Bennett lays at the door of his countrymen who command British and Khedivial troops. The Sirdar himself is included in his rigmarole of accusations. But whether dealing with particulars or the general course of events, Mr Bennett discloses that he has scarcely a nodding acquaintanceship with truth. He has said:

> This wholesale slaughter was not confined to Arab servants, (*i.e.*, killing wounded Dervishes.) The Sudanese seemed

to revel in the work, and continually drove their bayonets through men who were absolutely unconscious.... This unsoldierly work was not even left to the exclusive control of the black troops; our British soldiers took part in it.

On whatever ground Mr Bennett may seek to support these assertions, they are unwarranted and untruthful libels. There was no wholesale slaughter of wounded Dervishes, nor was there anything done in the least justifying or providing a decent pretext for that ferocious accusation. Very many thousands of Dervish wounded fell into our hands that day and later. Officers have written to the press, denying these charges and the rest of Mr Bennett's tale of monstrosity. The Sirdar himself has confirmed by a personal cablegram my refutation of them. Here is another of Mr Bennett's suggestions of evil-doing, by innuendo and assertion: "It was stated that orders had been given to kill the wounded." And, "If the Sirdar really believes that the destruction of the wounded was a military necessity," etc. Can colossal crassness go further? There is not and never was a scintilla of truth for the charge of wholesale slaughtering of wounded Dervishes, nor that the Sirdar ever issued such an order, or that any reputable person ever received it, or ever had it hinted to him. The accusation is an unmitigated untruth, and absolutely at variance with all that was said and done by the Sirdar before and during the course of the battle and the pursuit. I certainly never heard of the matter until Mr Bennett made the accusation, and I cannot trace its authorship beyond himself. From the Sirdar down, contradictions of the charge have deservedly been slapped in Mr Bennett's face.

But it is almost sheer waste of words to follow and refute line by line the article "After Omdurman." Other of Mr Bennett's accusations were: that the 21st Lancers, on the way to the front, robbed hen-roosts and stricken villagers; that once in Omdurman the Sudanese troops abandoned discipline, looted, ravished, and murdered the whole night long; that on land and water our cannon and Maxims were deliberately turned upon unarmed flying inhabitants, massacring, without pity, men, women, and children. And had these charges had been true, I should have hastened to denounce the culprits, whoever they were, in the interests of humanity and country. Happily, Mr Bennett's tale is utterly without foundation, whatever reflection that casts upon his condition. The Lancers passed through nothing but deserted villages, where there were neither natives nor roosts to rob, even had they been so disposed. As for the Sudanese troops, their discipline throughout was perfect; there was no looting, no ravishing nor murder done by them or any other divisions of the soldiery. Nor did our gunners on shore or afloat ever fire upon unarmed people. Let it be recalled that those whom Mr Bennett so flippantly accuses are honourable gentlemen and fellow-countrymen. Three things in this connection are worthy of special note. When the first Dervish attack upon our zereba was repulsed and Wad Melik's dead, dying and shamming warriors carpeted the north slopes of Jebel Surgham and the plain in front. "Cease fire" was sounded. Thereafter the Dervishes arose from the ground in hundreds and thousands and walked off, without awakening a renewal of our fire from cannon, Maxims, or rifles. At the entry into Omdurman the artillery and gunboats were ordered to be careful how they fired, and grave risks were incurred by the Sirdar and staff in personally counselling to friend and foe a cessation of fighting.

Inaccuracy and sensationalism Mr Bennett is welcome to, and to the sort of notoriety it has brought him. Cheap maudlin sentiment may profess a pity for those "Dervish homes ruined" by the successes of British arms. The Dervishes in their day had no homes. Nay, they made honest profession that their mission was to destroy other people's, and do without carking domesticity, as that detracted from the merit of preparation for paradise. As I have elsewhere said, one of the "fads" of the day is to hold that liberalism of mind is always characterised by being a friend to every country and race but your own. Exact truth is as illusive to discovery by that as other pernicious methods. That there may have been one or two instances of cruelty practised on the battle-field is possible. Something of the kind always takes place in warfare as in everyday life. But only the amateur would magnify a few instances into a catalogue of charges. Alas! you cannot eliminate from armies, any more than from ordinary communities, the foolish, insane, and criminal.

The Author
London
February, 1899

ALSO FROM LEONAUR
AVAILABLE IN SOFTCOVER OR HARDCOVER WITH DUST JACKET

WAR BEYOND THE DRAGON PAGODA by *J. J. Snodgrass*—A Personal Narrative of the First Anglo-Burmese War 1824 - 1826.

ALL FOR A SHILLING A DAY by *Donald F. Featherstone*—The story of H.M. 16th, the Queen's Lancers During the first Sikh War 1845-1846.

AT THEM WITH THE BAYONET by *Donald F. Featherstone*—The first Anglo-Sikh War 1845-1846.

A LEONAUR ORIGINAL

THE HERO OF ALIWAL by *James Humphries*—The days when young Harry Smith wore the green jacket of the 95th-Wellington's famous riflemen-campaigning in Spain against Napoleon's French with his beautiful young bride Juana have long gone. Now, Sir Harry Smith is in his fifties approaching the end of a long career. His position in the Cape colony ends with an appointment as Deputy Adjutant-General to the army in India. There he joins the staff of Sir Hugh Gough to experience an Indian battlefield in the Gwalior War of 1843 as the power of the Marathas is finally crushed. Smith has little time for his superior's 'bull at a gate' style of battlefield tactics, but independent command is denied him. Little does he realise that the greatest opportunity of his military life is close at hand.

THE GURKHA WAR by *H. T. Prinsep*—The Anglo-Nepalese Conflict in North East India 1814-1816.

SOUND ADVANCE! by *Joseph Anderson*—Experiences of an officer of HM 50th regiment in Australia, Burma & the Gwalior war.

THE CAMPAIGN OF THE INDUS by *Thomas Holdsworth*—Experiences of a British Officer of the 2nd (Queen's Royal) Regiment in the Campaign to Place Shah Shuja on the Throne of Afghanistan 1838 - 1840.

WITH THE MADRAS EUROPEAN REGIMENT IN BURMA by *John Butler*—The Experiences of an Officer of the Honourable East India Company's Army During the First Anglo-Burmese War 1824 - 1826.

BESIEGED IN LUCKNOW by *Martin Richard Gubbins*—The Experiences of the Defender of 'Gubbins Post' before & during the sige of the residency at Lucknow, Indian Mutiny, 1857.

THE STORY OF THE GUIDES by *G.J. Younghusband*—The Exploits of the famous Indian Army Regiment from the northwest frontier 1847 - 1900.

AVAILABLE ONLINE AT
www.leonaur.com
AND OTHER GOOD BOOK STORES

ALSO FROM LEONAUR
AVAILABLE IN SOFTCOVER OR HARDCOVER WITH DUST JACKET

A JOURNAL OF THE SECOND SIKH WAR by *Daniel A. Sandford*—The Experiences of an Ensign of the 2nd Bengal European Regiment During the Campaign in the Punjab, India, 1848-49.

LAKE'S CAMPAIGNS IN INDIA by *Hugh Pearse*—The Second Anglo Maratha War, 1803-1807. Often neglected by historians and students alike, Lake's Indian campaign was fought against a resourceful and ruthless enemy-almost always superior in numbers to his own forces.

BRITAIN IN AFGHANISTAN 1: THE FIRST AFGHAN WAR 1839-42 by *Archibald Forbes*—Following over a century of the gradual assumption of sovereignty of the Indian Sub-Continent, the British Empire, in the form of the Honourable East India Company, supported by troops of the new Queen Victoria's army, found itself inevitably at the natural boundaries that surround Afghanistan. There it set in motion a series of disastrous events-the first of which was to march into the country at all.

BRITAIN IN AFGHANISTAN 2: THE SECOND AFGHAN WAR 1878-80 by *Archibald Forbes*—This the history of the Second Afghan War-another episode of British military history typified by savagery, massacre, siege and battles.

UP AMONG THE PANDIES by *Vivian Dering Majendie*—An outstanding account of the campaign for the fall of Lucknow. This is a vital book of war as fought by the British Army of the mid-nineteenth century, but in truth it is also an essential book of war that will enthral.

BLOW THE BUGLE, DRAW THE SWORD by *W. H. G. Kingston*—The Wars, Campaigns, Regiments and Soldiers of the British & Indian Armies During the Victorian Era, 1839-1898.

INDIAN MUTINY 150th ANNIVERSARY: A LEONAUR ORIGINAL

MUTINY: 1857 by *James Humphries*—It is now 150 years since the 'Indian Mutiny' burst like an engulfing flame on the British soldiers, their families and the civilians of the Empire in North East India. The Bengal Native army arose in violent rebellion, and the once peaceful countryside became a battleground as Native sepoys and elements of the Indian population massacred their British masters and defeated them in open battle. As the tide turned, a vengeful army of British and loyal Indian troops repressed the insurgency with a savagery that knew no mercy. It was a time of fear and slaughter. James Humphries has drawn together the voices of those dreadful days for this commemorative book.

AVAILABLE ONLINE AT
www.leonaur.com
AND OTHER GOOD BOOK STORES

ALSO FROM LEONAUR
AVAILABLE IN SOFTCOVER OR HARDCOVER WITH DUST JACKET

THE JENA CAMPAIGN: 1806 *by F. N. Maude*—The Twin Battles of Jena & Auerstadt Between Napoleon's French and the Prussian Army.

PRIVATE O'NEIL *by Charles O'Neil*—The recollections of an Irish Rogue of H. M. 28th Regt.—The Slashers— during the Peninsula & Waterloo campaigns of the Napoleonic wars.

ROYAL HIGHLANDER *by James Anton*—A soldier of H.M 42nd (Royal) Highlanders during the Peninsular, South of France & Waterloo Campaigns of the Napoleonic Wars.

CAPTAIN BLAZE *by Elzéar Blaze*—Elzéar Blaze recounts his life and experiences in Napoleon's army in a well written, articulate and companionable style.

LEJEUNE VOLUME 1 *by Louis-François Lejeune*—The Napoleonic Wars through the Experiences of an Officer on Berthier's Staff.

LEJEUNE VOLUME 2 *by Louis-François Lejeune*—The Napoleonic Wars through the Experiences of an Officer on Berthier's Staff.

FUSILIER COOPER *by John S. Cooper*—Experiences in the 7th (Royal) Fusiliers During the Peninsular Campaign of the Napoleonic Wars and the American Campaign to New Orleans.

CAPTAIN COIGNET *by Jean-Roch Coignet*—A Soldier of Napoleon's Imperial Guard from the Italian Campaign to Russia and Waterloo.

FIGHTING NAPOLEON'S EMPIRE *by Joseph Anderson*—The Campaigns of a British Infantryman in Italy, Egypt, the Peninsular & the West Indies During the Napoleonic Wars.

CHASSEUR BARRES *by Jean-Baptiste Barres*—The experiences of a French Infantryman of the Imperial Guard at Austerlitz, Jena, Eylau, Friedland, in the Peninsular, Lutzen, Bautzen, Zinnwald and Hanau during the Napoleonic Wars.

MARINES TO 95TH (RIFLES) *by Thomas Fernyhough*—The military experiences of Robert Fernyhough during the Napoleonic Wars.

HUSSAR ROCCA *by Albert Jean Michel de Rocca*—A French cavalry officer's experiences of the Napoleonic Wars and his views on the Peninsular Campaigns against the Spanish, British And Guerilla Armies.

SERGEANT BOURGOGNE *by Adrien Bourgogne*—With Napoleon's Imperial Guard in the Russian Campaign and on the Retreat from Moscow 1812 - 13.

AVAILABLE ONLINE AT
www.leonaur.com
AND OTHER GOOD BOOK STORES

ALSO FROM LEONAUR
AVAILABLE IN SOFTCOVER OR HARDCOVER WITH DUST JACKET

CAPTAIN OF THE 95th (Rifles) *by Jonathan Leach*—An officer of Wellington's Sharpshooters during the Peninsular, South of France and Waterloo Campaigns of the Napoleonic Wars.

BUGLER AND OFFICER OF THE RIFLES *by William Green & Harry Smith* With the 95th (Rifles) during the Peninsular & Waterloo Campaigns of the Napoleonic Wars

BAYONETS, BUGLES AND BONNETS *by James 'Thomas' Todd*—Experiences of hard soldiering with the 71st Foot - the Highland Light Infantry - through many battles of the Napoleonic wars including the Peninsular & Waterloo Campaigns

THE ADVENTURES OF A LIGHT DRAGOON *by George Farmer & G.R. Gleig*—A cavalryman during the Peninsular & Waterloo Campaigns, in captivity & at the siege of Bhurtpore, India

THE COMPLEAT RIFLEMAN HARRIS *by Benjamin Harris as told to & transcribed by Captain Henry Curling*—The adventures of a soldier of the 95th (Rifles) during the Peninsular Campaign of the Napoleonic Wars

WITH WELLINGTON'S LIGHT CAVALRY *by William Tomkinson*—The Experiences of an officer of the 16th Light Dragoons in the Peninsular and Waterloo campaigns of the Napoleonic Wars.

SURTEES OF THE RIFLES *by William Surtees*—A Soldier of the 95th (Rifles) in the Peninsular campaign of the Napoleonic Wars.

ENSIGN BELL IN THE PENINSULAR WAR *by George Bell*—The Experiences of a young British Soldier of the 34th Regiment 'The Cumberland Gentlemen' in the Napoleonic wars.

WITH THE LIGHT DIVISION *by John H. Cooke*—The Experiences of an Officer of the 43rd Light Infantry in the Peninsula and South of France During the Napoleonic Wars

NAPOLEON'S IMPERIAL GUARD: FROM MARENGO TO WATERLOO *by J. T. Headley*—This is the story of Napoleon's Imperial Guard from the bearskin caps of the grenadiers to the flamboyance of their mounted chasseurs, their principal characters and the men who commanded them.

BATTLES & SIEGES OF THE PENINSULAR WAR *by W. H. Fitchett*—Corunna, Busaco, Albuera, Ciudad Rodrigo, Badajos, Salamanca, San Sebastian & Others

AVAILABLE ONLINE AT
www.leonaur.com
AND OTHER GOOD BOOK STORES

ALSO FROM LEONAUR
AVAILABLE IN SOFTCOVER OR HARDCOVER WITH DUST JACKET

DOING OUR 'BIT' *by Ian Hay*—Two Classic Accounts of the Men of Kitchener's 'New Army' During the Great War including *The First 100,000* & *All In It*.

AN EYE IN THE STORM by *Arthur Ruhl*—An American War Correspondent's Experiences of the First World War from the Western Front to Gallipoli and Beyond.

STAND & FALL by *Joe Cassells*—A Soldier's Recollections of the 'Contemptible Little Army' and the Retreat from Mons to the Marne, 1914.

RIFLEMAN MACGILL'S WAR by *Patrick MacGill*—A Soldier of the London Irish During the Great War in Europe including *The Amateur Army, The Red Horizon* & *The Great Push*.

WITH THE GUNS by *C. A. Rose & Hugh Dalton*—Two First Hand Accounts of British Gunners at War in Europe During World War 1- Three Years in France with the Guns and With the British Guns in Italy.

EAGLES OVER THE TRENCHES by *James R. McConnell & William B. Perry*—Two First Hand Accounts of the American Escadrille at War in the Air During World War 1-Flying For France: With the American Escadrille at Verdun and Our Pilots in the Air.

THE BUSH WAR DOCTOR by *Robert V. Dolbey*—The Experiences of a British Army Doctor During the East African Campaign of the First World War.

THE 9TH—THE KING'S (LIVERPOOL REGIMENT) IN THE GREAT WAR 1914 - 1918 by *Enos H. G. Roberts*—Like many large cities, Liverpool raised a number of battalions in the Great War. Notable among them were the Pals, the Liverpool Irish and Scottish, but this book concerns the wartime history of the 9th Battalion – The Kings.

THE GAMBARDIER by *Mark Severn*—The experiences of a battery of Heavy artillery on the Western Front during the First World War.

FROM MESSINES TO THIRD YPRES by *Thomas Floyd*—A personal account of the First World War on the Western front by a 2/5th Lancashire Fusilier.

THE IRISH GUARDS IN THE GREAT WAR - VOLUME 1 by *Rudyard Kipling*— Edited and Compiled from Their Diaries and Papers Volume 1 The First Battalion.

THE IRISH GUARDS IN THE GREAT WAR - VOLUME 2 by *Rudyard Kipling*— Edited and Compiled from Their Diaries and Papers Volume 2 The Second Battalion.

AVAILABLE ONLINE AT
www.leonaur.com
AND OTHER GOOD BOOK STORES

www.ingramcontent.com/pod-product-compliance
Lightning Source LLC
Chambersburg PA
CBHW031600170426
43196CB00031B/271